THE SINGLE GOSPEL

Icon of Jesus, St. Catherine's Monastery, Sinai
Photo: Gianni Dagli Orti / The Art Archive at Art Resource, NY

THE SINGLE GOSPEL

Matthew, Mark, Luke and John
Consolidated into a Single Narrative

Neil Averitt

Foreword by Ian Markham

RESOURCE *Publications* · Eugene, Oregon

THE SINGLE GOSPEL
Matthew, Mark, Luke and John Consolidated into a Single Narrative

Resource Publications
An Imprint of Wipf and Stock Publishers
199 W. 8th Ave., Suite 3
Eugene, OR 97401

www.wipfandstock.com

ISBN 13: 978-1-4982-2158-0

Manufactured in the U.S.A.   09/17/2015

CONTENTS

III. The Early Ministries

IV. The Galilee Ministry
Teaching and Healing

V. The Galilee Ministry
Building a Movement

VI. The Galilee Ministry
Moving into Opposition

VII. The Jerusalem Ministry

VIII. The Last Itinerant Ministry

IX. Holy Week

X. Trial and Crucifixion

XI. The Resurrection

FOREWORD

In the end Christianity is about Jesus Christ. Everything that Christians want to claim about God is captured in that life that Christians believe is the "Word made flesh." Jesus is the Eternal Wisdom embodied; Jesus is the utterance of God that shows us God; Jesus is the definitive revelation of God to humanity.

Christians are called to witness to Christ. We are obligated to share the story of his life, death, and resurrection with the world. We want to share our excitement about this remarkable life which is followed by over a third of the world's population. But all encounters with that life have a major problem: what do you do with the four differing portraits of Jesus in the four different Gospels?

In practice most Christians work with a 'single Gospel.' The Church Calendar tells the drama of Jesus Christ as one narrative. Movies tell the story of Jesus Christ as one narrative. When we pray, reflect, and think about Jesus, we create a continuous narrative from birth to baptism to ministry to the last week of his life to the joy of his resurrection. In our heads we have a 'single Gospel,' but nowhere does that 'single Gospel' exist.

Neil Averitt has spent much of the last decade working on a project that initially I thought was impossible, but as I have read and looked at this remarkable book I am persuaded he has pulled it off. He is revisiting the neglected and dying genre of a harmonized gospel. Such projects were all the rage in the 19th century, and then in the 20th they went completely out of fashion. The line taken by most contemporary New Testament scholars is that each Gospel needs to be honored on its own (with its distinctive theology and worldview). Neil Averitt then came along (fortunately not inside the New Testament guild) and just had an intuition that harmonization is still possible. So he set about to do it.

And this is the result. Neil Averitt has created the single Gospel that the Church Calendar assumes and most Christians have in their devotional life. And it works. The narrative is a delight to read. It combines the best of scholarship with an accessible tone. Wisely, he uses the most familiar phrases from the King James Version. Footnotes helpfully illuminate some of the mysteries of the text. He really is quite brilliant.

Do linger over the Introduction. The impulse behind this project is beautiful. Neil Averitt wanted to solve the puzzle of the motivation behind the extraordinary medieval churches of Europe. What was it that drove men and women to create such places of extraordinary elegance and assertion? The answer of course is the magic and radiance of Jesus Christ. His goal is that this life might touch afresh all our lives. Truly Soli Deo Gloria.

Ian Markham
Dean, Virginia Theological Seminary

INTRODUCTION

This book grows out of my own spiritual travels.

Like many Americans today, I grew up with religion playing very little part in my childhood life. This was a change from family tradition, because my ancestors had always had a strong Christian bent. Some members of the family were Huguenots—French Protestants who endured prosecution for the sake of their faith and eventually fled to England. Others were English Puritans, who suffered a different kind of persecution for their own faith and eventually fled to Jamestown in the new colony of Virginia. Once here, people in one branch of the family embraced the Church of Jesus Christ of Latter-day Saints—the Mormons—and braved the wilderness with Brigham Young to make new homes in the western desert. All were willing to endure great sacrifices for the sake of their beliefs.

This same religious commitment continued into more recent times. The family has produced many ministers and preachers. Some of them helped to found Averett College, a Baptist-affiliated school in southern Virginia. Another, the Rev. James Battle Avirett, was the Episcopal chaplain of Turner Ashby's cavalry regiment during the Civil War. Working for the success of the other side in the same conflict, my own great grandfather served as a doctor in the Union Army and then went on to spend the rest of his life in the ministry in Kentucky.

We were an educated family, however, and the Age of Reason had a strong influence on our thinking. By the time I was born, religion had gone out of style in America. My parents were scientists—geologists who were more inclined to study what they could see and measure, the stones and rock formations that make up the physical universe. They were fair-minded people and respectful of religion, but not religious themselves. And so I grew up virtually without a religious education.

We seldom went to church. From time to time my parents took us to services in the little Mormon farming towns of southern Utah, where my father spent summers doing geologic work. Back home in Washington they took me to a local church one Palm Sunday when I was in grade school. There I saw children my own age waving palm fronds; I recognized some of them as my classmates, but had little idea what their actions meant. Once when I was very young I had been asked by an elderly relative if I understood the meaning of Easter, and responded that I certainly did. It was the day, I explained gravely, when they nailed George Washington to the cross.

On other subjects, however, I was able to give better answers, and so I went to Harvard, the London School of Economics, and Harvard Law School. Religion remained absent in all these places. I spent my time amid throngs of intelligent people who were trying and often failing to find meaning in their lives. I enjoyed the sight of Memorial Church, a building that dominates the center of Harvard Yard and faces the main library; but I went inside only to see the lists of the Harvard men who had gone before me, and who had died in the First World War.

I also traveled during those student years, riding a motorcycle through Europe. One day I visited Mont Saint-Michel in France, and was struck by its beauty. A thin spire rose high above the cloister of the monastery, and its proportions reminded me of Memorial Church. But here too my response was just an aesthetic one—I thought it was a beautiful building with glorious architecture. Then later that day I had a serious accident. I hit a break in the pavement of the road, flipped the motorcycle, and broke my collarbone. A kindly motorist picked me up and took me to a nearby hospital affiliated with the Catholic Church. At the end of the day the nuns paced down the hallway chanting something beautiful and otherworldly. I couldn't understand the words, but for the first time I had an inkling that the world might contain other sets of values.

Visiting the cathedral of Notre Dame while recuperating, I looked with interest at the frieze of sculptures around the choir showing biblical scenes. It wasn't until many years later that someone explained that these depicted episodes in Jesus' life, designed to tell the Christian story to people of the Middle Ages who were illiterate. Here I was, a highly educated man, but I was less able to read that story than a person who could not read at all.

I sometime paused to think that this cathedral—and the churches of my own country—represented a huge investment of the time and wealth of earlier generations. Clearly they were expressing some message that those people had thought was vitally important to hand down to us. But the message wasn't reaching me.

As I moved into adult life, however, it became increasingly clear that our contemporary world was missing something that had been central to successful cultures and to successful individual lives in the past. I thought back to the European towns I had seen on my travels, and the classic American towns with churches at their center, and realized they had helped to build a sense of community that was no longer with us. The rational secular laws I had studied in law school didn't seem to be providing a similar structure for people's lives or making them particularly happy. There were a lot of alienated strivers in our world. But what was the alternative?

One alternative began to appear when I first encountered a true community of faith, and saw what lives lived in Christian understanding might look like. This experience could happen to a person anywhere, but in my case it happened on a visit to a place in Greece called Mount Athos.

Mount Athos is in Greece but not really of it. It is a self-governing, largely autonomous monastic republic in the northern part of the country, literally a piece of the old Byzantine Empire, a part of the doubly unfamiliar world of the Eastern Orthodox churches. It occupies a remote, mountainous peninsula that reaches thirty-five miles out into the Aegean, terminating in the steep-sided peak of Mount Athos itself, which rises seven thousand feet directly out of the ocean. No road connects the peninsula with the mainland, so it is for all practical purposes an island. Scattered across this isolated landscape are twenty large monasteries, a few small towns, innumerable farmhouses and hermitages, and about 2000 monks. Even the buildings themselves are dramatic, built of stone and fortified, with Byzantine and medieval influences predominating, the monasteries sometimes standing near the sea and sometimes clinging to crags a thousand feet above it. The entire community functions as a religious republic—a sort of "Christian Tibet"—under a charter granted by the Byzantine Emperor in the year 972. For the first-time visitor like me, the experience was as strange as being suddenly dropped down on Mars.

Although Mount Athos was undeniably exotic, it did not seem likely to be the place of my spiritual awakening. After all, I had gone there as a cultural tourist, to see the architecture and the unique institutions surviving from the classical world. I was a visitor.

Once there, however, I found faith in forms that I had not seen before. For one thing, the monks did not have, as one might have expected, a dour and burdened attitude toward their austere lives. Instead, the life they had chosen for themselves seemed to have made them calm and cheerful, and at peace with the world. The country lanes around some of the monasteries were so quiet that you could hear the sound of birds' wings and of bees in the trees, and a sense of age-old peace lay over the land. One of the monks recommended to me a line from the Psalms, "Be still and know that I am God."

The monks' faith was not just a response to a tranquil environment. It was grounded, not in a freedom from aggravation, but in a sense of continuing communion with something larger. Every act, it seemed, was imbued with religious significance and done for the greater glory of God. The monks rose for services at 3:30 in the morning, and prayed steadily for about four hours as the night gave way to dawn. At one monastery even the gardener's wheelbarrow was decorated with a cross painted on the side.

Where all these elements came together, it seemed to me, was in the lamps that lit the nighttime services. These burned olive oil and were dimmer than our paraffin candles of today, and the light was further muted by shining through bowls of colored glass, often red. They were calm and intimate, close at hand. And they symbolized, at least to me, a different way of looking at God—not distant, transcendent, remote, but rather as something personal and close by. They conveyed a sense that the infinite was accessible by looking within yourself.

But if this was the experience at the monasteries, what were my own beliefs? What elements of faith did I take away from the experiences?

In some senses the answer to this question is easy. The Nicene Creed and similar pledges have long defined the essential elements of Christianity—belief in the Trinity, in Jesus' incarnation as both God and man, in the resurrection, and in a number of other basic tenets. Yet while these are all key elements of the Christian faith, they do not all present themselves in exactly the same way to every person. Some elements have come to me more forcibly than others and have presented themselves with special vividness.

One particularly clear connection has been with Jesus in his earthly incarnation as the Son of Man. I find it easy to picture Jesus the human teacher walking the paths of his native Galilee, gathering disciples and teaching, and eventually making his way to the final confrontation in Jerusalem. His lessons speak fundamentally to the human heart, and they carry wisdom to our own day. When he tells us to "Love your enemies," and to seek out "treasures in heaven," he is giving a profoundly corrective message in a strife-ridden and materialistic world.

Another close connection has been with the third element in the Trinity—the Holy Spirit. Jesus described the Spirit as the Counselor, who will "bring to your remembrance all that I have said to you." The Spirit is more abstract than the other persons of the Trinity. But this abstract quality also makes it all-pervasive, helping us feel our connection with all the parts of the material world, and also helping us shape our own judgments in accordance with the teachings of Jesus, making us better able to sense and to *intuit* the proper path in life.

I had come to realize that I wanted to know more about Jesus and his life. And as I came to learn more, I found that my own truths had changed.

For one thing, the Christian teachings have made me more patient with the other people around me. I have become more willing to accept each of them for who they are, rather than looking for who I wish they would be—to see them, insofar as I am able, as God sees them. The words from the Sermon on the Mount have not encouraged me to set aside my judgments, but rather not to judge in the first place: For your heavenly Father "is kind even to the ungrateful and the selfish."

For another thing, faith has opened the door to a different way of looking at all the business and practical dealings of daily life. It made it suddenly clear that it is possible to live in the world by different values, and to perceive both troubles and opportunities in ways very different from our society's customary practices. A follower of Jesus might "live in this world but be a citizen of heaven."

And so, because of these values, I have become more at peace with myself and with the wider world. All things are related, and all things are sacred. The red lamps, which symbolized for me the presence of the Holy Spirit, also symbolize this universal, unifying presence of God. The calm, low, inward-turning focus of the lamps ultimately leads, somewhat counterintuitively, to a connection with the whole world. The Seventh Century church father, St. Isaac the Syrian, expressed this connection well:

> Be at peace with your own soul; then heaven and earth will be at peace with you. Enter eagerly into the treasure house that is within you, and so you will see the things that are in heaven; for there is but one single entry to them both. The ladder that leads to the kingdom is hidden within your own soul. Flee from sin, dive into yourself, and in your soul you will discover the stairs by which to ascend.

And so, at long last, I had relearned what had once been so well known in my family that it seemed to be in our DNA. And I had come to feel that the gospel story was something that I needed to work through, absorb, put into more understandable form, and make available to a general readership.

I therefore began a seven-year study of the history and theology involved in the various English versions of the gospels. I also acquired a working knowledge of Greek through various studies, including a course taught by the Dominicans. Then I considered whether it would be possible to build on the work of the earlier editions of the gospels by bringing some new skills that have not been a prominent part of religious publishing in the past. By profession I am an antitrust lawyer and a former editor of my school's law review. I could bring to the task an editor's ear for language, and a lawyer's ability to combine a variety of authorities into a coherent whole. Those seemed to be the relevant skills for the new kind of volume that was most needed; and thus this book.

*****

This version of the gospels strives to make the original material more readable in two different ways. First, the story is now arranged in a clean chronology, with the episodes following a single timeline and all the details of each incident or teaching collected in one account. Second, a new translation ensures that the text is clear and self-explanatory, while at the same time taking care that it preserves familiar passages and the key turns of phrase that are valued by one or another part of the Christian community.

The main challenge posed by the four gospels has always been that they are fragmented in ways that make them hard to understand. The pieces of the story are not set out in chronological order. After one book of the gospels has given what appears to be a complete life of Christ, another book will provide some new incident, which must be mentally inserted back into the story at the appropriate place. Luke describes the birth at Bethlehem, but then Matthew adds the visit of the Magi. Even more daunting, some important episodes, such as the resurrection, are described in tantalizing fragments over the course of all four gospels, with no one account presenting more than a fraction of the story.

This book provides a solution to these difficulties. It puts the incidents of Christ's life into one sequence that theological scholars call a "harmony." The birth is now followed, as the story intends, by the visit of the Magi. This chronological arrangement also brings together the different accounts of incidents into one complete description of each. The basic concept is *additive*. I take the view that each fact reported in one of the gospels is an integral part of the story as a whole. The text therefore includes all of the unique facts that are offered. A good example is the account of the Holy Spirit descending on Jesus in the form of a dove after he has been baptized in the Jordan. The gospel of Luke tells us that this occurred as Jesus emerged from the water and "was praying;" Mark tells us that the heavens were "torn open" to permit the passage of the dove; and Matthew tells us that the dove ended by "alighting on him." Once the overlaps are omitted, the unique phrases from each account can go into a single sentence: "And when Jesus came up out of the water, and was praying, straightaway he saw the heavens torn open and the Spirit of God descending in bodily form like a dove and alighting upon him."

This book also brings together the three different approaches to translation that are found in most of today's Bibles. It refers back to the original Greek and presents a new translation, which adjusts its tone according to the needs and context of a particular passage. Most often it preserves the general tone of the King James Version, but in a form that has been inconspicuously updated with wording more accessible to the modern reader. Sometimes, where necessary, it conveys particularly difficult descriptions through use of more informal and contemporary language. And at other times it stays with the grand and familiar language of the original King James itself.

Some phrases from the King James Version are so familiar to everyone from the traditional Christmas story or the Sermon on the Mount that any great departure from them would be jarring. For example, some recent but overly-literal translations have the angels announce the birth of Jesus by saying something like, "Glory to God in the highest, and on earth peace to men on whom his favor rests." This contrasts oddly with the more familiar account which says, "And on earth peace, good will toward men." There is really no substitute for the resonance of the older language, and that language has, through long usage, acquired its own legitimacy in the Christian community. Use of the King James is also appropriate where particular phrases have become familiar terms of speech. Thus certain unappreciated invitations "fall by the wayside," and last-minute arrangements are made "at the eleventh hour."

In the task of translation I have had invaluable help from many prior works. This is a new translation in the sense that I have looked continuously for new ways to express thoughts in traditional language that will make sense to modern readers. This volume was not written on a blank slate, however. The Revised Standard Version is still the best modern update of the King James, and has provided an essential model to style and expression, as well as to narrative interpretation. The New International Version provides scholarly insights on more modern language. And, of course, the King James Version remains the gold standard for the received traditional voice. None of these works bears responsibility for any shortcomings in the preparation of this volume. Nonetheless, I gratefully acknowledge my debt to all of them.

At the end of the day, my goal has been to create a Platonic form of the Bible story—not something with the shine of novelty, but something comfortable and familiar, the biblical narrative as it exists in our minds, and as we think we remember it.

I hope that the story in this form will speak to several different groups of readers. It may speak, first of all, in the language of faith. It does so in a form that is accessible to everyone. The teachings of Jesus do not focus on the particulars of ritual and doctrine. They address instead the wonderment of mankind's relationship to the infinite, the self-knowledge that comes from a study of the human heart, and the true community that binds together all the parts of God's creation. All these teachings present themselves with a new clarity and immediacy through a consolidated text.

This book should also be useful to secular readers as an accessible way to reconnect with one of the central narratives of Western civilization. The gospels are not only the foundation of the Christian faith, but also, as I learned at Notre Dame, the source of innumerable references in art and literature. One cannot understand the command to "turn the other cheek," or fully understand the life of Jesus for its historical significance, or view a painting like Rembrandt's *Descent from the Cross*, or read the O. Henry short story about *The Gift of the Magi*, without understanding their roots in the gospel narrative. Yet the details of this background are becoming less familiar to contemporary people, who are often less regular churchgoers than their parents and grandparents had been.

In the process of integrating the gospel accounts for a general readership I have followed several principles of composition. As already mentioned, I have followed the additive principle of including each distinctive fact, and the principle of familiarity when retaining certain well-loved phrases from the King James Version. A number of other principles also emerged during the course of the work. These address more specific issues, such as how to treat apparently identical events that are described at different times in the chronology, or how to handle the occasional points where the gospel accounts disagree with one another, or how broadly or narrowly to translate references to "the Jews." For the reader who is interested in these details of the drafting, they are described in an appendix on "Principles of Composition."

These kinds of judgments mean, of course, that the present work is no longer a holy text. Inevitably there will be errors in the editorial process. The resulting work should therefore be thought of as an interpretation or a study guide. When an authoritative source is needed, readers can consult the original underlying gospel texts for a given point; those references are given at the start of each chapter.

The editorial process has also tended to blur the distinctive character of the four individual gospels. Their distinctive purposes and points of view are necessarily lost in the course of creating a single narrative.

This "smoothing out" of the four gospel accounts is actually one of the main virtues of a consolidated story, however. While there may be four authoritative gospel accounts, there is only one underlying gospel. There was only one life of Jesus, and only one core body of Christian belief. The four gospels illuminate this one underlying reality from their four different vantage points, but bringing those four accounts together will give us our most rounded and nuanced portrait of Jesus and his life. A harmony is likely to come closer to this single underlying truth than any one incomplete gospel can do. To point out this fact does not imply a challenge to the historical scholarship that has been devoted to the individual gospels. Understanding the individuality of the four sources is a later and more advanced area of study, however, and many readers may feel that this is something that is best undertaken after an initial grounding in the core narrative.

My goal here has been to present the best possible consolidated text of the four gospels. I have taken the gospels themselves as a given. I have not attempted to look behind them to interpret their theology or to judge their status as historical documents. Those are tasks for other works and for individual churches. I have, however, included a number of basic footnotes in the body of the book, in order to ensure that the sense and context of a particular passage is clear, and that the reader will always understand at least the letter of what is being said. On particularly complex topics a footnote will end with an asterisk. That indicates that a fuller discussion of the subject can be found in the endnotes at the back of the book. Some narrower and more technical issues will be discussed only in the endnotes.

My hope is that this volume will make the life of Jesus more accessible to a wider audience. For some readers this text may itself be sufficient for their needs, and for others it may be the start of a more detailed study of the underlying individual evangelists.

Whichever road is taken, may you go with God.

Alexandria, Virginia
2015

THE GOSPEL

I. THE DEDICATIONS OF MARK AND LUKE
Mark 1:1; Luke 1:1–4

1. Here begins the gospel of Jesus Christ, the Son of God.

2. Many have undertaken to set forth a narrative of those things which have taken place among us, just as the accounts were handed down to us by those who from the first were eyewitnesses and ministers of the Word. Since I myself have carefully investigated everything from the beginning, it seemed good to me also to write an orderly account,[1] so that you may know the truth of the things you have been taught.

2. IN THE BEGINNING
John 1:1–6, 14–18

1. In the beginning was the Word. The Word was with God, and the Word was God.

2. The Word existed in the beginning with God. All things were made through him, and God created nothing except through him. In him was life, and this life brings light to all mankind. The light shines in the darkness, and the darkness has not overcome it.

3. And the Word was made flesh and dwelt among us, full of truth and kindness; we have beheld his glory, the glory of the only begotten Son of the Father. And from the abundance of Jesus' grace we have all

---

1. At this point Luke directly addresses the person for whom his account was first prepared, "for you, most excellent Theophilus." Because Luke's gospel now reaches a much wider audience, the original term of address is presented here only in footnote.*

1

received blessing upon blessing. For the law was given through Moses; grace and truth came through Jesus Christ.[2] No one has seen God at any time; but the only Son, who is closest to the Father's heart, has made him known to us.

4. And there was a man sent from God, whose name was John. John bore witness *to the eternal life of Jesus*[3] when he cried out, "This is the one of whom I said, 'He who comes after me ranks before me, because he existed before me.'"

---

2. The term "grace" refers to the assistance that God offers to help people toward spiritual understanding and salvation. It is a free gift, and it neither can nor needs to be earned. The underlying Greek word, *charis*, also has the secondary meaning of "kindness." Because the word appears three times in this verse, it is translated on one occasion in this latter sense.

3. Words in italics are not a part of the biblical text, but have been added to clarify its meaning. See the appendix on Principles of Composition.

Annunciation (San Marco), by Fra Angelico
Photo: Erich Lessing / Art Resource, NY

I. BACKGROUND AND BIRTH OF JESUS

3. AN ANGEL PROMISES THE BIRTH OF JOHN THE BAPTIST
Luke 1:5–25

1. *John the Baptist was born in the following way.* In the days of Herod, king of Judea, there was a priest[4] named Zechariah, of the priestly order of Abijah. He had a wife who was from the family of Aaron, and her name was Elizabeth. They were both righteous before God, walking blamelessly in all the commandments and ordinances of the Lord. But they had no child, because Elizabeth was barren, and they both were now well stricken in years.

2. One day when Zechariah's group was on duty and he was serving as a priest before God, he was chosen by lot, according to the custom among the priests, to enter the temple of the Lord and burn incense. At the time for the burning of incense, all the assembled worshipers were praying outside. Then an angel of the Lord appeared to Zechariah, standing on the right-hand side of the incense altar. Zechariah was shaken when he saw the angel, and fear fell upon him. But the angel said to him, "Do not be afraid, Zechariah, for your prayer has been heard, and your wife Elizabeth will bear you a son, and you shall call his name John.

3. "And you will have joy and gladness, and many will rejoice that he was born; for he will be great in the eyes of the Lord, and he shall drink neither wine nor strong drink, and he will be filled with the Holy Spirit,

---

4. These priests were officiants at the temple in Jerusalem, where they offered prayers and carried out sacrifices and other religious services. Their role was different from that of rabbis, whose authority was based on learning and scholarship.

even from his mother's womb. And he will turn many of the children of Israel back to the Lord their God, and he will go as a forerunner before the Lord in the spirit and power of Elijah, to turn the hearts of fathers to their children, and the disobedient to the wisdom of the righteous, and to make ready a people prepared for the Lord."

4. Zechariah said to the angel, "How can I know this? For I am an old man, and my wife is well stricken in years." And the angel answered him, "I am Gabriel, who stands in the presence of God; and I was sent to speak to you, and to bring you this good news. Now behold, you will be silent and unable to speak until the day that these things come to pass, because you did not believe my words, which will be fulfilled in their proper time."

5. Meanwhile the people were waiting for Zechariah, and they wondered why he was so long in the temple. When he came out, he could not speak to them, and they understood that he had seen a vision there; for he kept making signs to them but remained mute. And when his time of service was completed, he returned to his home.

6. After this his wife Elizabeth conceived, and for five months she kept herself in seclusion. "The Lord has done this for me," she said. "Now he has shown his favor and taken away the reproach I have endured among the people."

4. THE ANNUNCIATION TO MARY
Luke 1:26–38

1. In the sixth month *of Elizabeth's term* the angel Gabriel was sent by God to a town in Galilee called Nazareth, to a virgin betrothed to a man whose name was Joseph, of the lineage of David; and this maiden's name was Mary. Gabriel came to her and said, "Hail, O favored one, the Lord is with thee!"

2. Mary was greatly troubled at these words, and wondered what this greeting might mean. But the angel said to her, "Do not be afraid, Mary, for you have found favor with God. And behold, you will conceive in your womb and bear a son, and you shall call his name Jesus. He will be great, and will be called the Son of the Most High; and the Lord God will give to him the throne of his father David, and he will

rule over the house of Jacob forever, and his kingdom will have no end."

3. Mary said to the angel, "How can this be, since I have never known a man?" And the angel replied to her, "The Holy Spirit will come upon you, and the power of the Most High will overshadow you; therefore the child to be born will be holy, and he will be called the Son of God. For see, your kinswoman Elizabeth in her old age has also conceived a son; and this is now the sixth month for her who had been called barren. For with God nothing is impossible."

4. Mary said, "Behold, I am the handmaid of the Lord; let it be unto me according to thy word." And the angel departed from her.

5. MARY'S VISIT TO ELIZABETH
Luke 1:39–56

1. Then Mary arose and went with haste into the hill country, to a town of Judea, and she entered the house where Zechariah lived, and greeted *Zechariah's wife* Elizabeth. When Elizabeth heard Mary's greeting, the babe leaped in her womb; and Elizabeth was filled with the Holy Spirit and she gave a loud cry and exclaimed, "Blessed art thou among women, and blessed is the fruit of thy womb! But why is this granted me, that the mother of my Lord should come to me? For when the sound of your greeting reached my ears, the babe in my womb leaped for joy. And blessed is the woman who has believed, for the things that the Lord has spoken to her will be accomplished."

2. Mary responded,

> My soul doth magnify the Lord,[5]
> and my spirit rejoices in God my Savior,
> for he has shown favor to his humble handmaiden.[6]
> Behold, henceforth all generations will call me blessed;
> for he who is mighty has done great things for me,
> and holy is his name.
> For those who fear him, his mercy abides
> from generation to generation.
> He has shown might in his arm;

---

5. In the Latin, "Magnificat anima mea Dominum." This song has been frequently set to music as the "Magnificat."

6. In the King James Version, "he hath regarded the low estate of his handmaiden."

he has scattered those who are haughty in their inmost thoughts;
he has put down the mighty from their thrones,
and exalted those of low degree.
He has filled the hungry with good things,
and the rich he has sent empty away.
He has helped his servant Israel,
and remembered to be merciful
to Abraham and his posterity forever,
even as he promised to our fathers.

And Mary remained with Elizabeth for about three months, and then she returned to her home.

6. THE BIRTH OF JOHN THE BAPTIST
Luke 1:57–79

1. Then the time came for Elizabeth to be delivered, and she bore a son. Her neighbors and relatives heard that the Lord had shown her great mercy, and they rejoiced with her. And on the eighth day they came to circumcise the child; and they would have named him Zechariah after his father, but his mother said, "Not so; he shall be called John." And they said to her, "There is no one in your family who bears this name." So they made signs to the father, asking what he wished to have him called. And Zechariah motioned for a writing tablet, and wrote, "His name is John." And they were all astonished.

2. At once Zechariah's mouth was opened and his tongue freed, and he began to speak, praising God. And awe came upon all their neighbors. These things were talked about through all the hill country of Judea; and all who heard about them wondered what they meant, saying, "What then is this child going to be?" For the hand of the Lord was surely with him.

3. Then his father Zechariah was filled with the Holy Spirit, and he prophesied, saying,

> Blessed be the Lord God of Israel,
> for he has visited and redeemed his people,
> and he has raised up a rock of salvation for us
> in the house of his servant David,
> as he promised through his holy prophets from long ago.
> Thus we shall be saved from our enemies,

and from the hand of all who hate us.
The Lord has shown the mercy promised to our ancestors,
and he has remembered his holy covenant,
the oath which he swore to our father Abraham, to grant
that we, being delivered from the hand of our enemies,
might serve him without fear,
in holiness and righteousness before him all the days of our life.

And you, my child, will be called the prophet of the Most High;
for you will go ahead of the Lord to prepare the way for him,
to give his people knowledge of salvation
by the forgiveness of their sins.
Through the tender mercy of our God,
a new day shall dawn upon us from on high,
to give light to those who sit in darkness and in the shadow of death,
and to guide our feet into the way of peace.

7. THE ANNUNCIATION TO JOSEPH
Matthew 1:18b–25a

1. After Mary had been betrothed to Joseph, but before they came together, she was found to be with child by the Holy Spirit; and her husband Joseph, being a just man and unwilling to put her to public disgrace, resolved to send her away quietly.

2. But as he considered these things, an angel of the Lord appeared to him in a dream, saying "Joseph, son of David, do not fear to take Mary as your wife, for the child within her is conceived of the Holy Spirit. She will bear a son, and you shall call his name Jesus, for he will save his people from their sins."[7] All this took place to fulfill what the Lord had spoken through the prophet: "Behold, the virgin shall conceive, and shall bear a son, and they shall call his name 'Emmanuel,' which means, God is with us."

3. When Joseph woke from sleep, he did as the angel of the Lord commanded him; he took Mary as his wife, but did not know her until she had borne a son.

---

7. The name "Jesus" is a Greek form of the traditional Hebrew name Joshua, which means "Yahweh saves" or "Jehovah saves."

8. THE BIRTH OF JESUS
Matthew 1:18a; Luke 2:1–7

1. Now the birth of Jesus Christ took place in this way. In those days a decree went out from Caesar Augustus that all the world should be taxed. This was the first census taken while Quirinius was governor of Syria. All went to be enrolled, each to his own city. And Joseph went up from Galilee, out of the town of Nazareth, to Judea, to the city of David, which is called Bethlehem, because he was of the house and lineage of David, to be enrolled with Mary, his betrothed wife, who was great with child.

2. And while they were there, the time came for her to be delivered. And she brought forth her first-born son and wrapped him in swaddling cloths, and laid him in a manger, because there was no room for them in the inn.

9. THE ANGELS' PROCLAMATION TO THE SHEPHERDS
Luke 2:8–20

1. In that same region there were shepherds abiding in the fields, keeping watch over their flocks by night. And lo, an angel of the Lord appeared to them, and the glory of the Lord shone round about them, and they were sore afraid. But the angel said to them, "Be not afraid; for behold, I bring you good tidings of great joy, which will be for all the people; for unto you is born this day in the city of David a Savior, who is Christ the Lord. And this is how you shall know him: you will find a babe wrapped in swaddling cloths and lying in a manger." And suddenly there appeared with the angel a great multitude of the heavenly host, praising God and saying,

> Glory to God in the highest,
> and on earth peace, good will to men.

2. When the angels had gone away from them into heaven, the shepherds said to one another, "Let us go to Bethlehem and see this thing that has come to pass, which the Lord has made known to us." So they went quickly, and found Mary and Joseph, and the babe lying in a manger. When they saw this they spread the word of what they had been told

about this child; and all who heard it were astonished at what the shepherds told them.

3. But Mary treasured up all these things, pondering them *quietly* in her heart. And the shepherds returned to their flocks, glorifying and praising God for all the things they had heard and seen, which were just as the angel had told them.

10. PATERNAL GENEALOGY OF JESUS
Matthew 1:1–17

1. The record of the genealogy of Jesus Christ, the son of David, the son of Abraham, *through his father Joseph*:[8]

2. Abraham was the father of Isaac,
    Isaac the father of Jacob,
    Jacob the father of Judah and his brothers,
    Judah the father of Perez and Zerah by Tamar,
    Perez the father of Hezron,
    Hezron the father of Ram,
    Ram the father of Amminadab,
    Amminadab the father of Nahshon,
    Nahshon the father of Salmon,
    Salmon the father of Boaz by Rahab,
    Boaz the father of Obed by Ruth,
    Obed the father of Jesse,
    and Jesse the father of David the king.

3. And David was the father of Solomon by the woman who had been the wife of Uriah,
    Solomon the father of Rehoboam,
    Rehoboam the father of Abijah,
    Abijah the father of Asa,
    Asa the father of Jehoshaphat,
    Jehoshaphat the father of Joram,
    Joram the father of Uzziah,
    Uzziah the father of Jotham,

---

8. The gospels contain two different genealogies of Jesus, which are set out in this chapter and the next. The traditional explanation for the variance is that the first gives the legal genealogy of Jesus through his supposed father Joseph, while the second gives his actual human ancestry through his mother Mary.*

Jotham the father of Ahaz,

Ahaz the father of Hezekiah,

Hezekiah the father of Manasseh,

Manasseh the father of Amon,

Amon the father of Josiah,

and Josiah the father of Jechoniah and his brothers, about the time they
were carried away into Babylon.

4. And after they were carried away into Babylon,

Jechoniah was the father of Shealtiel,

Shealtiel the father of Zerubbabel,

Zerubbabel the father of Abiud,

Abiud the father of Eliakim,

Eliakim the father of Azor,

Azor the father of Zadok,

Zadok the father of Achim,

Achim the father of Eliud,

Eliud the father of Eleazar,

Eleazar the father of Matthan,

Matthan the father of Jacob,

and Jacob the father of Joseph the husband of Mary, of whom was born
Jesus, who is called the Christ.

5. So all the generations from Abraham to David are fourteen generations, and from David until the carrying away into Babylon are fourteen generations, and from the carrying away into Babylon until the
Christ are fourteen generations.

I I. MATERNAL GENEALOGY OF JESUS
Luke 3:23b–38

1. *The record of the genealogy of Jesus Christ, through his mother Mary.*

2. Jesus was the son (as was supposed) of Joseph,

the son-*in-law*[9] of Heli, the son of Matthat,

the son of Levi, the son of Melchi,

the son of Jannai, the son of Joseph,

---

9. The previous genealogy states that the father of Joseph was Jacob. Joseph's biological father therefore cannot also be Heli. But Heli could be Joseph's father in some
other sense, such as being his father-in-law. This could be the case if the second genealogy traces Jesus' human ancestry through his mother.

the son of Mattathias, the son of Amos,
the son of Nahum, the son of Esli,
the son of Naggai, the son of Maath,
the son of Mattathias, the son of Semein,
the son of Josech, the son of Joda,
the son of Joanan, the son of Rhesa,
the son of Zerubbabel, the son of Shealtiel,
the son of Neri, the son of Melchi,
the son of Addi, the son of Cosam,
the son of Elmadam, the son of Er,
the son of Joshua, the son of Eliezer,
the son of Jorim, the son of Matthat,
the son of Levi, the son of Simeon,
the son of Judah, the son of Joseph,
the son of Jonam, the son of Eliakim,
the son of Melea, the son of Menna,
the son of Mattatha, the son of Nathan,
the son of David,[10] the son of Jesse,
the son of Obed, the son of Boaz,
the son of Salmon, the son of Nahshon,
the son of Amminadab, the son of Arni,
the son of Hezron, the son of Perez,
the son of Judah, the son of Jacob,
the son of Isaac, the son of Abraham,
the son of Terah, the son of Nahor,
the son of Serug, the son of Reu,
the son of Peleg, the son of Eber,
the son of Shelah, the son of Cainan,
the son of Arphaxad, the son of Shem,
the son of Noah, the son of Lamech,
the son of Methuselah, the son of Enoch,
the son of Jared, the son of Mahalalel,
the son of Cainan, the son of Enos,
the son of Seth, the son of Adam,
the son of God.

---

10. Thus Mary as well as Joseph was a descendant of David. This record ensured that Jesus would be from the bloodline of the ancient king even if Joseph were not recognized as his biological father.*

I2. CIRCUMCISION AND NAMING
Matthew 1:25b; Luke 2:21

1. On the eighth day it was time to circumcise the infant.

2. Joseph named him Jesus, the name the angel had given him before he had been conceived in the womb.

I3. PRESENTATION IN THE TEMPLE
Luke 2:22–39a

1. And when the period for their purification according to the law of Moses had been completed,[11] Joseph and Mary brought Jesus up to Jerusalem to present him to the Lord and to offer the sacrifice required by the law of the Lord, a pair of turtledoves, or two young pigeons. For as it is written in the law of the Lord, "Every male that is the first-born child of its mother shall be dedicated to the Lord."

2. Now there was a man in Jerusalem, whose name was Simeon. He was righteous and devout, and looking forward to the Messiah who would rescue Israel, and the Holy Spirit was upon him. It had been revealed to him by the Holy Spirit that he should not see death before he had seen the Lord's Christ.[12] Moved by the Spirit, he went into the temple; and when the parents brought in the child Jesus, to carry out for him the requirements of the law,[13] he took the child up in his arms and blessed God and said,

> Lord, now allow thy servant to depart in peace,
> according to your promise.
> For mine eyes have seen the salvation
> which you have prepared for the use of all peoples—
> a light to reveal God to the Gentiles,
> and to be the glory of thy people Israel.

---

11. Under traditional law, new mothers were ceremonially unclean for a certain number of days after childbirth.*

12. The words "Messiah" and "Christ" are Hebrew and Greek respectively; both mean "the anointed one."

13. Throughout the gospels, the "Law" being referred to is not the secular law of the Judean or Roman states, but the Jewish religious law, traditionally understood to have been declared by Moses, set out in the first five books of the Old Testament. These five books are known in Hebrew as the Torah, and in Greek as the Pentateuch.

The child's father and mother were amazed at what was being said about him; and then Simeon blessed them and said to Mary his mother,

> This child is destined to cause the rise or the fall of many in Israel,
> and to be a sign from God, although many will oppose him.
> Through him the thoughts of many hearts will be revealed,
> and a sword will pierce your own soul too.

3. And there was a prophetess, Anna, the daughter of Phanuel, of the tribe of Asher. She was of great age, having lived with her husband seven years after her marriage, and as a widow until she was eighty-four. She never left the temple, but worshiped night and day with fasting and prayer. Coming up to them at that moment, she gave thanks to God and spoke about the child to all who were waiting for the redemption of Jerusalem.

4. And *then* they had performed everything according to the law of the Lord.

I4. GIFTS OF THE MAGI
Matthew 2:1–12

1. After *these things had taken place,* wise men from the East came to Jerusalem, asking, "Where is the child who has been born king of the Jews? For we have seen his star in the East, and have come to worship him."

2. When Herod the king heard this, he was deeply troubled, and all Jerusalem with him. Calling together all the chief priests and scribes of the people, he asked them where the Messiah was to be born. "In Bethlehem of Judea," they told him, "for thus it is written by the prophet:

> And thou Bethlehem, in the land of Judah,
> are by no means least among the ruling towns of Judah;
> for out of you shall come a ruler
> who will be the shepherd of my people Israel.

Then Herod secretly summoned the wise men and learned from them the exact time when the star had first appeared, and he sent them to Bethlehem, saying, "Go and search diligently for the child, and when you have found him bring me word, so that I too may go and do him homage."

3. After they had heard the king, the magi[14] went on their way; and lo, the star which they had seen in the East went before them, until it came and stood over the place where the child lay. When they saw the star, they rejoiced with exceedingly great joy; and going into the house[15] they saw the child with Mary his mother, and they knelt down and worshiped him. Then they opened their treasure chests and offered him gifts—of gold, and frankincense, and myrrh.

4. And being warned in a dream that they should not return to Herod, they departed for their own country by another way.

15. FLIGHT INTO EGYPT AND MASSACRE OF THE INNOCENTS
Matthew 2:13–18

1. After the magi had departed, an angel of the Lord appeared to Joseph in a dream and said, "Rise, take the child and his mother, and flee to Egypt, and remain there until I bring you word; for Herod intends to search for the child, to destroy him." So Joseph arose and took the child and his mother, and departed to Egypt by night,[16] and remained there until the death of Herod. This was to fulfill what the Lord had spoken through the prophet, "Out of Egypt I called my son."

2. When Herod saw that he had been outwitted by the wise men he was filled with rage, and he sent out orders to kill all the male children in Bethlehem and the surrounding region who were two years old or under, in accordance with the time he had learned from the wise men. Thus the words spoken by the prophet Jeremiah were fulfilled:

> A voice was heard in Ramah,
> with wailing and loud lamentation,
> Rachel weeping for her children;
> and she would not be comforted,
> because they were no more.

---

14. Magi were priests of the Zoroastrian religion, which at the time was the dominant faith of Persia. Their name survives in our word "magician."

15. The magi would not have been able to reach Bethlehem until some time after the star first appeared. By this time Joseph and Mary had found more regular lodgings in a house.

16. This was a significant journey. From Bethlehem to the closest part of the Nile delta is about 225 miles.

16. RETURN TO NAZARETH
Matthew 2:19–23; Luke 2:39b

1. After Herod died, an angel of the Lord appeared in a dream to Joseph in Egypt, saying, "Rise, take the child and his mother, and go into the land of Israel, for those who sought the child's life are dead." And Joseph arose and took the child and his mother, and went to the land of Israel.

2. But when he heard that Archelaus was ruling over Judea in place of his father Herod, Joseph feared to go there.[17] Being warned in a dream, they returned *instead* to the district of Galilee, and settled in their own town of Nazareth, so that what was spoken by the prophets might be fulfilled, "He shall be called a Nazarene."

---

17. Like his father, Archelaus had a reputation for cruelty. See notes on Chapters 151 and 191.

The Baptism of Christ, by Gustave Dore
Photo: HIP / Art Resource, NY

II. YOUTH AND PREPARATION

17. THE YOUNG JESUS CONFERS WITH THE TEACHERS
Luke 2:40–50

1. The child Jesus grew and waxed strong in spirit, filled with wisdom; and the grace of God was upon him.

2. Now his parents went to Jerusalem every year for the feast of the Passover. When Jesus was twelve years old they *took him with them* when they went up, according to the custom of the feast; but after the celebration was over, and they were returning home, the boy Jesus stayed behind in Jerusalem. His parents did not know this, but supposing him to be in their traveling party they went a day's journey, and then they looked for him among their kinsfolk and acquaintances. When they did not find him, they returned to Jerusalem to search for him.

3. After three days they found him in the temple, sitting in the midst of the teachers, listening to them and asking them questions; and all who heard him were amazed at his understanding and his responses. When his parents saw him they were astonished; and his mother said to him, "Son, why have you treated us this way? Your father and I have been anxiously looking for you." And Jesus said to them, "Why did you need to search for me? Did you not know that I must be in my Father's house?"

4. But they did not understand the significance of these words.

18. JESUS GROWS TO MANHOOD
Luke 2:51–52

1. After that, Jesus went back down to Nazareth with his parents, and was obedient to them; but his mother stored away the memory of these events in her heart.

2. And Jesus increased in wisdom and in stature, and in favor with God and men.

19. JOHN THE BAPTIST GROWS TO MANHOOD
Matthew 3:4; Mark 1:6; Luke 1:80

1. John *also* grew and became strong in spirit.

2. *He went into the wilderness, and there* he wore a garment of camel's hair, and a leather belt around his waist; and his food was locusts and wild honey. And he was in the wilderness until the day he showed himself to Israel.

20. JOHN THE BAPTIST BEGINS TO PREACH
Matthew 3:1–3, 5–6; Mark 1:2–5; Luke 3:1–6; John 1:7–8

1. In the fifteenth year of the reign of Tiberius Caesar,[18] when Pontius Pilate was governor of Judea, and Herod *the younger*[19] was ruler of Galilee, and his brother Philip was ruler of the region of Ituraea and Trachonitis, and Lysanias was ruler of Abilene, during the high-priesthood of Annas and Caiaphas, the word of God came to John the son of Zechariah in the wilderness.

2. And so John the Baptist appeared, and he went through all the region around the river Jordan, preaching a baptism of repentance for the

---

18. The events of the gospels took place when the Roman Empire was at its height, and the entire Mediterranean basin was under one government and linked by good communications. These things would later help Jesus' disciples spread the new religion of Christianity.

19. Another son of King Herod the Great.

forgiveness of sins.[20] In the wilderness of Judea he preached, "Repent, for the kingdom of heaven is at hand."[21]

3. John came to bear testimony, to bear witness to the light, so that through him all might believe. He himself was not the light, but he came to testify about the light. For he was the one spoken of by the prophet Isaiah when he said,

> Behold, I will send my messenger ahead of you,
> who shall prepare thy way before thee,
> with a voice shouting in the wilderness:
> 'Prepare the way for the Lord,
> make his paths straight!
> Every valley shall be filled in,
> and every mountain and hill shall be brought low;
> the crooked roads shall be made straight,
> and the rough ways shall be made smooth;
> and all mankind shall see the salvation that God provides.'

4. And people went out to John from Jerusalem and all the country of Judea and all the region along the Jordan; and they were baptized by him in the river Jordan, confessing their sins.

2 I. JOHN DEMANDS TRUE REPENTANCE
Matthew 3:7–10; Luke 3:7–14

1. But when John saw many of the Pharisees and Sadducees[22] coming for baptism, he said to them, "O generation of vipers! Who warned

---

20. Or, in King James Version, "for the remission of sins."

21. We know little about the details of John's teaching. It appears from the descriptions here and in the next chapter that the "kingdom of heaven" was to be understood in two different senses. It had an inward element, as people became conscious of their own sins and learned to seek forgiveness. And it had an outward element, as God's demanding and rigorously just rule on earth became a more immediate prospect. We do not know enough to state the balance between these two elements. However, John's pointed references to "the wrath to come," in the next chapter, suggest that his views had a strong apocalyptic component. It appears that expectations of apocalypse and of a messiah's arrival were in the air at the time, as the Jewish people grew restive under Roman rule.*

22. These were the two principal sects or schools of religious thought in the country. The Pharisees served the needs of more rural Jews, and emphasized the close observance of the Law of Moses in the course of daily life. Their main rivals for influence were the Sadducees, a more cosmopolitan, more Greek-influenced group tied to the

you to flee from the wrath to come? Bear fruit in keeping with true repentance, and do not think it is enough to say to yourselves, 'We have Abraham as our father.' I tell you, God is able from these very stones to raise up more children to Abraham. Even now the ax is laid to the root of the trees; and every tree that does not bear good fruit will be cut down and cast into the fire."

2. The crowds asked him, "What then should we do?" And he answered them, "He who has two shirts, let him share with him who has none; and he who has food, let him do likewise."

3. Tax-gatherers—*collaborators and revenue agents for the Romans*[23]— also came to be baptized, and they asked him, "Teacher, what should we do?" And he said to them, "Collect no more than you are entitled to." Soldiers asked him, "And we, what should we do?" And he said to them, "Take no money by force or by false accusation, and be content with your wages."

22. JOHN ANNOUNCES THE COMING OF THE MESSIAH
Matthew 3:11–12; Mark 1:7–8; Luke 3:15–18; John 1:19–28

1. The people were filled with expectation and all were wondering in their hearts whether John might perhaps be the Messiah.[24]

---

elite of the country, who emphasized instead the formal worship in the central temple at Jerusalem. A third significant sect, the Essenes, were more withdrawn and monastic, and are not mentioned in the gospels.*

23. This is the sense of the Greek word *telones*. The word is commonly translated as "tax collector," but is rendered here as "tax gatherer." These people engaged in tax farming as well as simple collection of revenues. Tax farmers bid for the right to collect the Roman taxes in a certain area, with any successful excess exactions being their profits. Because *telones* were seen as economic opportunists and sympathizers with the occupying power, they were held in considerably more disrepute than an ordinary "tax collector" would be.*

24. Belief in the eventual coming of the Messiah is an essential tenet of Judaism. God had made a promise to King David that his dynasty and family line would rule forever; at some point a descendant of David must therefore return to Jerusalem to reinstate the kingship. This descendant was expected to be a strong and righteous ruler, probably clothed with special powers from God. When Jesus spoke of himself as coming "with great power and glory," see Chapter 173:18, he was within terms of messianic expectations. In other respects he was quite different, however. The Messiah was not expected to be divine himself, and he was certainly not expected to submit to arrest and execution.*

2. But when the Jews of Jerusalem sent priests and Levites to ask him, "Who are you?," this was John's response. He confessed—he did not deny, but confessed—"I am not the Messiah." And they asked him, "What then? Are you Elijah?"[25] He said, "I am not." "Are you the prophet?" And he answered, "No." So they said to him, "Then who are you? Let us have an answer for those who sent us. What do you say about yourself?"

3. He said, "I am the voice of one shouting in the wilderness, 'Make straight the path of the Lord,' as the prophet Isaiah said." Now those who had been sent were from the Pharisees, and they asked him, "Then why are you baptizing, if you are neither the Messiah, nor Elijah, nor the prophet?"

4. John answered all of them with these words: "I baptize you with water for repentance, but among you stands one whom you do not know. He who is coming after me is mightier than I, whose sandals I am not fit to carry, and the strap of whose sandals I am not worthy to stoop down and unloose. I have baptized you with water, but he will baptize you with the Holy Spirit and with fire. His winnowing fork is in his hand, and he will clear his threshing floor and gather the wheat into the barn, but the chaff he will burn up with unquenchable fire."

5. This took place in Bethany beyond the Jordan, where John was baptizing. And with many other words he exhorted the people and preached the good news to them.

23. THE BAPTISM OF JESUS
Matthew 3:13–17; Mark 1:9–11; Luke 3:21–22

1. At that time, when all the people were being baptized, Jesus came from Nazareth in Galilee to the Jordan, to also be baptized by John. John tried to dissuade him, saying, "I need to be baptized by you, and instead you are coming to me?" But Jesus answered him, "Permit it for now; for in this way we each carry out the work that God has given us to do."

2. Then John consented, and Jesus was baptized by John in the Jordan.

---

25. Elijah was a prophet in the 9th Century B.C. His return to earth was thought to be the surest sign of the impending arrival of the Messiah. In the final verses of the Old Testament, it is said that he will return "before the great and terrible day of the Lord comes." Malachi 4:5.*

3. And when Jesus came up out of the water, and was praying, straightaway he saw the heavens torn open and the Spirit of God descending in bodily form like a dove and alighting upon him. And a voice came from heaven, "Thou art my beloved Son; with thee I am well pleased." *And the voice spoke also to the crowd, saying,* "This is my beloved Son, with whom I am well pleased."[26]

24. JOHN DECLARES JESUS TO BE THE CHRIST
John 1:29–34

1. The next day John saw Jesus coming toward him, and said, "Behold, the Lamb of God,[27] who takes away the sin of the world. This is the one of whom I said, 'After me there comes a man who ranks before me, because he existed before me.' I did not recognize him *as the Messiah*; but it was for this that I came baptizing with water, so that he might be revealed to Israel."

2. And John declared, "I saw the Spirit descend from heaven like a dove, and it remained upon him. I would not have known who he was; but the one who sent me to baptize with water said to me, 'He upon whom you see the Spirit descend and remain, this is the one who will baptize with the Holy Spirit.' I have seen this, and I testify that this is the Son of God."

---

26. Mark and Luke report the words addressed to Jesus. Matthew reports the more public words addressed to the crowd.

27. In the Latin, "Agnus Dei." This is a reference to Jesus' future role as an offering for the benefit of humanity. Animal sacrifice was a prominent part of Jewish practice at the time. Lambs were sacrificed twice a day at the temple in Jerusalem, and on Yom Kippur two goats were sacrificed or driven into the wilderness to atone for the sins of the community. By his voluntary self-sacrifice on the cross, Jesus will take on some part of these roles, making further animal sacrifice unnecessary in Christianity. Judaism later abandoned the practice as well, after the Romans destroyed the temple that was the only proper site for the ceremonies.*

25. TEMPTATION IN THE WILDERNESS
Matthew 4:1–11; Mark 1:12–13; Luke 4:1–13

1. Jesus returned from the Jordan full of the Holy Spirit. The Spirit immediately sent him out into the wilderness. He was in the wilderness forty days and forty nights, and was tempted there by Satan; and he was among the wild beasts.

2. Jesus ate nothing in those days; and when they were ended, he was hungry. Then the tempter came and said to him, "If you are the Son of God, command these stones to become loaves of bread." But Jesus answered, "It is written, 'Man shall not live by bread alone, but by every word that proceeds from the mouth of God.'"

3. Then the devil took him to the holy city, and set him on the highest point of the temple. "If you are the Son of God, throw yourself down from here; for it is written, 'He will give his angels charge over thee, to protect thee,' and 'On their hands they will bear you up, lest you strike your foot against a stone.'" But Jesus said to him, "It is also written, 'Thou shalt not test the Lord thy God.'"

4. And then the devil took Jesus up onto a very high mountain, and showed him all the kingdoms of the world in a single glance, and the splendor of them; and he said to him, "To you I will give all the power and glory of these kingdoms, for it has been delivered to me, and I can give it to whom I will. Therefore if you will fall down and worship me, all this shall be yours." But Jesus said to him, "Get thee behind me, Satan! For it is written, 'Thou shalt worship the Lord thy God, and him only shall you serve.'"

5. And when the devil had finished every temptation, he departed to wait for another opportunity, and angels came and ministered to Jesus.

26. JESUS BEGINS HIS MINISTRY
Luke 3:23a; John 1:9–13

1. Jesus was about thirty years of age when he began his ministry.

2. *And so* the true light that enlightens every man had come into the world. He was in the world, and the world had been made through him, yet the world did not recognize him. He came to his own land, and his own people did not receive him. But to all who did receive

him, who believed in his name, he gave the right to become children of God—children who were born, not of blood, or of the will of the flesh, or of the will of man, but of God.

Christ and the Samaritan Woman (detail), by Henryk Siemiradzki
Lvov Picture Gallery

III. THE EARLY MINISTRIES

27. JESUS FINDS HIS FIRST DISCIPLES
John 1:35–42

1. *When Jesus returned from the wilderness,*[28] John the Baptist was standing with two of his disciples; and he looked at Jesus as he walked by, and said, "Behold, the Lamb of God!"

2. When the two disciples heard John say this, they followed after Jesus. Jesus turned, and saw them following him, and said to them, "What are you looking for?" And they said to him, "Rabbi"—which means Teacher—"where are you staying?" He said to them, "Come, and you will see." It was then about the tenth hour of the day.[29] So the disciples went and saw where Jesus was staying; and they remained with him that day.

3. Andrew, Simon Peter's brother, was one of the two who had heard what John said and followed Jesus.[30] *Afterwards* Andrew hurried to find his brother Simon and tell him, "We have found the Messiah"— which means the Christ. He brought Simon to Jesus. Jesus looked at

---

28. The gospel of John does not describe the temptation in the wilderness or say when it took place. Putting it here, and starting a new sequence of days with Jesus' return, will place the miracle of Cana on "the third day," as it is described in Chapter 29:1.

29. The usual timekeeping conventions in the eastern Mediterranean, including Judea, counted the hours from dawn. This would make the time here about four o'clock in the afternoon.

30. The other disciple is not named, but was probably John the Evangelist, who wrote this account. John generally refrains from mentioning himself by name.

him, and said, "So you are Simon the son of John? You shall be called
Cephas"—which, when translated, is Peter.[31]

28. JESUS FINDS TWO MORE DISCIPLES
John 1:43–51

1. The next day Jesus decided to leave for Galilee. He found Philip and
   said to him, "Follow me." Now Philip was from Bethsaida, the city of
   Andrew and Peter. Philip *in turn* found Nathaniel, and said to him,
   "We have found the one about whom Moses wrote in the law, and the
   prophets also wrote—Jesus of Nazareth, the son of Joseph."

2. Nathaniel said to him, "Can any good thing come out of Nazareth?"
   Philip replied, "Come and see."

3. Jesus saw Nathaniel coming toward him and said, "Behold, here is a
   true Israelite, in whom there is nothing false!" "Where do you know
   me from?," Nathaniel asked him. Jesus answered, "I saw you when you
   were under the fig tree, before Philip called you." And Nathaniel exclaimed, "Rabbi, you are the Son of God! You are the King of Israel!"[32]

4. Jesus said, "You believe just because I told you that I saw you under the
   fig tree? You will see greater things than that." And he said, "I tell you
   truly, you will see heaven opened, and the angels of God going up and
   coming down unto the Son of Man."[33]

29. THE FIRST MIRACLE: CHANGING WATER INTO WINE
John 2:1–11

1. On the third day there was a marriage at Cana in Galilee. The mother
   of Jesus was there; and Jesus and his disciples had also been invited
   to the wedding. When the wine ran short, Jesus' mother said to him,

---

31. The name Cephas is Hebrew, and Peter is Greek; both mean "Rock."

32. Nathaniel's reaction is surprisingly strong. Most probably he had taken some
private action under the fig tree, which confirmed his sound character, but left him
amazed that Jesus had been able to perceive it.

33. Jesus is saying, in other words, that he will serve as the bridge between the two
worlds of heaven and earth.

"They have no more wine." And Jesus said to her, "*Good* woman,[34] does that need to concern us now? My hour has not yet come." But his mother said to the servants, "Do whatever he tells you."

2. Standing nearby were six stone water jars, of the kind used for the Jewish customs of ceremonial washing, each holding from twenty to thirty gallons. Jesus said to the servants, "Fill the jars with water;" so they filled them up to the brim. Then he said to them, "Now draw some out, and take it to the steward of the feast;" and so they took it. The steward tasted the water, which had now become wine, and did not know where it came from, although the servants who had drawn the water knew. Then the steward called the bridegroom aside and said to him, "Everyone serves the good wine first, and afterwards, when the guests have drunk freely, the poorer wine; but you have kept the best wine until now."

3. This, the first of the miraculous signs that confirmed his mission,[35] Jesus did at Cana in Galilee. He thereby revealed his glory; and his disciples believed in him.

30. A FEW DAYS AT THE LAKESHORE
John 2:12

1. After this Jesus went down to the town of Capernaum, *on the shore of the Sea of Galilee,*[36] with his mother and his brothers and his disciples.

2. There they stayed for a few days.

---

34. Jesus addresses his mother literally as "Woman." This term has an abruptness in English that is not necessarily implied by the Greek, however. After his resurrection, Jesus addresses Mary Magdalene in the same way.

35. This phrase spells out the full implication of the single word *semeion*. For better readability, however, the word will usually be translated as simply "miracles" or "signs."

36. The Sea of Galilee is a freshwater lake in northern Israel, measuring about 8 by 13 miles. It is fed by the Jordan River, which enters at the north end, exits from the south, and from there flows to the Dead Sea.

31. READING HEARTS IN JERUSALEM
John 2:13, 23–25

1. Then the Passover feast of the Jews drew near, and Jesus went up to Jerusalem.[37] When he was there, many trusted in his name when they saw the miracles that he did.

2. But Jesus did not entrust himself to them; because he knew all men. He needed no one to bear testimony to him about mankind, for he himself knew what was in each man.

32. "YOU MUST BE BORN AGAIN"
John 3:1–21

1. *In Jerusalem* there was a man named Nicodemus, a Pharisee and a leader among the Jews. This man came to Jesus by night and said to him, "Rabbi, we know that you are a teacher sent from God; for no one could do these miracles that you do, unless God is with him."

2. Jesus answered him, "Verily, verily, I say unto you,[38] unless a man be born again, he cannot see the kingdom of God." Nicodemus said to him, "How can a man be born when he is old? Can he enter a second time into his mother's womb and be born?" Jesus answered, "I tell you truly, unless one is born of water and the Spirit, he cannot enter the kingdom of God. That which is born of the flesh is flesh, and that which is born of the Spirit is spirit. Do not marvel that I said to you, 'You must be born again.' The wind blows where it wills, and you can

---

37. The passage of John 2:14–22, which occurs at this point, describes Jesus' cleansing of the temple at Jerusalem. The other three gospels all describe this cleansing as taking place later, during Holy Week, the last week of Jesus' life. It is possible that the temple was cleansed on two separate occasions. It seems more likely, however, that it happened only once, late in Jesus' ministry, and that John was describing the event out of its chronological sequence. The actions seem best suited to someone who has an established following and sense of impending crisis. All of the descriptions are therefore collected later, in Chapter 158.*

38. This is the familiar phrase from the King James Version. "Verily, verily" is ultimately derived from the Hebrew religious expression, "amen, amen." The word "amen" means "certainly" or "so be it." The repetition of the word gives the speaker a way to highlight the importance of a particular statement. The doubled phrase is frequently used in the gospel of John. For contemporary ears, however, it will usually be translated here in the more idiomatic form, "I tell you truly."

hear the sound of it, but you cannot tell where it comes from or where it is going; so it is with every one who is born of the Spirit."[39]

3. Nicodemus said to him, "How can these things be?" Jesus answered him, "Are you a teacher of Israel, and yet you still do not understand these things? I tell you truly, we speak of what we actually know, and bear witness to what we have actually seen; but you people do not accept our testimony. If I have told you of earthly things and you do not believe, how can you believe if I tell you of heavenly things? No one has ever ascended into heaven except the one who came down from heaven, the Son of Man. And just as Moses lifted up the serpent in the wilderness, likewise must the Son of Man be lifted up, so that whoever believes in him may have eternal life."[40]

4. For God so loved the world that he gave his only begotten Son, that whosoever believes in him should not perish, but have everlasting life. God did not send his Son into the world to condemn the world, but so that through him the world might be saved. He who believes in the Son is not condemned; but he who does not believe is condemned already, because he has not believed in the name of the only begotten Son of God.

5. And this is the reason for the condemnation: The light has come into the world, but men have long loved darkness rather than light, because their deeds have been evil. Every one who does evil hates the light, and does not come to the light, lest his deeds should be exposed. But he who lives by the truth comes into the light, so that it may be clearly seen that his deeds have been wrought in God.

---

39. In other words, the effects of religious enlightenment on the individual are clear, even if we do not fully understand how the Spirit brings those effects about, any more than we understand the operation of the wind.

40. The phrase "Son of Man" occurs frequently in the Old Testament, with the general meaning of "human being" or "mortal." In the New Testament, Jesus changes the sense of this term and uses it to refer more specifically to himself. He sometimes juxtaposes it with the term "Son of God" so as to make clear his two natures, both fully human and also fully divine.

33. JOHN THE BAPTIST TRANSFERS LEADERSHIP
John 3:22-36

1. After this, Jesus and his disciples *left Jerusalem and* went into the countryside of Judea; and there he spent time with them and performed baptisms. John also was baptizing at Aenon near Salim, because there was ample water there. People *continued to* come to John and were baptized, for he had not yet been cast into prison.

2. Then a question arose between the disciples of John the Baptist and a certain observant Jew over a matter of ceremonial washing. So John's disciples went to him and said, "Rabbi, the man who was with you beyond the Jordan—the one of whom you testified—now he is performing baptisms himself, and everyone is going to him." John answered, "No one can receive anything unless it is given to him from heaven. You yourselves are my witnesses that I said, 'I am not the Christ, but I have been sent ahead of him.' The bride belongs to the bridegroom.[41] The friend of the bridegoom, who stands by and listens for him, is overjoyed to hear the bridegroom's voice. That joy is mine, and it is now complete. He must become greater; and I must become less."

3. He who comes from above is above all. He who is of the earth belongs to the earth, and of the earth he speaks. But he who comes from heaven is above all else. He bears witness to what he has seen and heard, yet so few accept his testimony. But the one who does accept it affirms that God is truthful. He whom God has sent speaks the words of God, for God gives the Spirit without limit. The Father loves the Son, and has given all things into his hand. He who believes in the Son has everlasting life; and he who rejects the Son shall not see life, but the wrath of God shall rest upon him.

34. JOHN THE BAPTIST SCOLDS HEROD
Matthew 14:3-5; Mark 6:17-20; Luke 3:19-20

1. *Soon afterwards* John the Baptist reproved Herod the tetrarch[42] for marrying Herodias, his brother Philip's wife. John said to him, "It is

---

41. And, by analogy, the church belongs to Jesus.*
42. This is Herod Antipas, the ruler of Galilee. He was one of the children of King

not lawful for you to have thy brother's wife."[43] He also rebuked Herod for all the other evil things that he had done.

2. *For this, Herod's wife* Herodias bore a grudge against John, and wanted to see him dead. But she could not act, for Herod was in awe of John, knowing that he was a righteous and holy man, and he kept him safe. When Herod heard John speak he was greatly troubled in his mind, and yet he enjoyed listening to him. *Moreover, even when* Herod wanted to put John to death,[44] he feared the people, because they held John to be a prophet.

3. But to his other sins Herod now added this above all: he sent men who seized John, bound him, and shut him up in prison.

35. THE DECISION TO RETURN TO GALILEE
Matthew 4:12; Mark 1:14a; John 4:1–3

1. *Soon afterwards* Jesus heard that John had been arrested. And he learned that the Pharisees had become aware that he was making and baptizing more disciples than John—even though the fact was that Jesus himself did not baptize, but only his disciples.

2. When the Lord learned of these things, he left Judea and set out back to Galilee.[45]

Herod the Great, the man who had ordered the Massacre of the Innocents when Jesus was an infant. At the older Herod's death, three of his sons divided up the kingdom, each receiving what was conventionally although imprecisely referred to as a quarter-share or a "tetrarchy." Jesus' home province of Galilee was the principal part of the younger Herod's share.

43. This marriage grew out of a visit that Herod Antipas had made to his half-brother Philip, sometimes also known as Herod Philip or Herod II, while he was on a trip to Rome. Along the way he met and began a liaison with Philip's wife Herodias. The two subsequently divorced their original spouses and married each other. John the Baptist would have been offended not only by the termination of the first marriages, with the expedient and revocable concept of matrimony that this implied, but also by the close family ties that complicated the subsequent match.*

44. Mark describes Herod as sympathetic to John the Baptist, while Matthew reports that Herod "wanted to put him to death." The passage in italics balances those two reports. The two contradictory emotions might well coexist in an absolute monarch like Herod. He admired the sanctity of John, but was also angered by any person who felt free to speak his mind.*

45. Galilee is about 60 miles north of Jerusalem.

36. THE WOMAN AT THE WELL
John 4:4–44

1. *To get there* he had to pass through Samaria.[46] And so he came to a town in Samaria called Sychar, near the piece of land that Jacob gave to his son Joseph.[47] Jacob's well was there, and Jesus, tired from the long journey, sat down beside the well. It was about midday.

2. Then a woman of Samaria came to draw water. Jesus asked of her, "Give me something to drink." *He was alone at the time because* his disciples had gone into the city to buy food. The Samaritan woman said to him, "How is it that you, a Jew, ask for a drink from me, a woman of Samaria?" For Jews have no dealings with Samaritans.

3. Jesus answered her, "If you only knew the gift that God puts before you, and who it is that is saying to you, 'Give me a drink,' you would be asking him for the drink, and he would give you living water." The woman said to him, "But Sir, you have nothing to draw water with, and the well is deep; where would you get that living water? Are you greater than our father Jacob, who gave us this well, and drank from it himself, as did his sons and his cattle?"

4. Jesus said to her, "Every one who drinks of this water will become thirsty again, but whoever drinks of the water that I shall give him will never thirst; the water that I give will become a spring of water welling up within him and bringing eternal life." The woman said to him, "Sir, give me this water, so that I may not thirst, nor have to keep coming here to draw water."

5. Jesus said to her, "Go, call your husband, and come back." The woman answered him, "I have no husband." Jesus said to her, "You are right when you say, 'I have no husband.' You have had five husbands, and the man you now have is not your husband; this you said truly."

---

46. Samaria was a culturally distinct territory on the west bank of the Jordan, between Judea and Galilee. The Samaritans were related to the Israelites both ethnically and in their religion. They practiced a variant, perhaps older form of Judaism, however, and were not recognized by their neighbors as authentically Jewish. Relations between the two communities were strained.*

47. Jacob was the grandson of Abraham and one of the early patriarchs of Judaism. One night he wrestled with an angel until daybreak, and for this perseverance the angel gave him the new name of Israel, which probably means, "Contended with God." Jacob's twelve sons were the ancestors of the twelve tribes of Israel. Joseph was the favorite of these sons.*

6. The woman said to him, "Sir, I can see that you are a prophet. *So explain to me:* Our fathers worshiped on this mountain; why then do your people say that Jerusalem is the place where men ought to worship?"

7. Jesus said to her, "Woman, believe me, the hour is coming when you will worship the Father neither on this mountain nor in Jerusalem. You Samaritans worship what you do not know; we worship what we do know, for salvation is from the Jews. But a time is coming, and indeed is already here, when the true worshipers will worship the Father in spirit and truth, for these are the kind of worshipers the Father desires. God is spirit, and those who worship him must worship in spirit and in truth."

8. The woman said to him, "I know that the Messiah is coming—he who is called the Christ—and when he comes, he will explain all things to us." Jesus said to her, "I who speak to you am he."

9. Just then his disciples came back. They were surprised that he was talking with a woman, but none of them asked, "What do you want with her?" or, "Why are you talking with her?"

10. So the woman left her water jar, and went away into the town, and said to the people, "Come, see a man who told me all that I ever did. Can this be the Christ?" So they went out of the town and headed toward him.

11. Meanwhile his disciples were pleading with him, saying, "Rabbi, eat something." But he said to them, "I have food to eat that you know nothing of." So the disciples said to one another, "Has someone brought him food?" Jesus said to them, "My food is to do the will of him who sent me, and to finish his work.

12. "Do you not say, 'One must wait four months for the harvest'? But I tell you, lift up your eyes, and see how the fields are already ripe for harvest. Even now the reaper draws his wages, even now he harvests the crop for eternal life, so that the sower and the reaper may rejoice together. For here the saying is true, 'One sows and another reaps.' I have sent you to harvest a crop that you did not work for; others have labored, and now you can reap the benefits of their labor."[48]

13. Many Samaritans from that town believed in Jesus because of the woman's testimony, "He told me all that I ever did." So when the Samaritans came to him, they asked him to stay with them; and he stayed

---

48. In other words, earlier teachers, prophets, and John the Baptist all have prepared the ground for the disciples' ministry.

there two days. And many more came to believe because of his own words. They said to the woman, "It is no longer just because of your report that we believe, for now we have heard him ourselves, and we know that this is indeed the savior of the world."

14. After the two days Jesus departed to Galilee. *But he did not return directly to his childhood home in Nazareth,* for he himself had remarked that a prophet is not honored in his own town.

Mountain of the Beatitudes, traditional site of the Sermon on the Mount
Photo: Erich Lessing / Art Resource NY

IV. THE GALILEE
MINISTRY

Teaching and Healing

37. JESUS ARRIVES IN GALILEE
Luke 4:14–15; John 4:45

1. When Jesus returned to Galilee filled with the power of the Spirit, the Galileans made him welcome. They had seen all the things he had done in Jerusalem at the Passover feast, for they too had been there.

2. Reports about him went out through all the countryside. And he began to teach in the synagogues, and was praised by everyone.

38. HEALING AN OFFICIAL'S SON
John 4:46–54

1. One day Jesus went again to Cana in Galilee, where he had turned the water into wine. Now at that time there was a certain royal official whose son lay sick at *the lakeshore in* Capernaum. When this man heard that Jesus had arrived in Galilee from Judea, he went and begged him to come down and heal his son, for the boy was at the point of death.

2. Jesus said to him, "Unless you people see signs and miracles you will never believe." The official pleaded, "Sir, come down before my child

dies." Jesus said to him, "Go home, your son will live." The man believed this word that Jesus spoke to him and started on his way.

3. As he was going down *to Capernaum*, his servants met him and reported that his son was going to live. So he asked them the time when his son had begun to recover, and they said to him, "Yesterday at the seventh hour the fever left him." Then the father realized that this was the time when Jesus had said to him, "Your son will live." So he and all his household became believers.

4. This was the second miracle that Jesus performed, after coming from Judea to Galilee.

39. REJECTION AT NAZARETH
Luke 4:16–30

1. Later Jesus went to Nazareth, where he had been brought up, and he went to the synagogue, according to his custom, on the sabbath. He stood up to read; and the book of the prophet Isaiah was handed to him. He unrolled the scroll, and found the place where it was written,

> The Spirit of the Lord is upon me,
> for he has anointed me to preach the good news to the poor.
> He has sent me to heal the brokenhearted,
> to proclaim deliverance to the captives
> and recovery of sight to the blind,
> to set at liberty those who are oppressed,
> and to proclaim the year of the Lord's mercy.

And he rolled up the scroll, and gave it back to the attendant, and sat down; and the eyes of all in the synagogue were fixed on him.

2. Then he began to speak to them. "Today this scripture has been fulfilled by what you just heard me say." And all spoke well of him, and were amazed by the gracious words that came from his lips.

3. *But then they began to have doubts.* "Is this not Joseph's son?" they asked. And he said to them, "Doubtless you will quote to me this proverb, 'Physician, heal thyself!' And you will say, 'What we have heard you did at Capernaum, do the same things here in your own town.'" And he continued, "I tell you truly, no prophet is accepted in his own town. For I assure you, there were many *needy* widows in Israel in the days of *the prophet* Elijah, when no rain fell for three years and six

months, and a great famine came over all the land; yet Elijah was sent to none of those but only to a *foreign* widow at Zarephath in the land of Sidon. And there were many lepers in Israel in the time of the prophet Elisha; yet none of them was cleansed, but only Naaman the Syrian."

4. When they heard this, all the people in the synagogue were filled with fury.[49] They rose up and drove Jesus out of the city, and brought him to the brow of the hill on which their town was built, so that they might throw him down the cliff. But he passed through the midst of the crowd and went on his way.

40. STARTING THE MINISTRY IN CAPERNAUM
Matthew 4:13–17; Mark 1:14b–15

1. Leaving Nazareth, Jesus went and made his home in the town of Capernaum,[50] in Galilee, which was by the lake in the territory of Zebulun and Naphtali, so that what had been spoken by the prophet Isaiah might be fulfilled:

> In the land of Zebulun and the land of Naphtali—
> on the road to the sea, across the Jordan,
> in Galilee where so many foreigners live[51]—
> the people who lived in darkness
> have seen a great light;
> and for those who dwelt in the land and the shadow of death
> a light has dawned.

---

49. There were several reasons for the townspeople's fury. Jesus had suggested that they lacked the spiritual understanding to recognize a prophet in the first place. Moreover, he suggested that a true prophet's business might lie, not necessarily with his own people, but perhaps with people in the wider world of the Gentiles.*

50. Capernaum would become the base for Jesus' ministry. It was a fishing and trading town on the northwest shore of the Sea of Galilee, with a population in biblical times of about 1500. It was a larger and more cosmopolitan place than Nazareth, 25 miles away, which was relatively isolated and had a population of only about 450.

51. Literally, "Galilee of the Gentiles." Galilee was at the far northern end of the Jewish lands, and was not firmly or consistently under Jewish control. On occasion it was invaded and settled by other peoples. At the time of Jesus its population may have been predominately non-Jewish.*

2. From that time on, Jesus began preaching the good news of God, and saying, "The time has come, and the kingdom of heaven is close at hand; repent,[52] and believe in the gospel."[53]

41. THE GREAT CATCH OF FISH
Luke 5:1–10a, 11a

1. One day Jesus was standing by the Sea of Galilee, and the people were pressing hard about him to hear the word of God. Then he saw two boats lying at the water's edge. But the fishermen had gone out of them and were washing their nets.

2. Getting into one of the boats, which was Simon *Peter's*, Jesus asked him to push off a little way from the shore. Then he sat down and taught the people from the boat. When he had finished speaking, he said to Simon, "Put out into deep water and let down your nets for a catch." Simon answered, "Master, we toiled all night and caught nothing! But at your word I will let down the nets." And when they had done this, they enclosed such a great quantity of fish that their nets began to break. So they signaled to their partners in the other boat, James and John, the sons of Zebedee, to come and help them. And the partners came and filled up both the boats, so that they began to sink.

3. When Simon Peter saw this he fell down at Jesus' knees, saying, "Depart from me, Lord, for I am a sinful man." For he was astonished, as were all that were with him, at the number of fish they had taken. But Jesus said to Simon, "Do not be afraid," and they brought their boats to land.

---

52. Repentance was one of the central themes of Jesus' ministry. The concept is, however, more thoroughgoing than mere remorse for wrongdoing. The underlying Greek word is *metanoia*, which literally means a "change of mind" or "change of heart," and implies adopting a whole new way of thinking and behaving.

53. "Gospel" refers to the entire message of Jesus, which laid out a way of healing man's relationship with God. The word used in the Greek is *euangelion*, or, in Latinized form, *evangelion*, which means "good news." When translated into Old English, the phrase "good news" became "good speech" or "godspel." Our present word "gospel" is derived from that.

42. FISHERS OF MEN
Matthew 4:18–22; Mark 1:16–20; Luke 5:10b, 11b

1. *Later*, as Jesus was walking by the Sea of Galilee, he *again* saw the two brothers, Simon, who is called Peter, and Andrew, casting a net into the sea, for they were fishermen. And Jesus said to them, "Come, follow me, and I will make you fishers of men." At once they left their nets and followed him.

2. Continuing a little farther, Jesus saw the two other brothers, James the son of Zebedee and John his brother, in a boat with their father, mending their nets. And he called them, and immediately they left their father Zebedee in the boat with the hired men, left everything, and followed him.

43. HEALING THE SICK AND POSSESSED
Matthew 8:14–17; Mark 1:21–34; Luke 4:31–41

1. They went back into Capernaum; and on the next sabbath Jesus entered the synagogue and began to teach. The people were astonished at his teaching, for he taught them as one who had real authority, and not as the scribes.

2. In the synagogue there was a man who was possessed by a demon, an unclean spirit; and he suddenly cried out with a loud voice, "Let us alone! What business do you have with us, Jesus of Nazareth? Have you come to destroy us? I know who you are—the Holy One of God." But Jesus rebuked him, saying, "Hold thy peace, and come out of him." And when the demon had thrown the man down before them all, convulsing him and giving a loud scream, he came out of the man, without having done him any harm.

3. The people were all amazed, so that they asked each other, "What is this? A new teaching! With real authority he commands even the unclean spirits, and they obey him and depart." And at once news about Jesus began to spread through all the region of Galilee.

4. After they left the synagogue they went to the house of Simon Peter and Andrew, and James and John accompanied them. Now Simon Peter's mother-in-law[54] was lying sick with a high fever, and so they

---

54. This is the only reference in the gospels to a marriage involving the apostles. However, another passage, later in the New Testament, suggests that many or most

immediately told Jesus about her and asked him to help her. Jesus came and stood over her, rebuked the fever, took her by the hand, and helped her up. The fever left her, and at once she rose and served them.

5. That evening, after sundown,[55] the people brought to him all who were sick with various diseases or possessed by demons. The whole town was gathered about the door. Jesus laid his hands on every one of the invalids and healed them. He cast out the spirits with a word, and demons came out of many, crying, "You are the Son of God!" But he rebuked the demons, and would not permit them to speak, because they knew that he was the Christ.

6. This was to fulfill what had been spoken by the prophet Isaiah, "He took up our infirmities and bore our diseases."

44. THE MISSION TO OTHER TOWNS
Matthew 4:23–25; Mark 1:35–39; Luke 4:42–44

1. Very early in the morning, while it was still dark, Jesus rose and went out to a secluded place, and there he prayed.

2. Later Simon and his companions went to look for him, and when they found him they said to him, "Every one is searching for you." And the people came to Jesus, and would have prevented him from leaving them; but he said to them, "I must preach the good news of the kingdom of God to the other cities also; because that is why I was sent. So let us go on to the next towns."

3. Then he went throughout all Galilee, teaching in the synagogues and proclaiming the gospel of the kingdom and healing every kind of disease and infirmity among the people, and casting out demons.

4. So his fame spread through all Syria, and the people brought him all the sick, those suffering from various diseases and pains, the demon-possessed, epileptics, and the paralyzed; and he healed them. And

---

of the people around Jesus were married. There Paul asks, "Have we not the right to take a believing wife along with us, as do the other apostles, and the Lord's brothers, and Peter?"*

55. The timing here is significant. The Jewish sabbath ended at sunset, so Jesus and the people could then perform the work of healing without risk of violating the day of rest. This will become a point of dispute in later healings.

great crowds followed him—people from Galilee and the Decapolis[56] and Jerusalem and Judea, and from the lands beyond the Jordan.

45. CLEANSING A LEPER
Matthew 8:2–4; Mark 1:40–45; Luke 5:12–16

1. While Jesus was in one of the towns, a man full of leprosy came up; and when he saw Jesus he fell to his knees and begged him, "Lord, if you are willing, you can make me clean."

2. And being moved with compassion, Jesus stretched out his hand and touched him, and said to him, "I am willing; be clean." Immediately the leprosy left the man, and he was clean.

3. Jesus sent him away at once with a stern warning: "See that you say nothing to any one; but go, show yourself to the priest, and give for your cleansing the offering that Moses commanded, as a testimony that you are cured."[57]

4. But the man went out and began to talk freely about it, and to spread the news, so that the report about Jesus went abroad all the more; and great crowds gathered from every quarter to hear him and to be healed of their infirmities.

5. After that, Jesus could no longer openly enter a town. So he would withdraw to the wilderness and pray.

46. THE MAN ON THE PALLET AND A CHARGE OF BLASPHEMY
Matthew 9:1–8; Mark 2:1–12; Luke 5:17–26

1. After some days Jesus got into a boat, crossed over *the lake*, and came to his own town of Capernaum. The people heard that he had come home, and so many gathered that there was no room left, not even

---

56. A loose confederation of ten Greek and Roman cities, most of them clustered in an area about 30 miles across, east of the Jordan and south of the Sea of Galilee. Amman, Jordan, is the best-known of these cities today.

57. Literally, "for a testimony to them." This demonstration would have been significant for Jesus and his mission, as well as for the healed man, because the power to heal leprosy was one mark of divine agency.*

outside the door. Jesus was preaching the word to them; and the power of the Lord was with him to heal.

2. There were also scribes, Pharisees, and teachers of religious law sitting by, who had come from every town in Galilee, and from Judea and Jerusalem.

3. And some men came, bringing a paralyzed man to Jesus on a pallet carried by four of them. They sought to bring the man in and lay him before Jesus, but finding no way to get in, because of the crowd, they went up and removed part of the roof above Jesus. And when they had made an opening through the tiles, they let down the pallet on which the paralyzed man lay, into the midst of the crowd before him.

4. When Jesus saw their faith he said to the paralyzed man, "Take heart, son; your sins are forgiven." But some of the scribes and Pharisees sitting there began to question this, saying to themselves, "Who is this man, and why does he speak this way? It is blasphemy! Who can forgive sins but God alone?"

5. And immediately Jesus, perceiving in his spirit that this is what they were thinking within themselves, said to them, "Why do you have evil thoughts in your hearts? Which is easier, to say to the paralyzed man, 'Your sins are forgiven;' or to say, 'Arise, and take up your pallet, and walk'? But so that you may know that the Son of Man has authority on earth to forgive sins . . . ." And he said to the paralytic, "I say to you, arise, and take up your pallet, and go home." Immediately the man stood up before them all, took up that which he had been lying on, and went home praising God.

6. When the crowds saw this, they were amazed and filled with awe, and they glorified God who had given such authority to men, saying, "We have seen astonishing things today. We have never seen anything like this!"

47. MATTHEW BECOMES A DISCIPLE
Matthew 9:9; Mark 2:13–14; Luke 5:27–28

1. Then Jesus went out again beside the sea, and all the crowd gathered around him, and he taught them.

2. After this, as he continued on his way, he saw a tax-gatherer named Matthew Levi[58] the son of Alphaeus sitting at the tollhouse, and he said to him, "Follow me." And Matthew rose, left everything, and followed him.

48. JESUS' MISSION IS TO SINNERS
Matthew 9:10–13; Mark 2:15–17; Luke 5:29–32

1. Later Matthew Levi held a great banquet for Jesus at his house, and many collaborating tax-gatherers and other sinners came and sat with Jesus and his disciples; for there were many such among his followers. And when the Pharisees and the scribes[59] who belonged to their sect saw this, they complained to his disciples, asking, "Why does your master eat and drink with tax-gatherers and sinners?"

2. When Jesus heard this he answered them, "It is not the healthy who need a doctor, but the sick. Go and learn what this *scripture* means, 'I desire mercy, and not sacrifices.' For I have not come to call the righteous, but sinners to repentance."

49. LESS NEED FOR RITUAL FASTING
Matthew 9:14–17; Mark 2:18–22; Luke 5:33–39

1. One day the Pharisees and the disciples of John the Baptist were fasting, and John's disciples came to Jesus and asked, "Why do we and the disciples of the Pharisees often fast and pray, but your disciples continue to eat and drink?"

2. And Jesus said to them, "Can you make wedding guests mourn while the bridegroom is with them? As long as they have the bridegroom

---

58. Matthew reports that the tax-gatherer was named Matthew, while Mark and Luke give his name as Levi. The other details of the accounts are so similar that these were presumably two names of the same person.*

59. The two groups of the scribes and Pharisees represented the local-level religious establishment of rural Israel. The scribes were literate and educated members of the community who carried out a variety of quasi-legal functions, often guided by and applying religious law, that today would be entrusted to recorders, lawyers, and judges. The Pharisees were the school of local, often populist religious leaders who emphasized strict observance of the laws of Moses.*

with them, they cannot mourn. But the time will come when the bridegoom is taken away from them, and then they shall fast."

3. He also told them a parable: "No one tears a patch of unshrunk cloth from a new garment and sews it upon an old garment. If he does, he will have torn the new garment, and the new piece will pull away from the old garment, and a worse tear will be made. And the piece from the new garment will not match the old.[60]

4. "And no one puts new wine into old bottles or old wineskins. If he does, the new wine will burst the wineskins and the wine will spill out, and the wineskins will be ruined. New wine must be put into new wineskins, and then both are preserved. But no one who has become accustomed to drinking old wine immediately desires the new, for he says, 'The old is perfectly good.'"[61]

50. THE POOL OF BETHESDA
John 5:1–18

1. After this there came a festival day of the Jews, and Jesus went up to Jerusalem.[62]

2. Now in Jerusalem near the Sheep Gate there is a pool, which in Hebrew[63] is called Bethesda, and around which there are five covered porticos. In these lay a multitude of invalids—the blind, the lame, and the paralyzed—and they waited for the moving of the waters. For from time to time an angel would go down into the pool and stir up the water. Whoever stepped first into the pool after each such troubling of the waters would be cured of whatever disease he had.

---

60. And so, by analogy, the new doctrines of Jesus do not fit with the old doctrines of the Pharisees.

61. Literally, "And no one after drinking old wine desires the new, for he says, 'The old is serviceable.'" The point is that people who have grown up with the old doctrines will be slow to turn from them to new ones.

62. The identity of this festival is not specified. If it was a Passover, then four separate Passover celebrations will have been mentioned in the gospels, and Jesus' ministry would have lasted about three and a half years. If this was not a Passover, then the ministry was a year shorter.

63. In today's vocabulary this language would be identified more precisely as Aramaic—a related language that had come into increasing use, and was the common language among Jews at the time of Jesus.

3. One man there had been an invalid for thirty-eight years. When Jesus saw him lying there and learned that he had been ill for a long time, he said to him, "Would you like to get well?" The sick man answered him, "Sir, I have no one to put me into the pool when the water is troubled, and while I am trying to get there another steps in before me." Jesus said to him, "Stand up, take up your pallet, and walk." At once the man was healed, and took up his pallet and walked.

4. But that day was the sabbath. So the religious leaders among the Jews said to the man who had been cured, "It is the sabbath; it is not lawful for you to carry your pallet this day." But he answered them, "The man who made me well said to me, 'Take up your pallet, and walk.'" They asked him, "Who is this person who told you to take it up and walk?" But the man who had been healed did not know who it had been, for Jesus had slipped away into the crowd there.

5. Afterward, Jesus found him in the temple, and said to him, "See, you are well again! Sin no more, so that nothing worse may come upon you." The man went away and told the authorities that it was Jesus who had healed him. Therefore they began to persecute Jesus, because he did these things on the sabbath.

6. But Jesus answered them, "My Father is always at work, even until this very day, and I too am working." And this was why the Jewish leaders sought all the more to find a way to destroy him, because he not only broke the sabbath but also called God his father, making himself equal with God.

5 I. THE SON OF GOD
John 5:19–47

1. Jesus explained to the temple leaders, "I tell you truly, the Son can do nothing by himself, but does only what he sees the Father doing; because whatever the Father does the Son also does. For the Father loves the Son, and shows him all that he himself is doing; and he will show the Son even greater works to do than this, so that you will be astonished. For just as the Father raises the dead and gives them life, so also the Son gives life to whomever he chooses.

2. "The Father judges no one, but has entrusted all judgment to the Son, so that all may honor the Son, even as they honor the Father. Whoever

does not honor the Son does not honor the Father who sent him. I tell you truly, whoever hears my word and believes in him who sent me, he has everlasting life and will not be condemned; he has crossed over from death to life. I tell you truly, the hour is coming, and has now arrived, when the dead will hear the voice of the Son of God, and those who respond to it will live. For just as the Father has life in himself, so too he has granted the Son to have life in himself; and has also given him authority to pass judgment, because he is the Son of Man.[64] Do not marvel at this; for the hour is coming when all who are in the graves will hear his voice and come forth—those who have done good, to the resurrection of life; and those who have done evil, to the resurrection of damnation. By myself I can do nothing. As I hear *my Father*, I judge; and my judgment is just, because I seek to follow not my own will, but the will of him who sent me.

3. "If I were to testify about myself, my testimony would not be sufficient. But there is another who testifies about me, and I know that his testimony about me is true.

4. "You sent to John the Baptist, and he has borne witness to the truth. Now, I do not depend on human testimony; but I speak of this so that you may be saved. John was a burning and shining lamp, and for a little while you were willing to rejoice in his light.

5. "But the testimony supporting me is greater than that of John. The works which the Father has given me to accomplish, the very works that I am doing, bear witness that the Father has sent me. And the Father who sent me has himself testified about me. His voice you have never heard, his form you have never seen; and you do not have his word abiding in you, for you do not believe the one whom he has sent. You diligently study the scriptures, because you think that through them you will have eternal life. These are the very scriptures that testify about me, and yet you will not come to me to have life.

6. "I do not need praise from men. But I know you. I know that you do not have the love of God within you. I have come in my Father's name, and you do not accept me; but if another comes in his own name, him you will accept. How can you believe, when you accept honors from one another, yet make no effort to obtain the honor that comes from the only God?

---

64. Jesus' human nature as the Son of Man is particularly germane here, because his humanity makes him an appropriate judge of humans.*

7. "Do not think that I will be the one to accuse you before the Father. The one who accuses you is Moses, in whom you place your hope. If you believed Moses, you would believe me, for he wrote about me. But if you do not believe his writings, how will you believe my words?"

52. FOLLOWERS FROM MANY LANDS
Matthew 12:15–21; Mark 3:7–12; Luke 6:17b

1. Aware of *the hostility of the Jerusalem leadership*, Jesus and his disciples withdrew from there to the Sea of Galilee, and a great multitude from Galilee followed, and he healed all their sick. When they heard all that he was doing, many people also came to Jesus from all Judea and Jerusalem and Idumea, and from beyond the Jordan and from the seacoast of Tyre and Sidon.

2. And because of the crowd he told his disciples to have a boat ready for him, lest the people should crush him; for he had healed many, and now all who had diseases pressed upon him to touch him. And whenever the unclean spirits beheld Jesus, they fell down before him and cried out, "You are the Son of God."

3. But he gave strict orders to the spirits and to the crowds not to tell who he was. This was to fulfill what had been spoken by the prophet Isaiah:

> Behold my servant whom I have chosen,
> the one I love, with whom my soul is pleased;
> I will put my Spirit upon him,
> and he will proclaim justice to the Gentiles.
> He will not quarrel or cry out;
> no one will hear him shouting in the streets.
> A bruised reed he will not break,
> and a smoldering wick he will not snuff out,
> until he has led justice to victory.
> And in his name all the nations shall put their hope.

53. CALLING THE TWELVE APOSTLES
Matthew 10:1–4; Mark 3:13–19a; Luke 6:12–16

1. One day Jesus went up on a mountain to pray; and all night he continued in prayer to God. When morning came, he called his disciples, and they came to him, and he chose from them twelve whom he desired, whom he named apostles.[65] They were to accompany him, and to be sent out to proclaim the message. He gave them authority to cast out demons, and to heal all manner of disease and infirmity.

2. The names of the twelve apostles are these: first, Simon, who is called Peter; and Andrew his brother; James the son of Zebedee, and John his brother, to whom he gave the name of Boanerges, that is, the sons of thunder; Philip and Bartholomew; Thomas and Matthew the tax-gatherer; James the son of Alphaeus; Judas Thaddeus[66] from the family of James;[67] Simon who was called the Zealot;[68] and Judas Iscariot, who betrayed him.

---

65. The word "apostle" is based on a Greek word meaning "to send forth," and it denotes an ambassador or representative. Jesus selected the twelve apostles from among the larger number of his disciples or followers, as the ones he thought could most effectively carry his message.

66. The gospels agree on the names of eleven of the disciples. For the twelfth, however, Matthew and Mark give the name of Thaddeus, while Luke gives the name Judas. The reports can be reconciled on the assumption that these were the given name and the family name of the same individual.*

67. Luke identifies Judas simply as being "of James," a phrase that does not specify the exact nature of the relationship. Different translations have interpreted it to mean either "son" or "brother."

68. It is not clear whether this nickname was due to a general quality of commitment on Simon's part, or to membership in a more specific organized group. A sect called the Zealots became prominent about a generation later, devoted to driving the Romans out of Judea and restoring self-rule. The ruthlessness of the group's methods eventually gave it a bad name. The Zealots prolonged the six-month Roman siege of Jerusalem in A.D. 70 by killing those who advocated a negotiated surrender; and they are thought to have contributed to the disappearance of the cosmopolitan priestly class of the Sadducees by assassinating many of its members during the siege.*

54. PREPARATIONS FOR THE GREAT SERMON
Matthew 5:1–2; Luke 6:17a, 17c–20a

1. Jesus then came down with the apostles and stood on a level place, surrounded by a crowd of his disciples and a great multitude of people from *many lands*, who came to hear him and to be healed of their diseases. Those who were troubled by evil spirits were cured; and all the crowd sought to touch him, for power radiated out from him and healed them all.

2. Seeing the crowds, Jesus went up on the mountainside and sat down, and his disciples gathered around him. Then he lifted up his eyes to his disciples, and opened his mouth and taught them, *and his voice also carried to the crowd below.*[69]

55. THE SERMON ON THE MOUNT
Matthew 5:3—7:29; Luke 6:20b–38, 6:41—7:1a, 11:2b–4,
33–36; 12:22–30, 58–59

The Beatitudes

1. "Blessed are the poor and modest, for theirs is the kingdom of heaven.[70] Blessed are they that mourn, for they shall be comforted. Blessed are the meek, for they shall inherit the earth.

---

69. Before delivering this sermon Jesus first visits two different locations, first "on a level place" and later "up on the mountainside." These two places are separately described in Luke and Matthew respectively. Because the settings at first appear so different, some have thought that two different events are described, sometimes designated as "The Sermon on the Plain" and "The Sermon on the Mount" respectively. The actual contents of the sermons in Luke and Matthew are so similar, however, that the better interpretation seems to be that they were a single address. The different settings do not rule this out. Jesus could easily have started on the level ground at the foot of a hill, and then moved up the slope to get more private space to be with his disciples, and also a better vantage point from which to address the crowd that remained below. That he stayed in touch with the crowd is clear. The gospel of Matthew, which reports that he moved to the mountain, also reports at the end of the sermon that "the crowds were astonished at his teaching."

70. There is some variation between Matthew and Luke. Luke quotes Jesus as addressing his audience directly, "Blessed are you poor," while Matthew is traditionally translated as beginning the sermon more abstractly with, "Blessed are the poor in spirit . . . ." The phrase "poor in spirit" does not imply passivity or a lack of vital force. It instead implies humility and a wise awareness of one's shortcomings.*

Blessed are they that hunger and thirst after righteousness, for they
   shall be satisfied.
Blessed are the merciful, for they shall obtain mercy.
Blessed are the pure in heart, for they shall see God.
Blessed are the peacemakers, for they shall be called the children of
   God.
Blessed are those who are persecuted for righteousness' sake,
   for theirs is the kingdom of heaven.
Blessed are you that hunger now, for you shall be filled.
Blessed are you that weep now, for you shall laugh.
Blessed are you when men hate you, and when they exclude you and
   revile you, and falsely say all manner of evil against you for my
   sake. Rejoice in that day, and leap for joy, for behold, your reward
   in heaven is great; for so their fathers persecuted the prophets who
   were before you.

The task of the righteous

2. "You are the salt of the earth. But if the salt has lost its savor, how can
   it be made salty again? It is no longer good for anything except to be
   thrown out and trodden under foot by men.

3. "You are the light of the world. A city that is set upon a hill cannot be
   hid. Nor do men light a lamp and then put it away, or hide it under a
   bushel, but instead they put it on a lampstand, where it gives light to all
   that are in the house, so that those who enter may see the light. In the
   same way, let your light so shine before men, that they may see your
   good works and give glory to your Father who is in heaven.

Rules of conduct interpreted

4. "Do not think that I have come to abolish the law or the prophets; I
   have come not to abolish them but to fulfill them. For I tell you truly,
   until heaven and earth pass away, not even one letter, not a jot, will
   pass from the law until everything has been accomplished. Therefore,
   whoever relaxes even the least of these commandments and teaches
   others to do so, shall be called the least in the kingdom of heaven; but
   whoever practices and teaches these commandments shall be called
   great in the kingdom of heaven.[71]

---

71. By this Jesus promises to uphold at least the true spirit of the Law of Moses,
which provided instruction on ethics, sacrifices, and religious conduct generally. Jesus
had grown up within the Jewish tradition and had absorbed those rules. Later, however, he would set aside or reinterpret some of the more arbitrary rules, such as the

5. "For I tell you, unless your righteousness exceeds that of the scribes and Pharisees, you shall never enter the kingdom of heaven.

6. "You have heard that it was said to the people long ago, 'Thou shall not kill; and whoever kills shall be liable to judgment.' But I say to you that every one who is angry with his brother[72] will be liable to judgment, whoever insults his brother as empty-headed will be liable to the council, and whoever curses, 'You fool!' will be in danger of the fires of hell. So if you are offering your gift at the altar, and there remember that your brother has something against you, leave your gift there before the altar and be on your way; first be reconciled to your brother, and then come and offer your gift.

7. "Try to come to terms quickly with your adversary, while you are still on your way to court with him, lest he drag you to the judge, and the judge hand you over to the officer, and the officer put you in prison. I tell you truly, you will never get out of there until you have paid to the uttermost penny.

8. "You have heard that it was said, 'Thou shalt not commit adultery.' But I say to you that whoever looks upon a woman to lust after her has already committed adultery with her in his heart. If your right eye causes you to sin, pluck it out and throw it from you; it is better for you to lose one of your members than for your whole body to be thrown into hell. And if your right hand causes you to sin, cut it off and throw it from you; for it is better for you to lose one of your members than for your whole body to go into hell.

9. "It was also said, 'Whoever shall put away his wife, let him give her a certificate of divorce.' But I say to you that every one who divorces his wife, except on the ground of unfaithfulness, makes her an adulteress; and whoever marries a divorced woman commits adultery.

10. "Again you have heard that it was said to those of old time, 'Thou shalt not swear falsely, but shall perform unto the Lord thy oaths.' But I say to you, Swear not at all, neither by heaven, for it is God's throne, nor by the earth, for it is his footstool, nor by Jerusalem, for it is the city of the great King. And do not swear by your head, for you cannot make one hair white or black. Let your word be simply 'Yes' or 'No'; anything more than this is born of evil.

---

kosher rules of diet, see Chapter 84:7, thus beginning the break between Christianity and Judaism.

72. Some manuscripts add the qualification "without cause" at this point. However, the unqualified instruction seems more in keeping with the rest of the sermon.

11. "You have heard that it was said, 'An eye for an eye, and a tooth for a tooth.' But I say to you, Resist not evil. If any one strikes you on the right cheek, turn the other cheek to him also; and if any one wants to sue you to take your shirt, let him have your coat as well; and if any one forces you to assist him for one mile, go with him two miles. Give to every one who begs from you, and do not refuse the one who would borrow from you. If someone takes what belongs to you, do not insist on getting it back.

12. "You have heard that it was said, 'Thou shalt love thy neighbor, and hate thine enemy.' But I say to you that hear me, Love your enemies, do good to those that hate you, bless those who curse you, and pray for those who mistreat you, so that you may be the children of your Father who is in heaven. For he makes his sun to rise on the evil and on the good, and sends rain on the just and on the unjust.

13. "If you love those who love you, what credit is that to you? Do not even sinners and tax-gatherers do the same? And if you do good to those who do good to you, what credit is that to you? For even sinners do the same.

14. "And if you are courteous only to your brethren, what are you doing more than others? Do not even the pagans do the same? And if you lend only to those from whom you can expect repayment, what credit is that to you? Even sinners lend to sinners, to receive as much in return.

15. "But love your enemies, and do good to them, and lend, expecting nothing in return; and your reward will be great, and you will be the children of the Most High; for he is kind even to the ungrateful and the selfish.

16. "Be perfect, therefore, even as your heavenly Father is perfect.

Simplicity in religious observance: the Lord's Prayer

17. "Be careful not to practice your piety in front of men in order to be seen by them; for then you will have no reward from your Father who is in heaven. Therefore, when you give alms, sound no trumpet before you, as the hypocrites do in the synagogues and in the streets, so that they may be praised by men. Truly, I say to you, that will be their only reward. When you give to the poor, do not let your left hand know what your right hand is doing. Thus your giving will be in secret; and your Father who sees even what is done in secret will reward you.

18. "And when you pray, do not be like the hypocrites; for they love to stand and pray in the synagogues and on the street corners, so that they may be seen by men. Truly, I say to you, that will be their only reward. But when you pray, go into your inner room and shut the door and pray to your Father in secret; and your Father who sees what is done in secret will reward you.

19. "And in praying do not endlessly repeat empty phrases as the heathen do; for they think that they will be heard for their many words. Do not be like them, for your Father knows what things you have need of, even before you ask him. Pray then like this:

> Our Father who art in heaven,
> hallowed be thy name.
> Thy kingdom come,
> Thy will be done,
> on earth as it is in heaven.
> Give us this day our daily bread;
> and forgive us our trespasses,[73]
> as we forgive those who trespass against us.
> And lead us not into temptation,
> But deliver us from evil.
>
> For thine is the kingdom and the power and the glory
> for ever and ever. Amen.[74]

20. "For if you forgive others their trespasses, your heavenly Father will also forgive you; but if you do not forgive others their trespasses, neither will your Father forgive your trespasses.

21. "And when you fast, do not be of a somber countenance, like the hypocrites, for they neglect their appearance to show men they are fasting. Truly, I say to you, that will be their only reward. But when you fast, anoint your head and wash your face, so that your fasting will not be seen by others but only by your Father who is unseen; and your Father who sees what is done in secret will reward you.

---

73. The English word "trespasses" is suggested here by the context of the following verse, where that word most naturally suggests itself as part of the discussion of forgiveness of sins. Other, more literal translations use "debts" and "debtors."

74. These last two lines are a doxology—a short hymn of praise added at the end of a longer prayer. These particular lines appear in many editions of the Bible in footnote, because they come from later manuscripts. Some denominations include them in their services as part of the Lord's Prayer, others recite them separately from the prayer itself, and still others use a variant wording.

Spiritual values are the most important

22.   "Woe to you who are rich,
for you have already had your comfort.
Woe to you that are well fed now,
for you shall go hungry.
Woe to you who laugh now,
for you shall mourn and weep.
And woe to you when all men speak well of you,
for so their fathers treated the false prophets.

23.   "Do not lay up for yourselves treasures on earth, where moth and rust corrupt and where thieves break in and steal, but lay up for yourselves treasures in heaven, where neither moth nor rust corrupts and where thieves do not break in and steal; for where your treasure is, there your heart will be also.

24.   "The eye is the lamp of the body. So, if your eye is clear, your whole body will be full of light; but if your eye is not sound, your whole body will be full of darkness. Therefore be careful lest the light within you be darkness. For if the light in you is darkness, how great is that darkness! But if your whole body is full of light, having no part dark, it will be wholly bright, as when the bright shining of a lamp shall give you light.

25.   "No man can serve two masters; for either he will hate the one and love the other, or he will be devoted to the one and despise the other. You cannot serve both God and mammon. Therefore I tell you, do not be anxious about your life, about what you shall eat or what you shall drink, nor about your body, what you shall put on. Is not life more than food, and the body more than clothing?

26.   "Consider the ravens, and the birds of the air: they neither sow nor reap, nor do they gather the harvest into storehouse or barns, and yet your heavenly Father feeds them. Are you not of more value than they? Yet which of you by being anxious can add a single hour to his span of life? And if you are not able to do even so small a thing as that, why are you anxious about the rest?

27.   "And why be anxious about clothing? Behold the lilies of the field; consider how they grow. They toil not, neither do they spin; yet I tell you, even Solomon in all his glory was not arrayed like one of these. But if God so clothes the grass of the field, which today is alive and tomorrow is cast into the fire, will he not much more clothe you, O ye of little faith?

28. "Do not be of anxious mind, saying 'What shall we eat?' or 'What shall we drink?' or 'What shall we wear?' For all the nations of the world are eager for these things; and your heavenly Father knows that you have need of them all. But seek first his kingdom and his righteousness, and all these things shall be added to you as well.

29. "Therefore do not worry about tomorrow, for tomorrow will worry about itself. Sufficient unto each day are the troubles thereof.

Do not judge

30. "Be merciful, even as your Father is merciful.

31. "Judge not, that ye be not judged; for by the rule you apply to others you will be judged yourself. Condemn not, and you will not be condemned. Forgive, and you will be forgiven. Give, and it will be given to you. A good measure—pressed down, shaken together, running over—will be put into your lap. For the measure you give will be the measure you receive in return.

32. "And why do you see the speck of sawdust that is in your brother's eye, but do not notice the whole chip of wood that is in your own eye? How can you say to your brother, 'Brother let me take out the speck that is in your eye,' when all the while there is a chip in your own eye? You hypocrite, first take the chip out of your eye, and then you will see well enough to take the speck out of your brother's eye.

Seek out the godly life: the Golden Rule

33. "Do not give to dogs that which is holy; and do not cast your pearls before swine, lest they trample them underfoot and turn to attack you.

34. "Ask, and it shall be given to you. Seek, and ye shall find. Knock, and it shall be opened unto you. For every one who asks receives, and he who seeks finds, and to him who knocks the door will be opened.

35. "Which one of you, if his son asks him for bread, will give him a stone? Or if he asks for a fish, will give him a serpent? If you then, who are evil, know how to give good gifts to your children, how much more will your Father who is in heaven give good things to those who ask him?

36. "So in all things whatsoever, do unto others as you would have them do unto you, for this sums up all of the law and the prophets.

Flee from evil

37. "Enter by the narrow gate. For wide is the gate, and broad is the road that leads to destruction, and many are those who enter through it. But strait is the gate, and narrow is the way which leads to life, and few there are that find it.

38. "Beware of false prophets, who come to you in sheep's clothing, but inwardly they are ravening wolves.

39. "You will recognize them by their fruits, for every tree is known by its own fruit. Are grapes gathered from thornbushes, or figs from thistles? Every sound tree bears good fruit, but the rotten tree bears bad fruit. A good tree cannot produce bad fruit, nor can a bad tree produce good fruit. Every tree that does not bear good fruit is cut down and thrown into the fire. Therefore by their fruits you shall know them.

40. "The good man out of the good treasure in his heart brings forth good, and the evil man out of the evil treasure in his heart brings forth evil. For it is from the contents of the heart that the mouth speaks.

41. "Why do you call me Lord and not do what I tell you? Not every one who says to me, 'Lord, Lord,' will enter into the kingdom of heaven, but only the one who truly does the will of my Father who is in heaven. On judgment day many will say to me, 'Lord, Lord, did we not prophesy in your name, and cast out demons in your name, and do many miracles in your name?' And then I will declare before all the world, 'I never knew you; depart from me, you breakers of God's law!'

42. "Every one who comes to me and hears my words and follows them, I will tell you what he is like: he is like the wise man building a house, who dug deep, and laid the foundation upon the rock. The rain fell, and the floods came, and the winds blew and beat upon that house, but it did not fall, for it was founded upon a rock.

43. "But he who hears these words of mine and does not follow them is like the foolish man, who built his house upon the sand without a foundation. The rain fell, and the winds blew, and the floods came, and the torrent struck that house, and immediately it fell; and great was the fall of it."

44. When Jesus finished saying these things, the crowds were astonished at his teaching, for he taught them as one who had real authority, and not as their scribes.

Multiplication of the Loaves and Fishes, by Julius Schnorr von Carolsfeld
Photo: Foto Marburg / Art Resource, NY

V. THE GALILEE MINISTRY

Building a Movement

56. THE GENTILE CENTURION BELIEVES
Matthew 8:1, 5–13; Luke 7:1b–10

1. After Jesus came down from the mountain, great multitudes followed him, and he returned to Capernaum.

2. Now a centurion *there had* a servant whom he valued highly, who was sick and ready to die. When he heard about Jesus, he sent some elders of the Jews to him, asking him to come and heal this servant. And when the elders came to Jesus, they begged him earnestly, saying, "The centurion deserves to have you do this for him, for he loves our people, and he built us our synagogue. *And his* servant is lying paralyzed at home, in terrible distress."

3. Jesus said, "I will come and heal him;" and he went with them.

4. When Jesus was not far from the house, the centurion sent friends to him, saying to him, "Lord, do not trouble yourself, for I am not worthy to have you come under my roof; nor do I presume to come to you."

5. *But Jesus went on to the house, and when he arrived the centurion met him outside and said to him,*[75] "Just say the word, and my servant will

---

75. There is a divergence between the two gospel accounts of this story. Matthew reports that the centurion had a face-to-face conversation with Jesus, while Luke reports that the entire conversation was conducted through intermediaries. This work

be healed. For I too am in a chain of command, *and I know that words with authority bring results.* I have soldiers under me; and I say to one man, 'Go,' and he goes, and to another, 'Come,' and he comes, and to my slave, 'Do this,' and he does it."

6. When Jesus heard this he was amazed, and turned and said to the crowd that followed him, "I tell you truly, I have not found such great faith, not with anyone in Israel. I tell you, many will come from east and west and take their places at the banquet table with Abraham, Isaac, and Jacob in the kingdom of heaven. But *many Israelites,* the children of the kingdom, will be cast outside, into the outer darkness, where there shall be weeping and gnashing of teeth."

7. Jesus said to the centurion, "Go; let it be done for you as you have believed." And when *the man and* his messengers returned to the house, they found that the servant had been healed as of that very moment.

57. A WIDOW'S SON RAISED AT NAIN
Luke 7:11–17

1. Soon after this Jesus went to a town called Nain, and his disciples and a great crowd went with him. As he approached the gate of the town, he saw that a man who had died was being carried out. This man was the only son of his mother, and she was a widow; and a crowd from the town was with her.

2. When the Lord saw the widow, he had compassion for her and said to her, "Do not weep." And he went over and touched the bier, and those who carried it stood still. Then he said, "Young man, I say to you, arise." The dead man sat up and began to speak, and Jesus gave him back to his mother.

3. Fear seized all the people around; and they praised God, saying, "A great prophet has risen among us!" and "God has visited his people!" And this news about Jesus went out through the whole of Judea and all the surrounding country.

---

adopts a composite version, with the initial plea being made through messengers, but with Jesus and the centurion eventually meeting in person. This preserves the account of the deferential humility of the centurion, who did not presume to go to Jesus, which is the most prominent feature of the story, but it also follows the report of a direct conversation.

58. A LAST QUESTION FROM JOHN THE BAPTIST
Matthew 11:2–6; Luke 7:18–23

1. John's disciples visited him in prison and told him about the deeds that the Christ was performing. So John summoned two of the disciples and sent them to the Lord to ask, "Are you the one who is to come, or should we await another?" And when the men reached Jesus, they said, "John the Baptist has sent us to you to ask, 'Are you the one who is to come, or should we await another?'"

2. At that time Jesus was curing many people of diseases and plagues and evil spirits, and bestowing sight on many that were blind. So he answered the messengers, "Go and tell John what you have seen and heard here: the blind receive their sight, the lame walk, lepers are cleansed, the deaf hear, the dead are raised up, and the good news is preached to the poor. And blessed is he who can accept me for what I am!"

59. JESUS PRAISES JOHN AND CLAIMS HIS MANTLE
Matthew 11:7–19; Luke 7:24–35, 16:16–17

1. When the messengers from John had departed, Jesus began to speak to the crowds about him: "What did you go out into the wilderness to see? A reed swayed by the wind? If not, then what did you go to see? A man clothed in soft garments? No, those who are gloriously appareled and live in luxury are to be found in kings' courts. So what then did you go out to see? A prophet? Yes, I tell you, and much more than a prophet. This is the one of whom it is written, 'Behold, I will send my messenger ahead of you, who shall prepare thy way before thee.'

2. "I tell you truly, among those born of women there has risen no one greater than John the Baptist. Yet even the least one in the kingdom of heaven is greater than he. Before John came, all the prophets and the law were looking to the future. Since then, from the days of John the Baptist until now the good news has been preached, and the kingdom

of heaven has been strongly advancing, and determined people have been claiming their places in it.[76]

3. *These new opportunities do not mean that the law no longer governs our conduct.* It is easier for heaven and earth to pass away, than for one jot of the law to become void. But if you are willing to accept my words, John actually is Elijah, the one whom the prophets said would come.[77] He who has ears to hear, let him hear."

4. When they heard Jesus' words, all the people, even the tax-gatherers, agreed that God's ways were just, because they had been baptized by John. But the Pharisees and the experts in religious law rejected God's plan for themselves, for they had not been baptized by John.

5. Then Jesus said, "To what then shall I compare the people of this generation? What are they like? They are like children playing in the marketplace and complaining to one another,

> We played the flute for you, but you did not dance;
> we sang a dirge, but you did not weep.

6. "For John the Baptist came eating no bread and drinking no wine; and you say, 'He is possessed by a demon.' The Son of Man has come eating and drinking; and you say, 'Behold, a glutton and a drunkard, a friend of tax-gatherers and sinners!' Yet true wisdom is shown to be right by all her different children."

60. INVITING THE WEARY TO REST
Matthew 11:28–30

1. *In those days Jesus also said,* "Come unto me, all you who labor and are heavy-laden, and I will give you rest.

---

76. This is a difficult passage. This sentence is often translated to say that "the kingdom of heaven suffers violence, and violent men take it by force." However, that does not seem plausible; whatever the kingdom is precisely, is seems unlikely to be something that is vulnerable to direct attack. The more affirmative construction suggested here seems to fit the context better. John was a great prophet, and he effectively preached about the kingdom of God as a present opportunity, which became more attractive than before to many people, who then sought with renewed determination to become worthy of entering it.*

77. In other words, John carried out the same mission as Elijah, the prophet whose return would announce the coming of the Messiah; and Jesus is therefore the Messiah himself.

2. "Take my yoke upon your shoulders, and learn from me; for I am gentle and humble in heart, and you will find rest for your souls. My yoke is easy, and my burden is light."

61. THE PENITENT WOMAN
Luke 7:36–50

1. One of the Pharisees had invited Jesus to dine with him, and he went to the man's house and reclined at the table.

2. A woman of the city, who had lived a life of sin, learned that Jesus was eating at the Pharisee's house. She brought an alabaster flask of ointment and stood behind him at his feet, weeping.[78] She began to wet his feet with her tears, and wiped them with the hair of her head, and kissed them, and anointed them with the ointment.

3. Now when the Pharisee who had invited Jesus saw all this, he said to himself, "If this man were truly a prophet, he would know what sort of woman this is who is touching him, for she is a sinner."

4. Then Jesus answered his thoughts, "Simon, I have something to say to you." And Simon replied, "Teacher, say on." Jesus continued, "A certain moneylender had two debtors; one owed him five hundred denarii, and the other fifty. When they could not pay, he forgave both of them their debts. Now tell me, which one will love him more?" Simon answered, "The one, I suppose, to whom he forgave more." And Jesus said to him, "You have judged rightly."

5. Then he turned to the woman and said to Simon, "Do you see this woman? I came into your house, and you gave me no water to wash my feet, but she has wet my feet with her tears and dried them with her hair. You gave me no kiss, but from the time I came in she has kissed my feet continuously. You did not anoint my head with oil, but she has anointed my feet with ointment.

6. "Therefore I tell you, her sins, which are many, have been forgiven, for she has been showing much love; while he who has been forgiven little, loves little." And he said to her, "Your sins are forgiven."

---

78. Jesus was evidently dining in the classical manner, reclining on a couch at the table. This would make it possible for the penitent woman to stand behind him and still reach his feet.

7. Then the other guests began to say to one another, "Who is this, who even forgives sins?" And Jesus said to the woman, "Your faith has saved you; go in peace."

62. MARY MAGDALENE AND OTHER WOMEN SUPPORT JESUS' MINISTRY
Luke 8:1–3

1. Soon afterward Jesus set out again through cities and villages, preaching and proclaiming the good news of the kingdom of God. The twelve apostles were with him.

2. Also with him were certain women who had been healed of evil spirits and infirmities: Mary, called Magdalene,[79] from whom seven demons had come out; and Joanna the wife of Chuza, the manager of Herod's household; and Susanna; and many others. These women were helping to support the men out of their own means.[80]

63. THE SABBATH IS MADE FOR MAN
Matthew 12:1–8; Mark 2:23–28; Luke 6:1–5

1. One sabbath Jesus was going through the grainfields. As they walked along, his disciples became hungry and began to pluck some heads of grain, rubbing *off the husks* in their hands and eating the kernels. When some Pharisees saw this, they said to him, "Look, why are your disciples doing what is not lawful to do on the sabbath?"

---

79. This is our first explicit introduction to Mary Magdalene. We will not encounter her again by name until the time of the crucifixion and resurrection. How much we know about her actions and character will depend on whether some of the other passages in the gospels also refer to her and convey additional information. References to Mary of Bethany in Chapters 115 and 154, and to the penitent sinner in Chapter 61, may or may not be referring to Mary Magdalene. The accounts do not provide enough detail to let us know for certain whether they are describing one, two, or three separate women. The accounts contain tantalizing hints, however, and will support reasoned speculation, which has already produced a substantial literature.*

80. Jesus had an interest in the training and education of women that was unusual for the time. In accordance with the attitudes of the day, the women around him were not formally recognized as disciples. However, a number of them, particularly Mary Magdalene and the others who traveled with him, functioned very much as if they were disciples.*

2. But Jesus said to them, "Have you never read what David did, when he and his companions were in need and hungry? He entered the house of God, in the days when Abiathar was high priest, and ate the consecrated bread, which it is not lawful for any but the priests to eat, and also gave some of it to his companions.

3. "Or have you not read in the law how on every sabbath the priests in the temple violate the sabbath, and yet are guiltless?[81] And I tell you, something greater than the temple is here. So if you had known what these words mean—'I desire mercy, and not sacrifices'—you would not have condemned the innocent."

4. And he said to them, "The sabbath was made for man, not man for the sabbath; and so the Son of Man is lord even of the sabbath."

64. HEALING A HAND ON THE SABBATH
Matthew 12:9–14; Mark 3:1–6; Luke 6:6–11

1. On another sabbath, when Jesus entered the synagogue and taught, a man was there whose right hand was withered. The scribes and the Pharisees were looking for a reason to accuse Jesus, and so they asked him, "Is it lawful to heal on the sabbath?" And they watched him closely to see if he would do that thing.

2. But Jesus knew their thoughts, and he said to them, "What man among you, if he has a sheep and it falls into a pit on the sabbath day, will not lay hold of it and lift it out? And of how much more value is a man than a sheep! So it is lawful to do good on the sabbath."

3. Then he said to the man who had the withered hand, "Come up and stand before everyone." The man rose and came forward. Then Jesus said to the Pharisees, "I ask you, which is lawful on the Sabbath—to do good or to do harm, to save life or to destroy it?" But they were silent.

4. He looked around at all of them with anger, grieved at their hardness of heart, and said to the man, "Stretch out your hand." The man stretched it out, and his hand was restored, as sound as the other.

5. But the Pharisees were filled with fury, and went out and discussed what they might do to Jesus, and immediately began to conspire with the men around Herod about how to destroy him.

---

81. That is, on the sabbath the priests still carry out their work of conducting religious ceremonies.

65. JOHN THE BAPTIST IS BEHEADED
Matthew 14:6–13a; Mark 6:21–29

1. *Around this time Herod's wife, Herodias, found an opportunity to be revenged on John the Baptist.*

2. On his birthday Herod gave a great feast for his officials and army officers and the leading men of Galilee. The daughter of Herodias danced before them,[82] and she pleased Herod and his guests; and the king said to the girl, "Ask me for whatever you wish, and I will grant it." And he swore it to her: "Whatever you ask of me, I will give you, even unto half my kingdom."

3. And she went out and said to her mother, "What shall I ask for?" And Herodias said, "The head of John the Baptist." The daughter immediately hastened to the king and made her demand: "I want you to give me—at once—the head of John the Baptist on a platter."

4. Then the king deeply regretted his promise; but because of the oath made in public before his dinner guests he did not want to refuse her. So he called an executioner at once and commanded him to bring John's head. The man went, beheaded John in the prison, and brought his head back on a platter. He gave it to the girl; and the girl gave it to her mother.

5. When John's disciples heard of this, they came and took his body, and laid it in a tomb. Then they went and told Jesus. And when Jesus heard the news, he got into a boat and withdrew to a secluded place to be alone.

66. RESISTANCE FROM FAMILY AND FRIENDS
Matthew 12:22–23, 46–50; Mark 3:19b–21, 31–35; Luke 8:19–21, 11:14

1. *One day when Jesus was home with his disciples,* a crowd once again gathered, so that they could not so much as eat bread. And when his

---

82. This is Salome. She is not identified by name in the gospels, but her name and other details are given by the Roman-Jewish historian Josephus, who lived a generation later.*

family and friends heard of this, they started over to take custody of Jesus, for they said, "He is not in his right mind."

2. Then a man who was demon-possessed, and blind and mute, was brought to Jesus. Jesus cast out a demon that was mute; and when the demon had gone out, the mute man spoke and saw. All the people were amazed, and asked, "Might this possibly be the Son of David?"[83]

3. While Jesus was still speaking to the people *about the healing*, his mother and his brothers arrived, but they could not reach him because of the crowd. Standing outside, they sent a message in to him. A group was sitting around Jesus; and someone told him, "Your mother and your brothers and sisters are standing outside, asking to speak to you."

4. But he replied to the man who had told him this, "Who is truly my mother, and who are my brothers?" Then he looked at the disciples sitting in a circle around him, and motioning toward them, he said, "Here are my mother and my brothers! My mother and my brothers are those who hear the word of God, and follow it. For whoever does the will of my Father in heaven is my brother, and sister, and mother."

67. DENYING ALLIANCE WITH BEELZEBUB
Matthew 12:24–45; Mark 3:22–30; Luke 11:15–32, 12:10

1. When the Pharisees and the scribes who had come down from Jerusalem *saw the mute man cured and heard the crowd praise Jesus,*[84] they said, "He is possessed by Beelzebub! It is only with the help of Beelzebub, the prince of demons, that this man casts out demons."[85] And others, to try him, sought from him a sign from heaven.

2. Knowing their thoughts, Jesus called them to him, and said to them in parables, "How can Satan drive out Satan? If a kingdom or a city is divided against itself, it cannot stand. Every kingdom or city divided against itself is brought to ruin. A house divided against itself cannot

---

83. That is, the Messiah.

84. In the gospels of Matthew and Mark, the incident in this chapter is placed between the two halves of the incident involving Jesus' family in the previous chapter, after their expression of concern but before their arrival. The charge of an alliance with Beelzebub involves an important event that seems best presented in a chapter of its own, however.

85. The name Beelzebub probably means "Lord of the Flies." In Milton's *Paradise Lost*, Beelzebub is presented as the chief of the evil spirits around Satan.

stand. And if Satan drives out Satan, he is fighting against himself, and how then can his kingdom stand? It must come to an end.

3. "You say that I cast out demons by Beelzebub. But if I cast out demons with the help of Beelzebub, then with whose help do your own disciples cast them out? They will condemn you *for making that argument*. And if it is instead through the power of God that I cast out demons, then the kingdom of God has come close to you.

4. "Consider, when a strong man, fully armed, guards his own house, his possessions are safe. How can anyone enter *such* a man's house and plunder his goods, unless he first binds the strong man? But then indeed he may plunder the house. When one still stronger than the strong man assails him and overcomes him, he takes away the armor in which the man trusted, and distributes the plunder. *And in just this way I have overcome Beelzebub.*[86]

5. "He who is not with me is against me,[87] and he who does not gather *the flock* with me scatters it abroad. And I tell you truly, all sins will be forgiven the children of men, and all the blasphemies they utter. But blasphemy against the Spirit will not be forgiven. Whoever says a word against the Son of Man will be forgiven; but whoever speaks against the Holy Spirit will never be forgiven, either in this world or in the world to come. He is guilty of an eternal sin." Jesus said this because they kept saying, "He is in league with an evil spirit."

6. "Either admit that the tree is good, and its fruit good; or say that the tree is bad, and its fruit bad; for the tree is known by its fruit. *And the fruit of my actions has been good.*[88]

7. "You brood of vipers! How can you say anything good, when you are evil? For it is out of the abundance of the heart that the mouth speaks. The good man out of the good treasure in this heart brings forth good, and the evil man out of the evil treasure in his heart brings forth evil. I tell you, on the day of judgment men will render an account for every careless word they have uttered; for by your words you will be acquitted, and by your words you will be condemned.

---

86. Jesus implies something along the following lines: "Because I was able to recover this tormented person from the grip of the demons, I clearly had bound Satan through my strength and taken something from him that he valued—namely, his victim—and this shows that I am Satan's adversary rather than his follower."

87. Contrast this with the more tolerant view expressed in Chapter 99:5.

88. This argument also shows that Jesus has not conspired with Beelzebub; for he has obviously brought about good effects, and therefore he himself must be good.

8. "When an evil spirit comes out of a man, it roams through waterless places seeking rest, but finds none. Then the spirit says, 'I will return to the house from which I came.' And when he comes he finds the house empty, swept, and put in order. Then he goes and brings back with him seven other spirits more wicked than himself, and they enter and dwell there; and the final state of that man becomes worse than the first. So it shall also be with this evil generation."

9. As he said this, a woman in the crowd raised her voice and said to him, "Blessed is *your mother*—the womb that bore you and the breasts that nursed you!" And Jesus said, "Blessed, rather, are *all* those who hear the word of God and follow it!"

10. Then as the crowds were gathering around him, some of the scribes and Pharisees said to him, "Teacher, we wish to see a sign to prove who you are."

11. But he answered them, "An evil and adulterous generation demands a miraculous sign, but no sign will be given to it except the sign of the prophet Jonah. For as Jonah was three days and three nights in the belly of the whale, so the Son of Man will be three days and three nights in the heart of the earth.

12. "And just as Jonah became a miraculous sign to the people of Ninevah, so likewise the Son of Man will become a sign to this generation. On the day of judgment the men of Nineveh will arise, along with this generation, and they will condemn it; for they repented at the preaching of Jonah, and behold, something greater than Jonah is here, *and yet you do not repent.* And on the day of judgment the Queen of the South[89] will arise, along with this generation, and she will condemn it; for she came from the ends of the earth to hear the wisdom of Solomon; and behold, something greater than Solomon is here, *and yet you do not listen.*"

89. The Queen of Sheba.

68. PARABLES ABOUT THE KINGDOM OF GOD

Matthew 13:1–53; Mark 4:1–34; Luke 8:4–18, 13:18–21

1. That same day Jesus went out of the house and sat by the sea, and began to teach *about the kingdom of God*.[90] The crowd that gathered about him from all the towns was so great that he got into a boat and sat in it out on the water, while the people stood along the shore at the water's edge. And he taught them many things in parables.

Parable of sowing the seeds
Matthew 13:3–23; Mark 4:2–25; Luke 8:5–18

2. In his teaching he told this story: "Listen! A farmer went out to sow his seed. And as he sowed, some seeds fell by the wayside, where they were trodden under foot; and the birds of the air came and ate them up. Other seeds fell on stony ground, where they had not much soil; these shot up at once, because the soil was shallow, but when the sun rose they were scorched, and because they had no root or moisture they withered away. Still other seeds fell among thorns, and the thorns grew up with them and choked them, and they yielded no grain. But some seeds fell into good ground and brought forth grain, growing strongly and increasing and yielding thirty or sixty or a hundred times more than was sown." And after Jesus finished saying this, he called out, "He who has ears to hear, let him hear."

---

90. In this group of parables Jesus is teaching about a concept that was central to his ministry and to which he returns throughout the gospels. We know more about Jesus' views on the kingdom of God than we do about John the Baptist's. For Jesus the kingdom of God was clearly a two-part concept. The elements of divine rule and inner peace were both fully present. One part of the kingdom is external and future—a concrete realm centered on God. It is to be a time of God's sovereign reign on earth, more fully realized than it is today. This reign may begin with increased individual obedience to God, progress to a new age of greater peace and harmony, and at some point will include elements that are frankly apocalyptic. These last elements include a future rule in which strict justice is done: the righteous will be rewarded and the wicked punished. Verses 22 and 25 of this chapter, and the descriptions of the Second Coming and the Last Judgment in Chapter 173, describe this external aspect of the kingdom. In contrast, however, an equally important aspect of the kingdom of God is internal and present—an intangible, personal realm. It involves the condition in which an individual comes to sense the presence of God, and to be at peace with the world, with others, and with himself. Believers can attain this part of the kingdom of heaven immediately. Most of the parables in the present chapter, and teachings like the Sermon on the Mount in Chapter 55, describe this aspect of the concept. Scholars continue to debate the relationship between the two components and their relative importance in Jesus' thought.*

3. When he was alone, the twelve and his other followers came to him and asked, "Why do you speak to the people in parables?" And they asked what this parable meant. Jesus answered them, "To you it has been given to know the secrets of the kingdom of God, but to those outside it has not been given. This is why for those outside everything is said in parables, so that they may indeed see but not perceive, and may indeed hear but not understand; otherwise they might change their hearts, and be forgiven.[91] For with them indeed is fulfilled the prophecy of Isaiah which says:

> You shall indeed hear but never understand,
> and you shall indeed see but never perceive.
> For this people's heart has grown dull,
> and their ears are hard of hearing,
> and they have closed their eyes.
> Otherwise they might see with their eyes,
> and hear with their ears,
> and understand with their hearts,
> and turn, and I would heal them.

4. "But blessed are your eyes, for they see, and your ears, for they hear. I tell you truly, many prophets and righteous men longed to see the things that you see, and did not see them; and to hear the things that you hear, and did not hear them."

5. Then he said to them, "Do you not understand this parable? How then will you understand all the other parables? Listen then to what the parable of the sower means. The seed is the word of God. The farmer is the one who sows the word.

---

91. This is a startling remark, because at first sight it seems contrary to Jesus' declared mission of helping all people toward salvation. Several points may contribute to an explanation, however. The remark is a paraphrase from Isaiah, which is subsequently quoted in detail and is then presented again in Chapter 160:1. It might therefore be meant as a statement of fact or of prophecy about the nature of his audience, rather than as a statement of Jesus' own purpose. In this context the texts from Isaiah might be an explanation for why some people reject the gospel even while others accept it: they simply don't understand the message. Insofar as the remark expresses Jesus' own purposes, his goal may have been to slow people down, to give them time to reflect and repent properly, rather than to block them from repentance entirely. In these teachings there may also be an element of hidden knowledge accessible only by initiates, as a way of spurring his listeners to greater commitment. Ultimately the best explanation of these parables may be the one that appears in verse 19 of this chapter—that they were the best available way, in an imperfect world, to teach people "as they were able to understand."

6. "Some people are like the seed falling by the wayside. The word is sown
   in their hearts and they hear about the kingdom, but they do not understand it. Satan the evil one then immediately comes and snatches
   away the word, so that they will not believe and be saved.

7. "Others are like the seeds sown upon stony ground. When they hear
   the word, they receive it with joy; but these have no root. They believe
   for a while, but then, when tribulation or persecution arises on account of the word, or in time of temptation, they quickly fall away.

8. "And others are like seed sown among thorns. Such men are those who
   do hear the word, but as they continue on their way the cares of the
   world, the lure of riches, the pleasures of life, and the desire for other
   things enter into them and choke the word, and it bears no fruit.

9. "*But some people are like the seeds* in the good soil. They are those who,
   hearing and understanding the word, hold it fast in a good and honest
   heart, and bring forth fruit with patience, thirty and sixty and a hundred times what was sown."

10. And he said to them, "Is a lamp brought in to be hidden under a jar, or
    under a bed? No; instead a man puts it on a stand, so that all those who
    enter may see the light. For nothing is hidden that shall not be made
    manifest, nor is anything secret that shall not be known and come to
    light. If any man has ears to hear, let him hear."

11. And he said to them, "Consider carefully what you hear, and how you
    listen. The measure you give will be the measure you receive, and more
    will be given to you. To him who has *understanding*, still more will be
    given, and he will have an abundance; but from him who has not, even
    what he thinks he has will be taken away."

The wheat and the weeds
Matthew 13:24–30

12. Then Jesus presented another parable to them, saying, "The kingdom
    of heaven[92] may be compared to a man who sowed good seed in his
    field; but while men were sleeping, his enemy came and sowed tare
    weeds among the wheat, and then slipped away. So when the wheat
    came up and bore its grain, the weeds also appeared.

---

92. The term "kingdom of heaven" has essentially the same meaning as the "kingdom of God." It appears in the gospels as an alternative phrase most commonly in the
book of Matthew. Matthew was writing primarily for Jewish readers, and some of them
would have been uncomfortable with an explicit use of God's name.*

13. "The landowner's servants came and said to him, 'Master, did you not plant good seed in your field? Where then did the weeds come from?' He replied, 'An enemy has done this.' The servants said to him, 'Then do you want us to go and pull up the weeds?'

14. "But he said, 'No, for in pulling them up you may uproot the wheat along with them. Let both grow together until the harvest; and at harvest time I will tell the reapers, Collect the weeds first and bind them in bundles to be burned, but gather all the wheat into my barn.'"

The seed growing of itself
Mark 4:26-29

15. Jesus also said, "This is what the kingdom of God is like. A man scatters seed on the ground. Then day and night, whether he sleeps or wakes, the seed sprouts and grows, although he knows not how. For the earth brings forth fruit of herself—first the shoot, and then the ear, and then the full grain.

16. "But when the grain is ready, then he immediately puts the sickle to it, because the harvest time has come."

The mustard seed and the yeast
Matthew 13:31-35; Mark 4:30-34; Luke 13:18-21

17. And Jesus put another parable before them, saying, "With what can we liken the kingdom of God, or what parable shall we use to describe it? It is like a grain of mustard seed which a man took and planted in his garden. When sown upon the ground this is the smallest of all seeds; yet when it is planted it grows up and becomes the greatest of all garden herbs, and puts out large branches like a tree, so that the birds of the air can come and perch in their shade."

18. And he told them still another parable: "To what shall I compare the kingdom of heaven? It is like yeast, which a woman took and mixed in with a great bowl of flour, and yet this leavening worked its way through all the dough."

19. With many such parables he spoke to the crowds, teaching them as they were able to understand. And he said nothing to them without using a parable. This fulfilled what had been spoken by the prophet: "I will open my mouth in parables; I will utter things that have been kept secret since the foundation of the world." But he explained everything to his own disciples when they were alone.

The wheat and weeds explained
Matthew 13:36–43

20. After that, Jesus left the crowds and went back into the house. And his disciples came to him, asking, "Explain to us the parable of the weeds of the field."

21. He answered, "The one who sows the good seed is the Son of Man. The field is the world. The good seeds are the children of the kingdom. The weeds are the children of the evil one; and the enemy who sowed them is the devil. The harvest time is the end of the age; and the reapers are angels.

22. "Just as the weeds are gathered and burned in the fire, so it shall be at the end of the age. The Son of Man will send forth his angels, and they will winnow out of his kingdom everything that causes people to sin, and everyone who does evil, and shall throw them into the fiery furnace, where there will be weeping and gnashing of teeth. Then the righteous will shine like the sun in their Father's kingdom. He who has ears, let him hear!

Short parables about the kingdom of heaven
Matthew 13:44–53

23. "The kingdom of heaven is like treasure hidden in a field. A man found it and *quickly* covered it up again; then in his joy he went and sold all that he had and bought that field.

24. "Again, the kingdom of heaven is like a merchant searching for fine pearls, who, on finding one pearl of great price, went and sold all that he had and bought it.

25. "Or the kingdom of heaven is like a dragnet which was thrown into the sea and gathered fish of every kind. When it was full, men drew it ashore and sat down and sorted the good fish into baskets but threw away the bad ones. So it will be at the end of the age. The angels will come and separate the wicked men from the righteous, and will throw them into the fiery furnace, where there will be weeping and gnashing of teeth.

26. "Have you understood all these things?" Jesus asked. They said to him, "Yes, Lord." And he said to them, "Because of this, every scribe who has been instructed about the kingdom of heaven is like the master of a household who is able to bring out of his storeroom new treasures

as well as old ones." And when Jesus finished telling these parables he departed from that place.

69. CALMING THE WAVES OF GALILEE
Matthew 8:18, 23–27; Mark 4:35–41; Luke 8:22–25

1. Later that day, when evening had come, Jesus looked at the great crowds around him and said to his disciples, "Let us cross over to the other side of the lake." When he got into the boat, his disciples left the crowd and followed him. They took him with them in the boat, just as he was; and other boats were with him as well.

2. So they set out, and as they sailed he fell asleep.

3. Then there arose a great storm of wind on the lake, so that the waves broke over the boat, and they were filling with water, and were in great danger. But Jesus stayed asleep on the cushion in the stern.

4. The disciples went and woke him, saying, "Master, Master, save us! Do you not care that we perish?" And he said to them, "Why are you fearful, O ye of little faith?" Then he rose and rebuked the wind and the raging waves, commanding, "Peace! Be still!" And the wind ceased, and there was a great calm.

5. Then the men were filled with great fear, and they wondered at what they had seen, asking one another, "What manner of man is this, that he commands even the winds and the waves, and they obey him?"

70. THE DEMONS NAMED LEGION
Matthew 8:28–34; Mark 5:1–20; Luke 8:26–39

1. After this they came into the country of the Gadarenes, which is across the lake from Galilee.[93] When Jesus had stepped out of the boat and come ashore, he was met by two demon-possessed men coming from the tombs, so fierce that no one could pass that way.

2. *One of these men* was originally from the city, but for a long time he had worn no clothes, and he lived not in a house but in the tombs

---

93. Mark and Luke describe this as the country of the Gerasenes, a neighboring area.

instead. Many times the demon had seized him, and no one could hold him any more, even with a chain. For he had often been bound with shackles and chains, and kept under guard, but he wrenched the chains apart, and he broke the shackles in pieces, and no one had the strength to subdue him. *In the end* he was driven by the demon into solitary places. Night and day he was in the mountains, and among the tombs, screaming and cutting himself with stones.

3. When this man saw Jesus from a distance, he ran and fell on his knees before him. And crying out with a loud voice, he demanded, "What have you to do with us, Jesus, Son of the Most High God? I command you in God's name, do not torment me!"[94] For Jesus had said to him, "Come out of the man, you evil spirit!"

4. Then Jesus asked him, "What is your name?" And he replied, "My name is Legion; for we are many."

5. Many demons had entered him. Now they cried out, "Have you come here to torment us before the appointed time?" And they begged Jesus desperately not to command them to depart into the abyss.

6. A large herd of swine was feeding nearby on the hillside; and the demons begged Jesus, "If you cast us out, send us to the swine, and let us enter into them." He gave permission and said to them, "Go." So the evil spirits came out of the man and entered into the swine. And the whole herd, numbering about two thousand, rushed down the steep bank into the lake and drowned in the waters.

7. When the men tending the swine saw what had happened, they fled, and spread the news to the town and the surrounding countryside. Then people went out to see what had happened. They came to Jesus, and found the man from whom the legion of demons had gone out, sitting at his feet, clothed and in his right mind. And those who had seen it told them how the demon-possessed man had been healed, and what had happened to the swine.

8. Then all the people of the area were afraid, and when they met with Jesus they begged him to leave their territory. So he got into the boat and departed.

9. As Jesus was getting into the boat, the man who had been possessed by demons begged to go with him. But Jesus refused and sent him away, saying, "Return home to your own people, and tell them how much

94. With this statement the demons are, ironically enough, attempting to impose a spell on Jesus, using the traditional form of the ritual, but with the roles reversed.*

the Lord has done for you, and how merciful he has been to you." So the man went away and began to proclaim throughout the entire Decapolis how much Jesus had done for him. And all the people were amazed.

7 I. JAIRUS' DAUGHTER AND THE BLEEDING WOMAN
Matthew 9:18–26; Mark 5:21–43; Luke 8:40–56

1. When Jesus had crossed again in the boat to the other side of the lake, a great crowd gathered around him at the shore and welcomed him, for they had all been watching for him.

2. And there came a man named Jairus, who was a leader at the synagogue. Seeing Jesus, he knelt down before him, and begged him to come to his house, to save his only daughter, a girl about twelve years of age. "My little daughter lies at the point of death. *Perhaps* she has already died.[95] Come and lay your hands on her, so that she may be made well, and live." So Jesus rose and went with him, along with his disciples.

3. As Jesus was on his way there, a great crowd followed and pressed about him. And *among the people* there was a woman who had had a chronic flow of blood for twelve years, and who had suffered greatly under many physicians. She had spent all that she had, and was no better, but rather grew worse, and could not be healed by any one.

4. She had heard the reports about Jesus, and came up behind him in the crowd and touched the fringe of his cloak. For she said to herself, "If I touch even his clothes, I shall be made well." Immediately the hemorrhage ceased; and she felt in her body that she was healed of her affliction.

5. Jesus realized at once that power had gone out from him. He turned around in the crowd and demanded, "Who touched my garments?" When all denied it, Peter and the disciples said, "Master, you see the crowds surrounding you and pressing against you; how can you ask, 'Who touched me?'" But Jesus said, "Someone touched me, for I can

---

95. In Mark and Luke, Jairus tells Jesus that the girl is dying. In Matthew he says that she is already dead. It seems perfectly plausible that a distracted father would say both these things. This harmony preserves both the statements, putting the second one into tentative form to reflect Jairus' uncertainty and fear.

feel that power has gone forth from me." And he looked around to see who had done it.

6. Then the woman, knowing what had happened to her, and seeing that she had not escaped notice, came in fear and trembling and fell down before Jesus, and told him the whole truth. She declared before all the people why she had touched him, and how she had been immediately healed. And Jesus said to her, "Be of good heart, my daughter; your faith has made you well. Go in peace, and be healed of your disease."[96] And the woman was made whole from that moment.

7. While Jesus was still speaking, some men arrived from the house of Jairus, the synagogue leader, and said, "Your daughter is dead. Why trouble the Teacher any further?" But when Jesus heard what they said, he told Jairus, "Do not fear; only believe, and she shall be saved."

8. When he came to the house, he permitted no one to enter with him, except Peter, and James, and John the brother of James, and the father and mother of the child. Jesus saw the flute players and the noisy crowd, and people weeping and wailing loudly, mourning for her. He said to them, "Why all this commotion and tears? Depart and do not weep; for the girl is not dead but sleeping." And they laughed him to scorn, knowing that she was dead.

9. But he sent them all outside, and took the child's father and mother and his three disciples, and went in to where the child was. Taking her by the hand he said to her, "Talitha cumi," which means, "Young lady, I say to you, arise." Immediately her spirit returned, and she got up and walked. And her parents were overcome with amazement.

10. Jesus told them to give her something to eat. Then he strictly charged them that no one should know about what had happened. But the report about this spread through all that district.

---

96. Under traditional religious law, a woman having her period, or other continuing flow of blood, was in a state of ritual impurity. Jesus' engagement with this woman was another instance of his willingness to look past or moderate the arbitrary elements of the received law.*

72. HEALING ACCORDING TO THEIR FAITH
Matthew 9:27–34

1. When Jesus left that place, two blind men followed him, calling out, "Take pity on us, Son of David." After he entered the house *where he was staying,*[97] the blind men came in to him; and Jesus asked them, "Do you believe that I am able to do this?" They said to him, "Yes, Lord." Then he touched their eyes, saying, "According to your faith let it happen to you." And their eyes were opened.

2. Then Jesus sternly charged them, "See that you let no one know of this."[98] But they went out and spread his fame through all the district.

3. As they were on their way out, a man who was demon-possessed and could not speak was brought in to Jesus. When the demon had been cast out, the mute man spoke; and the crowds were astonished, saying, "Never has anything like this been seen in Israel." But the Pharisees *again* said, "It is through the prince of demons that he casts out demons."[99]

73. FINAL REJECTION AT NAZARETH
Matthew 13:54–58; Mark 6:1–6a

1. Then Jesus left there and went to the town where he had grown up; and his disciples accompanied him. And on the sabbath he began to teach in the synagogue; and the people who heard him were amazed, saying, "Where did this man get these things? What wisdom has been given to him, and what power in his hands to do miracles!"

97. This may have been Simon Peter's house, where he had healed Simon's mother-in-law.

98. Jesus frequently instructed witnesses not to speak of his miracles. This may have been purposeful, in that too much attention to the startling miracles might distract people from his more important spiritual messages of repentance and reform. See endnote on Chapter 25 (the Temptation in the Wilderness). On the other hand, on many other occasions Jesus appealed to his miracles as evidence for the truth of his status and mission. See Chapter 125:5 ("even though you do not believe me, believe the works").

99. The incident in this verse looks at first like a shortened version of the account in Chapter 67, above. But the two incidents are both described by Matthew, at different places, making it clear that they are separate events.

2. *But then, once again, they began to doubt.*[100] "Is this not just the carpenter—and the son of our carpenter?[101] Is this not the son of Mary?[102]
Aren't his brothers James and Joseph and Simon and Judas? Do not all
his sisters live here among us?[103] Where then would this man get such
powers?" And they took offense at him.

3. And Jesus said to them *once more,* "A prophet is not without honor,
except in his own town, and among his own relatives, and in his own
house." And he could not do many miracles there, because of their unbelief, except that he laid his hands upon a few sick people and healed
them. And their lack of faith amazed him.

74. A RICH HARVEST BUT FEW WORKERS
Matthew 9:35–38; Mark 6:6b

1. After this Jesus traveled through all the towns and villages, teaching in
the synagogues and proclaiming the good news of the kingdom, and
healing every disease and every infirmity.

2. When he saw the crowds that came he felt compassion for them, because they were harassed and wandering, like sheep that have no shepherd. And he said to his disciples, "Truly the harvest is plentiful, but

---

100. There is a marked change in the mood of the crowd at this point. Or perhaps
even their first lines were spoken with sarcasm, and the crowd was doubting from the
start.*

101. The Greek word here is *tekton,* which has a somewhat broader connotation
than the traditional "carpenter." A *tekton* was a journeyman artisan, who had some
familiarity with all the basic construction techniques used in rural towns. These skills
would begin with carpentry, but could also include things like masonry or metalwork.

102. This apparently innocuous line may have carried an insult. Jewish men were
commonly identified by their father's name—as in, Jesus the son of Joseph. To refer
to him instead as the son of Mary may suggest that his parentage and legitimacy were
questioned in his home town. This is possible: the explanatory angelic announcements
had been made only to Joseph and Mary, and not to the townspeople. But other, less
hostile explanations for the comment are also possible. Joseph may have died by this
time, and the townspeople may have simply been referring to Mary as the sole surviving parent known to her neighbors. Jesus is later referred to as the son of Joseph in
Chapter 82:7.*

103. The relationship between Jesus and these siblings has been much discussed.
They may have been other children of Joseph and Mary, born after Jesus. Or they may
have been children of Joseph from a prior marriage. Or they may have been more distant cousins, referred to as "brother" and "sister" as a form of familiar address. Different
churches favor different interpretations on this point.*

the workers are few; therefore pray to the lord of the harvest, that he
will send out workers into his field."

75. THE TWELVE APOSTLES ARE SENT OUT
Matthew 10:5–11:1; Mark 6:7–13; Luke 9:1–6, 12:6–7

1. So Jesus called the twelve together, and gave them power and author-
    ity over all demons, and to cure diseases. And he sent them out two by
    two, to preach the kingdom of God and to heal the sick.

Instructions for the journey

2. These were his directions: "Do not go in the way of the Gentiles, and
    enter no town of the Samaritans, but go rather to the lost sheep of the
    house of Israel. And as you go, preach this message: 'The kingdom of
    heaven is near.' Heal the sick, raise the dead, cleanse the lepers, cast out
    demons. Freely you have received; now freely give.

3. "Take nothing *special* for the journey—no bag, no extra tunic, no trav-
    elers' staves, no walking shoes. Take no bread, and no gold or silver or
    copper in your purses; for the laborer is worthy of his keep. Take noth-
    ing except the staff and the sandals *that you already have.*"[104]

4. And he said to them, "Whatever town or village you enter, find out
    who in it is worthy and stay with him. Whenever you enter a house,
    stay there until you depart from that town. As you enter the house,
    give it your blessing, saying, 'May peace be on this house.'[105] If the
    house proves worthy, let your blessing of peace remain upon it; but if
    it is not worthy, let your blessing return to you. And if any house or
    town will not receive you or listen to your words, shake the dust of it
    from your feet when you leave, as a testimony against them. I tell you
    truly, on the day of judgment it shall be more bearable for Sodom and
    Gomorrah than for that town.

---

104. The italicized words reconcile a potential difference among the gospels. All of
the listed items are prohibited in Matthew and Luke. In Mark, however, sandals and a
staff are permitted. These two instructions can be harmonized on the understanding
that expensive travelers' versions of these items were banned, while the ordinary daily
versions were permitted.*

105. The elaborating text, spelling out the words of the blessing, appears in only
some manuscripts and some older versions of the bible, such as the Douay-Rheims.
Virtually all commentators believe, however, that a blessing on these terms was at least
implied.

The need for steadiness

5. "Behold, I am sending you out as sheep in the midst of wolves; so you must be as cunning as serpents and innocent as doves.

6. "Beware of men, for they will deliver you up to their councils, and flog you in their synagogues, and you will be brought before governors and kings for my sake. But there you can bear testimony to them and the Gentiles. When they hand you over for trial, take no thought for how you are to speak or what you are to say. What you are to say will be given to you at that moment; for it is not you who will speak, but the Spirit of your Father speaking through you.

7. "You will be hated by all for my name's sake. But he that endures to the end will be saved. When you are persecuted in one town, flee to the next; for I tell you truly, you will not have finished going through all the towns of Israel before the Son of Man arrives.

8. "A disciple is not above his master, nor the servant above his lord; it is enough for the disciple to be like his master, and the servant like his lord. So if they have called the master of the house Beelzebub, by how much more will they defame the members of his household?

9. "But have no fear of them; for nothing is concealed that will not be revealed, or secret that will not be made known. What I tell you in the dark, speak in the daylight; and what you hear whispered in your ear, proclaim from the housetops.[106] And do not fear those who kill the body but cannot kill the soul; rather fear him who is able to destroy both soul and body in hell. Are not two sparrows sold for a penny? Are not five sold for two pennies? Yet not one of them shall fall to the ground without your Father's eye upon it. Even the very hairs of your head have all been numbered. So fear not, for you are of more value than many sparrows.

10. "Every one who acknowledges me before men, I will likewise acknowledge before my Father who is in heaven; but whoever denies me before men, I will likewise deny before my Father in heaven.

The need for passion

11. "Do not think that I have come to bring peace to the earth; I have not come to bring peace, but a sword. For I have come to set—

---

106. Village houses in Jesus' day had flat roofs, which could be accessed as additional living areas and as vantage points over the street.

a man against his father,
and a daughter against her mother,
and a daughter-in-law against her mother-in-law;
and a man's foes will be those of his own household.[107]

Brother will betray brother to death, and the father his child, and children will rise up against their parents and cause them to be put to death.[108]

12. "He who loves father or mother more than me is not worthy of me; and he who loves son or daughter more than me is not worthy of me; and he who does not take up his cross and follow me is not worthy of me. Whoever clings to his life will lose it, but whoever loses his life for my sake will find it.

13. "Whoever receives you receives me, and whoever receives me receives him who sent me. Whoever receives a prophet because he is a prophet shall receive the same reward as a prophet; and whoever receives a righteous man because he is a righteous man shall receive a righteous man's reward. And whoever gives even a cup of cool water to the least of my followers,[109] just because he is a disciple of mine, truly, I say to you, he shall not lose his reward."

14. When Jesus had finished instructing his twelve disciples, he went on to teach and preach in the towns of Galilee.

15. And so the apostles set out and went through the villages, preaching the gospel and proclaiming that all people should repent. They cast out many demons, and anointed with oil many that were sick,[110] and healed them.

---

107. This is a reference to Micah 7:6.

108. In most cases, however, the conflict anticipated by Jesus will probably not be this intense. He certainly expects that the initial spread of his new doctrines will lead to disputes between believers and non-believers, even within families. This is more likely to be a matter of verbal argument than of physical violence, however. In later teachings he uses a milder vocabulary to suggest that he will be bringing "division." See Chapter 122:2. However, the risk of persecution and martyrdom is always present for his followers.*

109. Literally, "to one of these little ones." The reference is not to children, however, but rather to the humility of Jesus' followers and their modest status by the standards of the world.

110. The anointing was usually done with olive oil.

76. HEROD GROWS WORRIED
Matthew 14:1–2; Mark 6:14–16; Luke 9:7–9

1. At this time Herod the tetrarch heard the reports about Jesus, and of all that he was doing, for Jesus' name had become well known.

2. And he was troubled, because it was said by some, "This is John the Baptist; he has been raised from the dead, and that is why these miraculous powers are at work in him." But others said, "It is Elijah." And still others said, "It is a prophet, like one of the prophets of old, who has come back to life."

3. When Herod heard all this, he said to his attendants, "John, whom I beheaded, has been raised from the dead! *Or else then*[111] who is this *other* person about whom I hear such things?" And he began trying to see Jesus.

77. THE APOSTLES RETURN
Mark 6:30–32; Luke 9:10; John 6:1

1. *After a while* the apostles returned to Jesus, and reported to him all they had done and taught.

2. And he said to them, "Let us go away by ourselves to a quiet place, and rest a while." For so many people were coming and going that they had no time even to eat. So he took them in a boat to the other side of the Sea of Galilee, also called the Sea of Tiberias, to a secluded place in the territory of the town called Bethsaida, where they might have a chance to be alone.

78. THE LOAVES AND FISHES
Matthew 14:13b–21; Mark 6:33–44; Luke 9:11–17; John 6:2–13

1. But many people saw Jesus and the disciples going *across the water*, and recognized them. The crowds ran after them on foot from all the

---

111. In Matthew and Mark, Herod believes that John has risen from the dead. In Luke he seems more confident that John remains dead, and so he is puzzled about the identity of the new teacher. The words in italics suggest how both these concerns might be present.

towns, because they had seen the miracles which Jesus performed on those who were sick, and they got *to the landing place* ahead of them.

2. As Jesus went ashore he saw the great throng. *But before addressing them* he went up into the hills, and there sat down with his disciples. It was almost time for the Jewish feast of the Passover.

3. When Jesus looked up and saw that the great multitude was coming toward him, he had compassion on them, because they were like sheep without a shepherd; and he began to teach them many things. He welcomed them, and spoke to them about the kingdom of God, and cured those who had need of healing.

4. Then when the day grew far spent, the disciples came to him and said, "This is a lonely place, and the hour is now late. Send the crowds away to go to the farms and villages round about, so they can find shelter and buy food for themselves."

5. But Jesus answered, "They do not have to go away; give them something to eat." And he asked Philip, "Where can we buy bread, so that these people may eat?" Jesus said this to Philip to test him, for he already knew what he would do. Philip answered him, "Eight months' wages would scarcely buy enough bread for each one to have even a little!" And the disciples asked, "Do you wish us to go and spend that much on bread for them?"

6. Jesus asked them, "How many loaves have you? Go and see." And when they had found out, one of his disciples, Andrew, Simon Peter's brother, reported to him, "There is a boy here who has five barley loaves and two small fish; but what are they among so many?"

7. Jesus said, "Bring them here to me." And he said to his disciples, "Have all the people be seated in groups, about fifty each." The disciples did so, and had them all sit down. Now there was an abundance of green grass in that place, and the men sat down on it in groups, by hundreds and by fifties.

8. Then taking the five loaves and the two fish, Jesus looked up to heaven and blessed the food, and broke the loaves, and gave the loaves to the disciples, and the disciples gave them to those who were seated. He did the same with the two fish, giving out as much as they wanted. And the people all ate and were filled.

9. When they had eaten their fill, he said to his disciples, "Gather up the fragments that remain, so that nothing may be wasted." They took them up, and they filled twelve baskets with pieces from the five barley

loaves and the fish, which were left over by those who had eaten. And those who ate were about five thousand men, besides women and children.

Curses Against the Pharisees (detail), by James Tissot
Brooklyn Museum

VI. THE GALILEE MINISTRY

Moving into Opposition

79. JESUS AVOIDS BEING MADE KING
Matthew 14:22–23; Mark 6:45–46; John 6:14–17a

1. When the people saw the miracle which Jesus had done, they began to say, "Surely this is the prophet who is to come into the world!" Realizing that the people were about to come and take him by force and make him their king, Jesus immediately instructed his disciples to get into the boat and go ahead of him to the other side of the lake, by way of Bethsaida,[112] while he dismissed the crowd.

2. And after he had sent the people away, he went up into the hills[113] by himself to pray.

3. When evening came, his disciples went down to the water, got into a boat, and started across the sea to Capernaum. But Jesus was still there in the hills alone.

---

112. Mark gives the detail that Jesus instructed his disciples to go to Bethsaida. This is puzzling, because that town was nearby and not on the far side of the lake. A likely explanation is that the weather was threatening, see Chapter 80:2, and Jesus was advising the disciples to stay close to shore, going toward and then past the town on their way around the end of the lake, and then on to their final destination.*

113. The hills rising above the eastern shore of the Sea of Galilee form the edge of the plateau known today as the Golan Heights.

95

80. WALKING ON THE WATER
Matthew 14:24–33; Mark 6:47–52; John 6:17b–21a

1. It was now dark, and the boat was in the midst of the sea, and Jesus was alone on the land, and had not yet come to them. And the sea rose because of a great wind that blew.

2. Jesus saw that the disciples were hard-pressed in rowing and were tossed by the waves, for the wind was against them. And in the fourth watch of the night, when they had rowed about three or four miles, he went out toward them, walking on the water.

3. He intended to go on past them, but when the disciples saw Jesus walking on the water and drawing close to the boat, they were all frightened and began to cry out, saying, "It is a ghost!" Then Jesus immediately spoke to them and said, "Take heart! It is I. Be not afraid."

4. And Peter answered him, "Lord, if it is you, command me to come to you on the water." Jesus said, "Come." So Peter got out of the boat and walked on the water toward Jesus. But when he saw the strength of the wind he was afraid; and, beginning to sink, he cried out, "Lord, save me!" Jesus at once reached out his hand and caught him, saying to him, "O ye of little faith, why did you doubt?"

5. Then the disciples were willing to take him into the boat. And when Jesus and Peter got into the boat with them, the wind ceased.

6. Then those in the boat worshiped him, saying, "Truly you are the Son of God." They were utterly amazed, for they had not understood the miracle of the loaves; their hearts had been hardened.

81. THE HEM OF THE GARMENT
Matthew 14:34–36; Mark 6:53–56; John 6:21b

1. After that, the boat soon reached the coast where they were heading. They came to land at Gennesaret,[114] where they moored to the shore. And when they got out of the boat, the people of that place recognized Jesus at once, and they ran through the whole neighborhood, and sent word out to all the region. And they began to carry sick people on their pallets to any place where they heard he was.

---

114. Gennesaret is a coastal plain along the west side of the Sea of Galilee, extending from Capernaum south to Magdala.

2. And wherever Jesus went—in villages, towns or the countryside—they laid the sick in the marketplaces, and begged him to let them touch even the hem of his garment;[115] and all who touched it were made well.

82. THE BREAD OF LIFE
John 6:22–59

1. *In the meantime* the people who remained on the other side of the sea realized that only one boat had been there, and that Jesus had not entered it with his disciples, but that the disciples had gone away without him. Then some boats from Tiberias arrived near the place where they had eaten the bread after the Lord gave thanks. Once the people realized that Jesus was no longer there, nor his disciples, they got into these boats and went to Capernaum, seeking him.

2. When they found Jesus on the other side of the sea, they asked him, "Rabbi, when did you get here?" Jesus answered them, "I tell you truly, you seek me, not because you saw the miracles, but because you ate the loaves, and were filled by them. Yet you should not work for food which spoils, but for the food which endures to eternal life, which the Son of Man will give to you; for on him God the Father has set his seal."

3. Then the people asked him, "What must we do, to be doing the work of God?" Jesus answered, "The work of God is this—that you believe in the one whom he has sent."

4. So they said to him, "Then what sign will you give us, so that we may see and believe you? What miracle can you perform? Our fathers ate manna in the wilderness; and so it is written, 'He gave them bread from heaven to eat.'" Jesus then said to them, "I tell you truly, it was not Moses who gave you the bread from heaven, but my Father. And now he gives you the true bread from heaven. For the bread of God is that which comes down from heaven, and gives life to the world." They said to him, "Lord, give us this bread always."

---

115. The reference is to the fringe of loose threads or tassels around the border of a garment. The tassels placed at the corners of outer garments had a particular significance to observant Jews, because they had been instructed to put these on their clothing to serve as a constant reminder to follow God's laws. See Numbers 15:37–41. The people may have been seeking to touch such tassels here. The fringe of his garment had also been touched by the bleeding woman in Chapter 71:4.*

5. Jesus said to them, "I am that bread of life; he who comes to me shall never hunger, and he who believes in me shall never thirst.

6. "But as I have told you, you have seen me and yet you still do not believe. All those that the Father gives me will come to me; and whoever comes to me I will certainly not turn away. For I have come down from heaven, not to do my own will, but the will of him who sent me. And the will of him who sent me is this: that I should not lose even one of those that he has given me, but should raise them up again on the last day. My Father desires that all those who look upon the Son and believe in him should have eternal life; and I will raise them up on the last day."[116]

7. Then the crowd began to grumble about him, because he said, 'I am the bread which came down from heaven.' They said, "Is this not Jesus, the son of Joseph, whose father and mother we know? How can he now say, 'I have come down from heaven'?"

8. Jesus answered them, "Do not complain about this. No one can come to me unless the Father who sent me leads him there; and that one I will raise up on the last day. It is written in the prophets, 'And they will all be taught by God.' Everyone who has heard the Father and learned from him comes to me. Not that any one has seen the Father except the one who is from God; but that one has seen the Father. I tell you truly, he who believes in me has everlasting life.

9. "I am the bread of life. Your fathers ate the manna in the wilderness, and yet they died. But here before you is the bread which comes down from heaven, so that a man may eat of it and not die. I am the living bread which came down from heaven. Whoever eats of this bread will live forever. And the bread that I will give is my flesh, which I give for the life of the world."

10. Then the people began to argue among themselves, saying, "How can this man give us his flesh to eat?" So Jesus said to them, "I tell you truly, unless you eat the flesh of the Son of Man and drink his blood, you will have no life in you. Whoever eats my flesh and drinks my blood has eternal life, and I will raise them up on the last day. For my flesh is food indeed, and my blood is drink indeed. Those who eat my flesh and drink my blood abide in me, and I in them. As the living Father sent me, and as I live because of the Father, so he who eats me will live

---

116. These teachings were a departure from traditional Judaism. The themes of life after death, resurrection, and immortality are mentioned only briefly in the Old Testament.*

because of me. This is the bread that came down from heaven. And unlike your fathers, who ate manna and are dead, he who eats this bread will live forever." Jesus said these things as he taught in the synagogue at Capernaum.

83. MANY DISCIPLES FALL AWAY
John 6:60–71

1. On hearing this, many of his disciples said, "This is a difficult teaching. Who can accept it?" And Jesus, knowing within himself that his disciples were troubled by it, said to them, "Does this offend you? Then what *would you think* if you were to see the Son of Man ascending to where he was before? It is the spirit that gives life; the flesh profits nothing. The words that I have spoken to you are spirit and life. But there are some among you that do not believe."

2. For Jesus knew from the beginning which ones of them did not believe, and who it was that would betray him. And he said, "This is why I told you that no one can come to me unless the Father makes it possible."

3. After this many of his disciples turned back and no longer followed him. Jesus said to the twelve, "You do not wish to leave me also, do you?" Simon Peter answered him, "Lord, to whom would we go? You have the words of eternal life; and we believe, and have come to know, that you are the Holy One of God." Jesus answered them, "Did I not choose you, the twelve? And yet one of you is a devil!" He had in mind Judas, the son of Simon Iscariot, for he, although one of the twelve, was going to betray him.

84. OLD DIETARY LAWS ARE SET ASIDE
Matthew 15:1–20; Mark 7:1–23; Luke 6:39–40

1. Later a group of Pharisees and scribes who had come from Jerusalem gathered around Jesus, and noticed some of his disciples eating their food with hands that were "impure," that is, unwashed. For the Pharisees, and all the Jews, do not eat unless they properly wash their hands, observing the tradition of the elders; and when they come from the

marketplace, they do not eat unless they first purify themselves with water. And they hold to many other traditions, such as the ceremonial washing or sprinkling[117] of cups, pitchers, cooking vessels and dining couches.

2. So the Pharisees and the scribes asked Jesus, "Why do your disciples not live according to the tradition of the elders,[118] but instead eat with impure hands? For they do not wash their hands before they eat."

3. Jesus answered them, "And why do you break the commandment of God for the sake of your tradition? You seem to think that is a fine thing! For God and Moses said, 'Honor thy father and thy mother;' and 'Whoever curses his father or mother must surely die.' But you say, 'If a man tells his father or his mother, Whatever support you might otherwise have received from me is Corban (that is, dedicated to God) then he is not to honor his father or his mother with it.' You no longer permit him to do anything for them. Thus you make void the command of God through the tradition which you have handed down. And you do many such things.

4. "You hypocrites! Isaiah spoke rightly when he prophesied about you:

> These people honor me with their lips,
> but their hearts are far away from me.
> In vain do they worship me,
> teaching as holy doctrines the precepts of men.

For you too have left the commandments of God, and hold fast to the tradition of men."

5. Then Jesus summoned the crowd to him, and said to them, "Hear me, all of you, and understand: It is not what goes into the mouth from outside that defiles a man, but what comes out of the mouth; that it what defiles a man."

6. When he had left the crowd and entered the house, his disciples came and said to him, "Do you know that the Pharisees were offended when

---

117. The Greek word here is *baptismos*, which normally implies a formal cleansing by immersion in water. Because dining couches cannot be submerged easily or without damage, however, it appears that other methods of cleansing may also be acceptable.*

118. The Pharisees engaged in a highly detailed elaboration of the law of Moses. Unlike the Sadducees, who accepted only the written scripture as authoritative, the Pharisees also valued oral interpretive traditions. These were deliberately made more restrictive than the law itself in order to provide a margin for error. Over the years this oral tradition became large and difficult to remember. Around A.D. 200 this material began to be written down and it eventually became the Talmud.*

they heard your words?" He answered, "Every plant which my heavenly Father did not plant will be rooted up. Keep clear of them; they are blind guides." And he told them this parable: "Can the blind lead the blind? Will they not both fall into the ditch? A disciple is not better than his teacher, but every student when he is fully taught will become like his teacher."

7. Then Peter and the other disciples said to him, "Explain the teaching to us." And Jesus said, "Do you too still understand so little? Do you not see that whatever goes into a man from outside cannot defile him? For whatever goes into the mouth enters, not the man's heart but his stomach, and so it passes on." In saying this, Jesus declared all foods clean.

8. And he said, "But what comes out of the mouth proceeds from the heart, and this is what can defile a man. For from within, out of the hearts of men, come evil thoughts—murder, adultery, promiscuity, theft, blasphemy, greed, wickedness, malice, deceit, sensuality, false witness, envy, arrogance, and folly. All these evil things come from within, and these are what defile a person. But to eat with unwashed hands does not defile."

85. A GENTILE WOMAN ASKS FOR THE CRUMBS FROM THE TABLE
Matthew 15:21-28; Mark 7:24-30

1. Leaving the place *where he had given this lesson*, Jesus went to the district of Tyre and Sidon. There he entered a house, and wished not to have any one know it, and yet he could not escape notice.

2. For immediately a woman from that region heard of his presence, and came and fell at this feet, and cried, "Have pity on me, O Lord, Son of David; my daughter is possessed and cruelly tormented by a demon."

3. Now the woman was a Gentile—*by territory* a Canaanite, and by nationality a Syro-Phoenician.[119] And she begged Jesus to cast the demon

119. "Canaan" was a general term for the land of Israel, but also had a more extensive connotation, which included some non-Jewish lands, such as the Phoenician territories to the north. Tyre and Sidon were coastal cities in this latter area, and were the heart of the old Phoenician state. The "Syro-Phoenician" woman would be member of the Phoenician community living along this coast, which was under the political control of Syria. In Mark this woman is further identified as a "Greek," but that term

out of her daughter. But he did not answer a word. His disciples came and urged him, "Send her away, for she is distracting us with her constant begging." And then he answered the woman, "I was sent only to the lost sheep of the house of Israel."

4. She came and knelt before him, saying, "Lord, help me." But he said to her, "No, first let the children eat their fill; for it is not right to take away the children's bread and throw it to the dogs."[120] She replied, "Yes, Lord; yet even the dogs under the master's table are allowed to eat the crumbs that the children drop."

5. Then Jesus said to her, "O woman, for that good answer you may go home content. Great is your faith. Let it be done for you as you desire; the demon has left your daughter." And her daughter was healed from that moment. The woman went home, and found her child lying in bed, and the demon gone.

86. JESUS DOETH ALL THINGS WELL
Mark 7:31–37

1. Soon after this Jesus departed from the area of Tyre, and went up through Sidon, and then returned to the Sea of Galilee and the region of the Decapolis. There some people brought to him a man who was deaf and had an impediment in his speech; and they begged him to lay his hand upon him.

2. Taking the man aside, away from the crowd, Jesus put his fingers into the man's ears, and he spat and touched the man's tongue; and looking up to heaven he sighed deeply, and said to him, "Ephphatha," which means, "Be opened." And straightaway the man's ears were opened, his tongue was released, and he spoke clearly.

3. Jesus charged the people to tell no one; but the more he charged them, with the more determination they proclaimed the news. For they were

---

was used by Jewish writers to refer generally to all non-Jewish inhabitants of the Middle East, among whom Greek was the common language. The term "Gentile" seems to better capture this designation.*

120. Jesus is speaking here in metaphor: The Jews are the children of Israel, and it would not be right to take their most valuable possessions—the teachings of their religion and the power of their prophets—and make them freely available to the non-Jewish world.

astonished beyond measure, saying, "He does all things well; he makes both the deaf to hear, and the mute to speak."

87. FEEDING THE FOUR THOUSAND
Matthew 15:29–38; Mark 8:1–9a

1. From there Jesus passed along by the Sea of Galilee. And he went up into the hills, and there he sat down.

2. Great crowds came to him, bringing with them the lame, the deformed, the blind, the mute, and many others. All these they put at his feet, and he healed them, so that the multitude marveled when they saw the mute speaking, the deformed made whole, the lame walking, and the blind seeing; and they praised the God of Israel.

3. Because the crowd grew very great, and they had nothing to eat, Jesus called his disciples to him, and said to them, "I have compassion for these people, because they have been with me for three days now, and have nothing left to eat. And I do not wish to send them away fasting to their homes, for fear that they may faint on the road, for some of them have come from far away."

4. His disciples answered him, "Where are we to get enough bread in this remote place to feed so great a crowd?" And he asked them, "How many loaves have you?" They said, "Seven, and a few small fish."

5. Then he told the crowd to sit down on the ground; and he took the seven loaves, and gave thanks, and broke them, and gave them to his disciples to set before the people; and the disciples gave them to the crowd. And having blessed the few small fish, he commanded that these also should be set before the crowd. And the people all ate and were filled.

6. Afterward the disciples took up seven baskets full of the broken pieces left over. Those who ate were about four thousand men, besides women and children.[121]

---

121. At first this looks like another description of the miracle of the loaves and fishes. Matthew and Mark both wrote separately about the original miracle, however, and so it is clear that they are reporting on a different event here. Moreover, the two accounts give different numbers for some specific details, such as the numbers of loaves, baskets of leftovers, and people attending.

88. THE SIGNS OF THE TIMES
Matthew 15:39–16:4; Mark 8:9b–13

1. After sending away the crowds, Jesus got into the boat with his disciples, and went to the region of Magdala[122] and Dalmanutha.

2. There the Pharisees and Sadducees came and began to question him; and to test him they asked him to show them a sign from heaven.

3. He answered them, "When evening comes, you say, 'It will be fair weather, for the sky is red.' And in the morning you say, 'It will be foul weather today, for the sky is red and lowering.' You know how to interpret the appearance of the sky, but you cannot interpret the signs of the times."

4. And he sighed deeply and asked, "Why does this evil and adulterous generation keep looking for a miraculous sign? I tell you truly, no sign shall be given to it except the sign of Jonah."[123] And so he left them, and getting back into the boat he departed for the other side.

89. "BEWARE THE LEAVEN OF THE PHARISEES!"
Matthew 16:5–12; Mark 8:14–21

1. Now the disciples had forgotten to bring bread, and they had only one loaf with them in the boat. When they reached the other side, Jesus cautioned them, saying, "Take heed, and beware of the leaven of the Pharisees and Sadducees, and the yeast of Herod." The disciples began to discuss this among themselves, saying, "It is because we have brought no bread."

2. Becoming aware of this, Jesus said, "O ye of little faith, why are you talking about having no bread? Do you still not perceive or understand? Are your hearts hardened? Do you have eyes and not see, and have ears and not hear?

---

122. This was the probable home town of Mary Magdalene. The town was sometimes also referred to as Magaden. It stood on the shore of the Sea of Galilee, about six miles south of Jesus' town of Capernaum.

123. Jonah's escape from the whale provided a model of Jesus' own later resurrection. See Chapter 67:11.

3. "And do you not remember? When I broke the five loaves for the five thousand, how many baskets full of broken pieces did you pick up?" They said to him, "Twelve." "And the seven loaves for the four thousand, how many baskets full of broken pieces did you pick up?" And they said to him, "Seven."[124]

4. And he said to them, "Do you still not understand? How can you fail to see that I was not speaking about bread when I told you to beware the yeast of the Pharisees and Sadducees!" Then they understood that he was not telling them to beware of the yeast used in making bread, but to beware of the teaching of the Pharisees and Sadducees.[125]

90. AN ERROR IN HEALING
Mark 8:22–26

1. Then they came to Bethsaida. There some people brought a blind man to Jesus and begged Jesus to touch him.

2. Jesus took the blind man by the hand and led him out of the town. When he had spit on the man's eyes and laid his hands upon him, Jesus asked him, "Can you see anything?" And the man looked up and said, "I see people; they look like walking trees."

3. Jesus put his hands on the man's eyes once more. Then the man's gaze was sharpened, his sight was restored, and he saw all things clearly. And Jesus sent him away straight to his home, saying, "Do not even go into the town."

91. THE KEYS OF THE KINGDOM
Matthew 16:13–20; Mark 8:27–30; Luke 9:18–21

1. Jesus and his disciples continued to the villages around Caesarea Philippi. Along the way, Jesus was praying one day in the absence of the crowds. The disciples were with him, and he asked them, "Who do the people say that I am?"

---

124. These numbers may have once had a symbolic meaning that is now forgotten.

125. In this context, "yeast" does not refer to the normal, wholesome leavening agent in bread. The reference is instead to "sour or fermenting dough, suggesting hidden corruption."*

2. And they answered, "Some say you are John the Baptist; others say Elijah; and still others, that Jeremiah or one of the prophets of old has come back to life."

3. He asked them, "But who do you say that I am?" Simon Peter replied, "You are the Christ, the Son of the living God."

4. And Jesus responded, "Blessed are you, Simon son of John! For this was not revealed to you by flesh and blood, but my Father who is in heaven. And I tell you, you are Peter, and upon this rock[126] I will build my church; and the gates of hell[127] shall not prevail against it. I will give unto you the keys of the kingdom of heaven, and whatever you bind on earth shall be bound in heaven, and whatever you loose on earth shall be loosed in heaven."[128]

5. Then he strictly ordered his disciples to tell no one that he was the Christ.

92. JESUS FORETELLS HIS DEATH AND RESURRECTION
Matthew 16:21–28; Mark 8:31–9:1; Luke 9:22–27

1. From that time Jesus began to teach his disciples that he must go to Jerusalem. He said, "The Son of Man must suffer many things from the elders and chief priests and scribes, and be rejected by them, and be killed, and on the third day be raised from death."[129] And he said this plainly.

---

126. This is a pun on Peter's name. In Greek, Peter is *Petros*, and rock is *petra*.

127. Literally, "the gates of Hades," the abode of the dead, from which no one emerges. This is a figure of speech meaning that "the power of death shall not prevail against it."

128. Peter later went to Rome and became the new church's bishop in the Imperial city. Popes today count themselves as the successors of Saint Peter in that office. The Pope is automatically the Bishop of Rome, and the governing apparatus of the Catholic Church, the Holy See, is technically the administrative office of the bishopric. Peter's crossed keys are prominent among the emblems of the Vatican. Jesus later conferred an additional power to bind and to loose on the apostles generally, in Chapter 100:2, in a passage that is cited by Protestant churches.

129. In Matthew and Luke, Jesus says that he will be raised "on the third day." Here and elsewhere in the gospels, Mark he says that he will be raised "after three days." The two expressions have the same meaning and merely reflect different conventions in counting. However, the expression used in the text seems to be the clearer of the two.

2. Peter took Jesus aside and tried to dissuade him from these thoughts, saying, "God forbid, Lord! This shall never happen to you." But when Jesus turned and looked at his disciples, he rebuked Peter and said, "Get thee behind me, Satan! You are only making my path more difficult,[130] for you are not thinking about the purposes of God, but the purposes of men."

3. And he called the crowd to him, along with his disciples, and said to them all, "If anyone wishes to come with me, he must deny himself and take up his cross daily and follow me. Whoever wishes to save his life will lose it; and whoever loses his life for my sake and the sake of the gospel will save it.

4. "For what does it profit a man to gain the whole world, if he loses his own soul? And what shall a man give in exchange for his soul?

5. "Whoever is ashamed of me and of my words in this adulterous and sinful generation, of him the Son of Man will also be ashamed, when he comes in his glory and in the glory of the Father and the holy angels. Then he will reward every man according to his deeds."[131]

6. And he said to them, "I tell you truly, there are some standing here who will not taste of death before they see the kingdom of God come with power, and the Son of Man coming in that kingdom."

---

130. Literally, "you are a stumbling-block to me."

131. This raises the recurring question of faith versus works. Does salvation come through interior faith and the unilateral grace of God, or through meritorious exterior actions such as charitable giving and religious observances? Jesus said things on both sides of this question, mentioning the importance of individual actions and deeds here, and the importance of grace somewhat more frequently, in passages such as Chapter 146:7. Various formulas have been proposed to understand the relationship between these two teachings. One is to say that a person is indeed saved by faith and grace alone, but that faith should then be followed by good works that confirm the vitality of the faith. Another formula explains that without God's grace, man *can* do nothing toward his salvation; but without man's efforts, God *will* do nothing.*

93. THE TRANSFIGURATION
Matthew 17:1–8; Mark 9:2–8; Luke 9:28–36a

1. Six days[132] after saying these things, Jesus took Peter, and James, and John the brother of James, and led them up a high mountain by themselves to pray.[133]

2. And as he was praying, the appearance of his countenance was changed, and he was transfigured before their eyes. His face began to shine like the sun, and his garments became glistening, brilliantly white, like the light or like snow, such as no cloth-worker on earth could bleach them.

3. And suddenly two men, Moses and Elijah, appeared in glorious splendor and began talking with Jesus. They spoke of his approaching death, which he would soon bring about at Jerusalem.

4. Peter and his companions had been heavy with sleep, but now they were fully awake, and they saw the glory of Jesus and saw the two men who stood with him.

5. And as the men were parting from Jesus, Peter said to him, "Master, it is good that we are here. Let us put up three temporary shelters, one for you and one for Moses and one for Elijah." He spoke in confusion, not knowing what he said, for they were exceedingly afraid.

6. Peter was still speaking when a bright cloud came and enveloped them; and they were afraid as they entered the cloud. And a voice came out of the cloud, saying, "This is my beloved Son, my Chosen One, with whom I am well pleased; listen to him!"

7. When the disciples heard this, they fell face down on the ground, and were filled with awe. But Jesus came and touched them, saying, "Rise, and have no fears." And suddenly, when they looked up, they no longer saw any one with them except Jesus only.

---

132. Matthew and Mark both specify six days; Luke says "about eight days."

133. The Mount of the Transfiguration is not identified in the gospels. Long Christian tradition, however, dating at least at least as far back as the Third Century, believes it to be Mount Tabor, a solitary and steep-sided hill, 11 miles southwest of the Sea of Galilee.

94. JOHN THE BAPTIST WAS ELIJAH
Matthew 17:9–13; Mark 9:9–13; Luke 9:36b

1. As they were coming down the mountain, Jesus instructed them, "Tell no one of this vision, until the Son of Man has been raised from the dead." So they kept it close and told no one, only discussing among themselves what "rising from the dead" might mean.

2. And they asked him, "Why do the scribes say that Elijah must return *before the Christ comes?*" And he said to them, "Elijah will indeed come first, and will make all things ready. But I tell you that Elijah has already come, and they did not recognize him, but did to him whatever they pleased, as it is written of him.

3. "And why do the scriptures say of the Son of Man, that he must suffer many things and be despised? Because the Son of Man will suffer at their hands in the same way."[134]

4. Then the disciples realized that he was speaking to them about John the Baptist. But they told no one at that time anything of what they had seen.

95. THE FAITH THAT MOVES MOUNTAINS
Matthew 17:14–21; Mark 9:14–29; Luke 9:37–43a, 17:5–6

1. On the next day, when they had come down from the mountain and returned to the other disciples, they saw a great crowd gathered around the disciples, and some scribes arguing with them. When the people saw Jesus they were greatly excited and they all ran at once to greet him.

2. He asked them, "What were you arguing about?" A man came up and kneeling before him said, "Lord, have mercy on my son, my only child. I beg you to look at him, for he is possessed by a spirit that has made him mute. He has seizures and suffers terribly. Whenever the spirit seizes him, he suddenly cries out; it convulses him and hurls him to the ground. He foams at the mouth and grinds his teeth and becomes rigid. Often he falls into the fire, and often into the water. The spirit scarcely ever leaves him and is wearing him away. And I brought the

---

134. This is probably a reference to the "suffering servant" passage in Isaiah. See Isaiah 52:13—53:12.

boy to your disciples, and begged them to cast the spirit out, but they could not."

3. And Jesus responded, "O contrary and unbelieving generation, how much longer must I be with you? How long am I to bear with you? Bring your son here to me." And they brought the boy to him.

4. While the boy was still approaching, the spirit saw Jesus and immediately it convulsed the boy, so that he fell on the ground and rolled about, foaming at the mouth.

5. Jesus asked the boy's father, "How long has he been this way?" "From childhood," the father answered, "and it has often thrown him into the fire or into the water, trying to kill him. But if you can do anything, take pity on us and help us."

6. "'If you can!'" Jesus repeated to him. "All things are possible for him who believes." Immediately the father of the child cried out and said, "I do believe, Lord; help me with my unbelief!"

7. When Jesus saw that a crowd was running to the scene, he rebuked the evil spirit, saying to it, "You spirit that makes this boy unable to hear or speak, I command you, come out of him, and enter into him no more!" And after screaming out and convulsing the boy terribly, the spirit came out of him.

8. The boy looked so much like a corpse that most bystanders said, "He is dead." But the boy was healed from that moment. Jesus took him by the hand and lifted him up, and he got to his feet; and Jesus gave him back to his father. And all were amazed at the majesty of God.

9. When Jesus had gone inside, his disciples asked him privately, "Why could we not cast it out?" And he said to them, "Because this kind can be driven out only with prayer and fasting, and you have little faith." The apostles said to the Lord, "Increase our faith!" And the Lord said, "I tell you truly, if you have faith, even as a grain of mustard seed, you could say to this mulberry tree, 'Uproot yourself, and plant yourself in the sea,' and it would obey you. Or you could say to this mountain, 'Move hence to yonder place,' and it will move; and nothing will be impossible to you."

96. AGAIN FORETELLS HIS DEATH AND RESURRECTION

Matthew 17:22–23; Mark 9:30–32; Luke 9:43b–45

1. Even while the people were marveling at all the things Jesus had done, he and his disciples left that place and passed through Galilee. And Jesus did not want anyone to know of their passage, for he was teaching the disciples.

2. He said to them, "Let these words sink into your ears: the Son of Man is going to be betrayed into the hands of men. They will kill him; but after he has been killed, on the third day he will rise again."

3. The disciples were greatly distressed. But they did not understand what Jesus meant. The meaning was concealed from them, so that they could not perceive it; and they were afraid to ask him about it.

97. THE TRIBUTE TO THE TEMPLE

Matthew 17:24–27; Mark 9:33a

1. When they came to Capernaum, the collectors of the two-drachma tax went up to Peter and asked, "Your teacher pays the temple tax, does he not?" "Indeed he does," Peter replied; and then he went into the house.

2. Before he could say anything, Jesus asked, "What do you think, Simon? From whom do kings of the earth collect tolls and taxes? From their own children, or from others?" "From others," Peter said to him. And Jesus said, "Then we, the children of God, should be exempt from the temple tax.[135]

3. "However, so as not to give offense to them, go to the sea and cast a hook, and take the first fish that comes up. When you open its mouth you will find a four-drachma coin; take that and give it to them for my tax and yours."

---

135. The original Greek here is considerably more terse: "Then the children are exempt." The language in the text attempts to convey the sense of this thought.

98. JESUS BEGINS TO THINK ABOUT LEAVING FOR JERUSALEM
John 7:1–9

1. After this Jesus went about only in Galilee, deliberately staying away from Judea because the leaders of the Jews there were waiting to take his life.

2. But when the time for the Jewish feast of Tabernacles drew near, his brothers said to him, "Leave here and go to Judea, so that your disciples may see the works you are doing. For no man works in secret if he wishes to become a public leader.[136] If you can actually do these great things, show yourself to the world." For even his brothers did not believe in him.[137]

3. Jesus said to them, "My time has not yet come, even if for you the time is always right. The world cannot hate you, but it hates me because I testify of it that its works are evil. Go up to the feast yourselves; I am not going yet, for my time has not yet fully come."

4. Saying this, he remained *a little while longer* in Galilee.

99. BEING GREAT AND BEING CHILDLIKE
Matthew 18:1–14; Mark 9:33b–50; Luke 9:46–50, 17:1–2

1. During those days an argument arose among the disciples as to which of them was the foremost. When Jesus was back at the house, he asked them, "What were you arguing about on the road?" But they were silent. Then they asked him, "Who is the greatest in the kingdom of heaven?"[138]

---

136. Judea was the most important center of Jewish culture, and its main city, Jerusalem, was the center of worship and the site of the temple. In comparison, Galilee was an outlying province.

137. Some members of Jesus' family later became important supporters of his cause. Their support was nonetheless limited in time, and it did not keep some apostles and later-recruited followers—rather than the blood relatives—from eventually coming to manage the development of the early church. This fact may have saved Christianity from the kind of schism that later appeared in Islam, where an enduring split formed between the followers of Mohammed's family (the Shiites), and the followers of the institutionalized leadership of the religion (the Sunnis).*

138. It appears that the apostles did not always understand the true nature of Jesus' mission, and sometimes acted with materialistic motives. If the kingdom of heaven

2. When Jesus perceived the thought that was in their hearts, he sat down, and called the twelve, and he said to them, "If any one desires to be first, he must be the last of all and the servant of all."

3. And he called a child, and had him stand among them; and then taking the child up in his arms he said to the disciples, "I tell you truly, unless you change and become as little children, you will never enter into the kingdom of heaven. Whoever humbles himself to be like this child, and is least among you all—he is the greatest in the kingdom of heaven.

4. "Whoever welcomes one such child in my name welcomes me; and whoever welcomes me, welcomes not only me but also the one who sent me."

5. John said to him, "Master, we saw someone casting out demons in your name, and we tried to stop him, because he is not one of us." But Jesus said, "Do not forbid him. No one who does a miracle in my name will be able to turn in the next moment and speak evil of me. And he that is not against us is for us.[139]

6. "I tell you truly, whoever gives you a cup of water to drink in my name because you are committed to Christ, he will by no means lose his reward. But whoever causes one of these little ones who believe in me to stumble, it would be better for him if a great millstone were fastened round his neck and he were drowned in the depths of the sea.

7. "Woe to the world for temptations toward sin! It is inevitable that temptations come, but woe to the man by whom they come!

8. "Therefore if your hand causes you to sin, cut it off and throw it from you; it is better for you to enter life maimed than to go to hell with two hands, into the fire that shall never die. And if your foot causes you to sin, cut it off; it is better for you to enter life lame than to have two feet and be cast into everlasting fire. And if your eye causes you to sin, pluck it out and throw it from you; it is better for you to enter the kingdom of God with one eye than with two eyes to be thrown into hell, where the worms *that consume the body* never die and the fire is never quenched.

---

were going to be instituted on earth, and instituted by Jesus, then the foremost of his disciples might expect to be entrusted with the greatest wealth and power.

139. Compare this with Chapter 67:5. As Jesus prepares to leave Galilee his attitude has apparently become more forgiving, or perhaps the circumstances here are simply less dire.

9. "Every heart will be prepared with fire, just as every sacrifice is prepared with salt. Salt is good; but if the salt has lost its flavor, how will you make it salty again? So cultivate the quality of saltiness within you, *and keep your heart always prepared*, and be at peace with one another.[140]

10. "Take heed that you do not look down on one of these little ones, for I tell you that in heaven their angels are always within reach of my heavenly Father. And the Son of Man has come to save that which was lost.

11. "So tell me! If a man has a hundred sheep, and one of them has gone astray, will he not leave the ninety-nine on the hills and go in search of the one that went astray? And if he finds it, I tell you truly, he rejoices over it more than over the ninety and nine that never went astray. So it is not the will of your heavenly Father that even one of these little ones should be lost."

100. FORGIVING YOUR BROTHER
Matthew 18:15–35; Luke 17:3–4

1. And Jesus said, "If your brother[141] sins against you, go and tell him his fault, between the two of you alone. If he listens to you, you have regained your brother.

2. "But if he will not listen, then take one or two others along with you, so that everything may be confirmed by the evidence of two or three witnesses. If he refuses to listen to them, take your complaint to the church. And if he refuses to listen even to the church, then let him be to you as a heathen or a tax-gatherer. I tell you truly, whatever you bind on earth will be bound in heaven, and whatever you loose on earth will be loosed in heaven.[142]

---

140. In literal terms this passage begins by saying that "every one will be salted with fire, and every sacrifice shall be salted with salt." The sense of it seems to be this: Every one will at some point be tested through the fires of temptation. He who passes this test is fit to be a servant of the Lord, just as a sacrifice, ritually sprinkled with salt, is fit to be presented to the Lord. The true disciple will internalize this discipline of preparation ("cultivating the quality of saltiness" within himself) and thereby will keep himself humble and at peace with all others.*

141. This term includes not only blood relatives, but also fellow members of the community of believers.

142. Thus, in this particular context, the apostles' judgment about how to treat quarreling brothers will be confirmed in heaven. The passage also has a more general

3. "Again, I tell you truly that if two of you on earth agree about anything you ask for, it will be done for you by my Father in heaven. For wherever two or three are gathered together in my name, there am I in the midst of them."

4. Then Peter came up and asked him, "Lord, how often can my brother sin against me, and I must forgive him? As many as seven times?" And Jesus said to him, "Be on your guard! If your brother sins, rebuke him, and if he repents, forgive him; and if he sins against you seven times in the day, and returns to you seven times, saying, 'I repent,' you must forgive him. I tell you, not seven times, but until seventy times seven.

5. "For the kingdom of heaven may be compared to a king who wished to settle accounts with his servants. When he began to do this, a man was brought to him who owed him a great sum of money; and as he could not pay, his lord ordered him to be sold, together with his wife and children and all that he had, to repay the debt.

6. "The servant fell on his knees before his master, begging him, 'Lord, be patient with me, and I will repay you everything.' And out of compassion for him the lord of that servant released him and forgave him the debt.

7. "But as that servant went out, he came upon one of his fellow servants who owed him a small sum; and seizing him by the throat he demanded, 'Pay me what you owe.' His fellow servant fell down at his feet and begged him, 'Have patience with me, and I will repay you.' But he refused and went and had the man put in prison until he should pay the debt.

8. "When the other servants saw this they were greatly offended, and they went and reported to their master all that had happened.

9. "Then the lord summoned the first servant and said to him, 'You wicked servant! I forgave you that huge debt because you begged me to. Should you not have had mercy on your fellow servant, even as I had mercy on you?' And in anger his lord handed him over to the jailers, to be tortured until he should pay all his debt.

10. "So likewise my heavenly Father will treat every one of you, if you do not forgive your brother or sister from your heart."

significance, however, in that it gives all of the apostles some of the authority over the church that had been previously granted to Peter alone. Compare Chapter 91:4.

IOI. JESUS LEAVES SECRETLY FOR JERUSALEM
Luke 9:51; John 7:10

1. As the time approached for him to ascend to heaven, Jesus set a determined face to go to Jerusalem.

2. And so after his brothers had gone up to the feast of Tabernacles, then he also went up, not openly, but as it were in secret.

I02. OVER-ZEALOUSNESS ON THE ROAD
Luke 9:52–56

1. Jesus sent messengers ahead of him, who went and entered a village of the Samaritans, to make things ready for him. But the people there would not welcome him, because he was on his way to Jerusalem.

2. When his disciples James and John saw this, they said, "Lord, do you want us to call down fire from heaven to consume them?"

3. But Jesus turned and corrected them; and he said, "You do not recognize what manner of emotion is driving you; for the Son of Man came not to destroy men's lives but to save them." And so they went on to another village.

I03. POTENTIAL RECRUITS ARE TESTED
Matthew 8:19–22; Luke 9:57–62

1. As they were walking along the road, a scribe came up and said to Jesus, "Master, I will follow you wherever you go." And Jesus said to him, "Foxes have their dens, and birds of the air have nests; but the Son of Man has nowhere to lay his head."

2. To another of the disciples he said, "Follow me." The disciple replied, "Lord, let me first go and bury my father." But Jesus said to him, "Follow me, and let the dead bury their own dead.[143] Your duty is to go and proclaim the kingdom of God."

---

143. In other words, leave to those who have remained at home and are deaf to the call—those who are spiritually dead—the job of burying those who are literally dead.*

3. Still another man said, "I will follow you, Lord; but let me first say fare-
well to those at my home." And Jesus said to him, "No one who puts his
hand to the plow and then looks back is fit for *service in* the kingdom
of God."

104. SEVENTY DISCIPLES ARE SENT AHEAD
Luke 10:1–12, 16; 12:4–5, 8–9, 11–12; John 13:20

1. After this, the Lord appointed seventy or seventy-two[144] other
disciples,[145] and sent them on ahead of him, two by two, into every
town and place that he intended to visit.

2. He said to them, "The harvest is plentiful, but the workers are few;
therefore pray to the Lord of the harvest, that he send more workers
into his field. Now go! And keep in mind, I am sending you out as
lambs in the midst of wolves."

3. *And he gave them a shorter version of the same instructions he had given
to the twelve:* "Carry no money, no bag, no walking shoes; and do not
stop to talk with anyone on the road. Whenever you enter someone's
home, first say 'Peace be on this house!' If a man of peace is there, your
peace shall rest upon him; but if not, it shall return to you. Remain
in the same house, freely eating and drinking what they provide, for
the laborer deserves his wages; but do not move about from house to
house.

4. "Whenever you enter a town and it welcomes you, eat what whatever
is set before you, heal the sick in it, and say to them, 'The kingdom of
God is near you now.' But whenever you enter a town and it does not
welcome you, go into its streets and say, 'Even the dust of your town
that clings to our feet, we brush off in testimony against you. Yet know
this: that the kingdom of God has come near.' I tell you, on the day of
judgment it will be more bearable for Sodom than for that town.

5. "I tell you, my friends, do not fear those who kill the body, and after
that can do nothing more. But I will warn you whom you should fear:

---

144. Different manuscripts and different Christian traditions preserve one or the
other number.

145. In the Orthodox tradition these messengers are commonly referred to as
"apostles;" and certainly they had been "sent out" as well. Using the title of "disciple"
here, however, seems less likely to create confusion with the original twelve apostles.

Fear him who, after killing the body, has also the power to cast you into hell. Yes, I tell you, fear that one!

6. "And when they bring you before the synagogues and the magistrates and the authorities, do not be anxious about how you are to defend yourself or what you should say; for the Holy Spirit will teach you in that very hour what you must say.

7. "I tell you truly, he who receives whomever I send receives me; and he who receives me receives him who sent me. But he who rejects you rejects me, and he who rejects me also rejects the one who sent me.

8. "And I tell you, every one who acknowledges me before men, the Son of Man will acknowledge before the angels of God; but whoever denies me before men will be denied before the angels of God."

105. DENOUNCING THE UNRECEPTIVE CITIES
Matthew 11:20–24; Luke 10:13–15

1. And Jesus began to denounce the cities where most of his great miracles had been performed, because they had not repented and changed their ways.

2. "Woe to you, Chorazin! Woe to you, Bethsaida! For if the mighty works done in you had been done in Tyre and Sidon, they would have repented long ago, sitting in sackcloth and ashes. But I tell you, on the day of judgment it will be more bearable for Tyre and Sidon than for you.

3. "And you, Capernaum, will you be lifted up to heaven? No, you shall be thrust down to Hades. For if the mighty works done in you had been done in Sodom, it would have remained there until this day. But I tell you, on the day of judgment it will be more bearable for the land of Sodom than for you."

106. THE SEVENTY RETURN WITH ENCOURAGING NEWS
Luke 10:17-20

1. *Later* the seventy returned with joy, saying, "Lord, even the demons obey us when we call upon your name!"

2. And he said to them, "Yes, I saw Satan fall from heaven like lightning. For indeed, I have given you authority to trample down serpents and scorpions, and over all the power of the enemy; and nothing shall harm you. Nevertheless do not rejoice because the spirits submit to you; but rather rejoice because your names are written in heaven."

107. CONTINUING TO JERUSALEM IN GOOD SPIRITS
Matthew 11:25-27; Luke 10:21-24

1. And in that moment Jesus was filled with joy through the Holy Spirit, and he said, "I thank thee, Father, Lord of heaven and earth, because you have hidden these things from the wise and learned, and revealed them to little children. Yes, Father, for this way was pleasing in your sight.

2. "All things have been entrusted to me by my Father. No one truly knows the Son except the Father; and no one truly knows the Father except the Son, and those to whom the Son chooses to reveal him."

3. Then turning to his disciples he said quietly, "Blessed are the eyes that see what you see! For I tell you, many prophets and kings longed to see the things that you see, and did not see them, and longed to hear the things that you hear, and did not hear them."

Jesus and the Adultress, by Harry Anderson

VII. THE JERUSALEM MINISTRY

108. THE PEOPLE LOOK FOR JESUS
John 7:11–13

1. The crowds *in Jerusalem* were looking for Jesus at the Feast of Tabernacles,[146] and saying, "Where is he?"

2. And there was much quiet argument about him among the people. While some said, "He is a good man," others said, "No, he is deceiving the people." Yet for fear of the chief priests and Pharisees no one spoke openly about him.

109. JESUS SHOWS HIMSELF AT THE TEMPLE
John 7:14–24

1. Then, midway through the festival, Jesus went up into the temple[147] courtyards and began to teach. The crowds marveled when they heard him, saying, "How did this man acquire such learning, when he has never been trained?"

---

146. Also known as Sukkot, this is a seven-day festival celebrated at a variable point between late September and late October. Its main feature is construction of simple outdoor shelters in memory of the years wandering in the wilderness. The final day of the festival is known as the Great Day.

147. The temple in Jerusalem was the center of Jewish religious practice. A predecessor temple had been built on the site by King Solomon. The building in Jesus' time was the Second Temple, dedicated in 515 B.C. and later extensively renovated by King Herod the Great. This building was later destroyed by the Romans in 70 A.D. at the end of the Jewish Revolt. Today the site is known as the Temple Mount and the Moslem shrine of the Dome of the Rock is located where the temple had been.

2. So Jesus answered them, "My teaching is not my own, but it comes from him who sent me. Anyone who desires to do God's will shall know whether my teaching is from God or whether I am only speaking on my own authority. He who speaks on his own authority seeks his own glory; but he who seeks glory for the one who sent him is a man of truth, and in him there is no falsehood.

3. "Has not Moses given you the law? Yet none of you keeps the law. Why do you want to kill me?" The people answered, "You are possessed! Who is trying to kill you?"

4. Jesus answered them, "I did one miracle, and you are all shocked *that I acted on the sabbath*.[148] But Moses gave you the teaching about circumcision (although that is not truly from Moses, but rather from the patriarchs) and so you circumcise a child even on the sabbath. Now if a child can be circumcised on the sabbath so that the law of Moses will not be broken, why are you angry with me because on the sabbath I healed a man's entire body? Do not judge according to appearances, but make a sound judgment."

110. "OUT OF GALILEE THERE ARISES NO PROPHET"
John 7:25—8:1

1. Then some of the people of Jerusalem began to ask, "Is this not the man they want to kill? And yet here he is, speaking openly, and they do not challenge him! Is it possible that the authorities actually know that this is the Messiah? Yet we know where this man comes from; and when the Messiah appears, no one will know where he is from."

2. So Jesus lifted his voice, as he taught in the temple, and he said, "Yes, you know me, and you know where I come from. But I have not come here on my own. He who sent me is true, and him you do not know. But I know him, for I come from him, and he has sent me."

3. Then they wished to seize Jesus; but no one laid a hand on him, because his time had not yet come. And many in the crowd believed in

---

148. The healing in the pool at Bethesda, described in Chapter 50:4, took place in Jerusalem on the sabbath in this way. Some of the people that Jesus is now addressing would probably have participated in denouncing it as impious. Even if not, then at least some among the citizens of Jerusalem as a whole had done so.

him. They said, "When the Christ appears, will he do more miracles than this man has done?"

4. The Pharisees heard the crowd whispering these things about Jesus, and the chief priests and Pharisees sent temple guards to arrest him. Jesus then said, "I shall be with you only a little longer, and then I am going back to the one who sent me; you will seek me and you will not find me; for where I am going you cannot come."

5. The people said to one another, "Where does this man intend to go that we shall not find him? Does he mean to go to the communities of Jews who live out among the Greeks, and teach the Greeks? What does he mean by saying, 'You will seek me and you will not find me,' and, 'Where I am going you cannot come'?"

6. On the last day of the feast, the Great Day, Jesus stood up and proclaimed, "If anyone is thirsty, let him come to me and drink. Whoever believes in me, as the scripture has said, 'Out of his heart shall flow streams of living water.'" In saying this, Jesus was referring to the Spirit, which would later be given to all those who believed in him; but at that time the Spirit was not yet given, because Jesus had not yet been glorified.

7. When they heard his words, some of the people said, "This is truly the prophet." Others said, "This is the Christ." But some said, "Surely the Christ is not to come from Galilee. Does not the scripture say that the Christ is to come from the line of David, and from Bethlehem, the town where David lived?" So the crowd was divided over him. Some of them wanted to arrest him, but no one laid a hand on him.

8. Then the temple guards went back to the chief priests and Pharisees, who asked them, "Why did you not bring him here?" The guards answered, "No man ever spoke the way this man does!" The Pharisees responded, "Have you been deceived as well? Have any of the authorities or the Pharisees believed in him? But this mob, which knows nothing of the law—they are accursed."

9. Nicodemus, who had once visited Jesus, and who was one of the ruling council, asked, "Does our law judge any man before it hears him and learns what he is doing?" They replied, "Are you too from Galilee? Search *the scriptures* and you will see: out of Galilee there arises no prophet."[149]

---

149. The implication was that no past prophets had come from Galilee, nor did the scriptures predict that any future prophets would do so. This was not correct as a matter of history. The prophet Jonah, among others, had been from Galilee. See 2 Kings 14:25.

10. Then each of them went to his own house. But Jesus went to the Mount of Olives.

I I I. THE WOMAN TAKEN IN ADULTERY
John 8:2–11

1. Early in the morning Jesus returned to the temple. All the people came to him, and he sat down and began to teach them.

2. Then the scribes and Pharisees brought in a woman who had been caught in adultery, and placing her in the midst of the group they said to him, "Teacher, this woman was taken in adultery, in the very act. Now, in the law Moses commanded us to stone such women to death. But what do you say?" They asked this to trap him, so that they might have some accusation to make against him.

3. Jesus bent down and wrote with his finger on the ground, *as though he had not heard them.* And as they continued to press him, he straightened up and said to them, "He among you who is without sin, let him cast the first stone at her." And then he bent down again and continued to write with his finger on the ground.

4. When the accusers heard this, they slipped away, one by one, beginning with the eldest, even to the last, until only Jesus was left, with the woman still standing before him.

5. Jesus stood up and asked her, "Woman, where are they? Has no one condemned you?" She said, "No one, Lord." And Jesus said, "Neither do I condemn you. Go, and sin no more."

I I 2. THE GOOD SAMARITAN
Luke 10:25–37

1. One day a specialist in religious law stood up to put Jesus to the test, asking, "Teacher, what must I do to inherit eternal life?" Jesus said to him, "What is written in the law? How do you read it?" The scholar answered, "'You shall love the Lord your God with all your heart, and with all your soul, and with all your strength, and with all your mind.'

But still less, in the opinion of the priests, was the Messiah likely to come from such a provincial place.

And *second*, 'you shall love your neighbor as yourself.'"[150] And Jesus said to him, "You have answered rightly; do this, and you will live."

2. But the scholar, wanting to justify his question, asked Jesus, "And who is my neighbor?"

3. Jesus replied *with this story*: "A man was going down from Jerusalem to Jericho, and he fell among thieves, who stripped him of his clothes and beat him, and departed, leaving him half-dead. Now it happened that a priest was going down the same road; but when he saw the injured man he passed by on the other side of the road. And likewise a Levite, when he came to the place and saw him, passed by on the other side.

4. "But a certain Samaritan,[151] as he journeyed, came to where the man was; and when he saw him, he had compassion on him, and went to him and bound up his wounds, pouring oil and wine on them. Then he put him on his own donkey and brought him to an inn, and cared for him. The next day *when he departed* he took out two silver coins and gave them to the innkeeper, saying, 'Take care of him, and whatever more you spend, I will repay you when I come back.'

5. "Which of these three, do you think," Jesus asked, "proved to be a neighbor to the man who fell among the thieves?" The scholar said, "The one who took pity on him." And Jesus said to him, "Go, and do likewise."

I I 3. THE LIGHT OF THE WORLD
John 8:12–30

1. Later Jesus spoke to the people again, saying, "I am the light of the world. He that follows me shall not walk in darkness, but shall have the light of life."

2. But the Pharisees challenged him, saying, "You are testifying about yourself; and your own testimony is not sufficient." Jesus answered, "Even if I do testify on my own behalf, my testimony is sufficient, for I know where I have come from and where I am going. You, however,

150. These are traditional Jewish principles. In his teachings, Jesus emphasized that their intended scope is universal rather than parochial.*

151. Samaritans were members of a separate and often hostile ethnic group, and many of them would not have recognized Jews as their "neighbors." See notes to Chapter 36:1.

do not know where I came from or where I am going. You judge by human standards; I judge no one.

3. "Yet even if I should judge, my judgment is just, for it is not I alone that judge, but both I and the one who sent me. In your law it is written that the testimony of two men is true. I am one witness for myself, and the Father who sent me is another."

4. So then they asked him, "Where is your Father?" Jesus answered, "You know neither me nor my Father; if you knew me, you would know my Father also." He spoke these words while he was teaching in the temple, in the section called the Treasury; but no one arrested him, because his time had not yet come.

5. He said to them once more, "I will soon go away, and then you will seek me, but you will die still in a state of sin. Where I am going, you cannot come." The people asked one another, "Surely he does not mean to kill himself, does he, since he says, 'Where I am going, you cannot come'?"

6. He said to them, "You are from below; I am from above. You are of this world; I am not of this world. I told you that you would die in your sins, for indeed you will die in your sins unless you believe that I am he." So they asked him, "Then who are you?" Jesus said to them, "Just what I have said to you from the beginning. I have much to say about you and much I could blame you for. But he who sent me is truthful, and I declare to the world only what I have heard from him." But they did not understand that he was speaking to them about the Father.

7. So Jesus said, "When you have lifted up the Son of Man, then you will know that I am he; and that I do nothing on my own authority, but I speak just as the Father has taught me. And he who sent me remains with me. He has not left me alone, for I always do what is pleasing to him." And as Jesus said these things, many came to believe in him.

114. EXASPERATION WITH THE COMPLACENT
John 8:31–59

1. Then Jesus said to those who believed in him, "If you continue in my word, then you are truly my disciples; and you shall know the truth, and the truth shall make you free."

2. Some Jews in the crowd answered him, "We are the descendants of Abraham, and have never been in bondage to any man. How can you say, 'You will be made free'?"

3. Jesus answered them, "I tell you truly, every one who commits sin is a slave to sin. Now a slave does not continue in a household forever; but a son remains always. So if the Son sets you free, you will be free indeed.

4. "I know that you are descendants of Abraham. Yet some of you are ready to kill me, because you have no place in your hearts for my word. I speak to you of what I have actually seen with my Father, and you are only doing what you have been told to do by your own fathers."

5. They answered him, "Abraham is our father." Jesus said to them, "If you were Abraham's children, you would do the things that Abraham did. But now you seek to kill me, a man who has told you the truth, which I heard from God. Abraham did not do such things. You are only doing what your own fathers once did."

6. They said to him, "We were not born of fornication.¹⁵² We have only one father, and that is God." Jesus said to them, "If God were your father, you would love me, for I proceeded and came forth from God; I have not come of my own accord, but because he sent me.

7. "Why do you not understand what I am saying? It is because you cannot bear to hear my word. For in reality you are the children of your father the devil, and your will is to do your *true* father's desires. He was a murderer from the beginning, and abode not in the truth, because there is no truth in him. When he speaks a lie, he speaks according to his nature, for he is a liar and the father of lies. And so, because I tell you the truth, you do not believe me.

8. "Who of you can accuse me of any sin? And if I speak the truth, why do you not believe me? He who belongs to God listens to the words of God; the reason why you do not listen is that you do not belong to God."

9. The crowd answered him, "Truly we are right when we say that you are a Samaritan and are possessed by a demon!"

10. Jesus answered, "I am not possessed; but I honor my Father, and you dishonor me. I do not seek glory for myself, but there is one who seeks

---

152. Jesus' opponents may have been making a sly insult here about his own unconventional parentage.

it for me, and he will be the judge. I tell you truly, if any one follows my teaching, he will never see death."

11. The crowd said to him, "Now we know that you are possessed! Abraham died, as did the prophets; yet you say, 'If any one follows my teaching, he will never taste death.' Are you greater than our father Abraham, who is dead? And the prophets are dead. Who do you make yourself out to be?"

12. Jesus answered, "If I glorify myself, my glory means nothing; but it is my Father who glorifies me, and you say that he is your God, although you do not know him. But I know him. If I said, I do not know him, I should be a liar like you; but I do know him and I keep his word. Your father Abraham rejoiced at the thought of seeing my day; he saw it and was glad."

13. The crowd then said to him, "You are not yet fifty years old, and you have seen Abraham?" Jesus said to them, "I tell you truly, even before Abraham was born, I am."[153] At this, the crowd took up stones to throw at him; but Jesus hid himself from their sight and went out of the temple.

I I 5. AT THE HOME OF MARTHA AND MARY
Luke 10:38–42

1. *One day as Jesus and his disciples were traveling in the countryside near Jerusalem,* he entered a village; and a woman named Martha invited him into her house. She had a sister called Mary, who sat at the Lord's feet and listened to his teaching.

2. But Martha was distracted with the labor of much serving, and she went to Jesus and said, "Lord, do you not care that my sister has left me to serve alone? Tell her then to help me."

3. But the Lord answered her, "Martha, Martha, you are worried and troubled about many things. But only one thing is needful. Mary has chosen that good part, and that shall not be taken away from her."

---

153. Jesus was here asserting not only that he was the Son of God, but also that he had a divine status himself. He was asserting a life much longer than the normal human lifetime; Abraham had lived in the second millenium B.C. More important, Jesus described himself with the simple phrase "I am"—a distinctive description and name also used for God.*

116. HEALING A MAN BORN BLIND
John 9:1–41

1. One day as Jesus was walking, he saw a man who had been blind from his birth. And his disciples asked him, "Rabbi, who sinned, this man or his parents, that he was born blind?"

2. Jesus answered, "It was not that this man sinned, or his parents, but so that the power of God might be displayed in his life. We must work the works of him who sent me, as long as it is daylight; the night comes, when no man can work. But as long as I am in the world, I am the light of the world."

3. After he had said this, Jesus spat on the ground and made clay with the saliva and anointed the man's eyes with the clay, saying to him, "Go, wash in the pool of Siloam"—a name which means Sent. So the man went and washed, and he came back seeing.

4. The neighbors and those who had seen him before as a beggar said, "Is this not the man who used to sit and beg?" Some said, "It is he;" others said, "No, he merely looks like him." But the man himself said, "I am that man."

5. So they asked him, "Then how were your eyes opened?" He answered, "The man called Jesus made clay and anointed my eyes and said to me, 'Go to the pool of Siloam and wash;' so I went and washed, and I received my sight."

6. They said to him, "Where is he?" He replied, "I do not know."

7. So they brought the man who had once been blind to the Pharisees. Now it was a sabbath day when Jesus made the clay and opened his eyes. The Pharisees also asked him how he had received his sight. And he said to them, "He put clay on my eyes, and I washed, and I can see."

8. Some of the Pharisees said, "This man is not from God, for he does not keep the sabbath." But others said, "How could a sinner perform such miracles?" So there was a division of opinion among them. Then they turned again to the blind man, "What do you say about him, since it was your eyes he opened?" The man said, "He is a prophet."

9. The Pharisees did not believe that the man had in truth been blind and had been given his sight, until they called his parents and asked them, "Is this your son, who you say was born blind? How then does he now see?" His parents answered, "We know that this is our son, and that

he was born blind. But how he now sees we do not know; and who opened his eyes, we do not know. Ask him; he is of age, and he can speak for himself."

10. His parents said this because they feared the religious authorities, for they had already agreed that if any one should acknowledge Jesus as the Christ, he was to be expelled from the synagogue. Therefore his parents said, "He is of age; ask him."

11. So for a second time the Pharisees called in the man who had been blind, and they said to him, "Give God the praise, for we know that this man is a sinner." He answered, "Whether he is a sinner, I do not know. One thing I do know: I was blind, but now I see."

12. They asked him, "But what did he do to you? How did he open your eyes?" The man answered them, "I have told you already, and you would not listen. Why do you want to hear it again? Do you too wish to become his disciples?"

13. At this the Pharisees turned on him in anger, saying, "You are his disciple, but we are disciples of Moses! We know that God spoke to Moses, but as for this man, we do not even know where he comes from." The man answered, "Why, this is strange indeed! You do not know where he comes from, and yet he opened my eyes. We know that God does not listen to sinners; he listens to the man who worships him and does his will. Never since the world began has any one opened the eyes of a man born blind. If this man were not from God, he could have done nothing." The Pharisees answered him, "You were born full of sin, and you would teach us?" And they threw him out.

14. Jesus heard that they had put the man out, and when he found him he asked, "Do you believe in the Son of Man?" The man answered, "And who is that, sir? Tell me so that that I may believe in him." Jesus said to him, "You have already seen him; he is the one who is speaking with you now." The man said, "Lord, I believe;" and he worshiped him.

15. Jesus said, "I have come into this world to prepare men for judgment—to give sight to the blind, and to show those who think they see clearly that they have been blind." Some of the Pharisees near him heard this, and they said to him, "Do you think that we too are blind?" Jesus said to them, "If you were truly blind, you would not be guilty of sin; but because you claim, 'We see,' your sin remains with you."

117. THE GOOD SHEPHERD
John 10:1–21

1. "I tell you truly," *Jesus continued*, "he who does not enter the sheepfold by the gate, but climbs in by some other way, that man is a thief and a robber; but he who enters through the gate is the shepherd of the sheep. The porter opens the gate for him; the sheep respond to his voice, and he calls his own sheep by name and leads them out. When he has brought out all his own, he goes on ahead of them, and the sheep follow him, for they know his voice. The sheep will not follow a stranger, but they flee from him, for they do not know the voice of strangers." Jesus used this image with the crowd around him, but they did not understand his meaning.

2. So Jesus spoke further to them, "I tell you truly, I am the gateway for the sheep. All who came before me are were thieves and robbers; and the sheep did not heed them. I am the gateway; and if any one enters through me, he will be saved. He will come in and go out freely, and will find pasture. The thief comes only to steal and kill and destroy; I have come so that they may have life, and have it abundantly.

3. "I am the good shepherd. The good shepherd lays down his life for the sheep. The man who is a hireling and not a shepherd, whose own the sheep are not, sees the wolf coming and leaves the sheep and flees; and the wolf catches up the sheep and scatters them. He flees because he is a hireling and cares nothing for the sheep. But I am the good shepherd. I know my own sheep and my sheep know me, just as the Father knows me and I know the Father. And I lay down my life for the sheep.

4. "And I have other sheep, which are not of this fold; I must bring them also.[154] They too will heed my voice, and there shall be one flock, and one shepherd.

5. "This is why the Father loves me, because I lay down my life, so that I may take it up again. No one takes it from me, but I lay it down of my own will. I have the power to lay it down, and I have power to take it up again; for this is the charge I received from my Father."

6. There was again a division of opinion among the people at these words. Many of them said, "He is possessed by a demon, and is mad; why do

---

154. This verse is a point of departure for the Church of Jesus Christ of Latter-day Saints, for whom the Book of Mormon provides an account of events among some of those "other sheep" in the New World.*

you listen to him?" Others said, "These are not the words of a possessed man. And can a demon open the eyes of the blind?"

118. INSTRUCTIONS ON PRAYER
Luke 11:1–2a, 5–13

1. One day Jesus was praying in a certain place, and when he was finished, one of his disciples said to him, "Lord, teach us to pray, as John
   taught his disciples." So Jesus said to them, "When you pray, *pray with
   persistence*."[155]

2. And he explained to them, "Imagine that you have a friend, and that
   you go to him at midnight and say to him, 'Friend, lend me three
   loaves of bread; for a friend of mine has arrived on a journey, and I
   have nothing to set before him.' And suppose the friend answers from
   inside, 'Do not bother me; the door is now shut, and my children are
   with me in bed; I cannot get up and give you anything.'

3. "I tell you, although the man inside the house will not get up and give
   anything to the man at the door just because he is his friend, yet because of his persistence he will rise and give him whatever he needs.

4. "So I tell you, Ask, and it shall be given to you; seek, and ye shall find;
   knock, and it shall be opened unto you. For every one who asks receives, and he who seeks finds, and to him who knocks the door will
   be opened.

5. "For what father among you, if his son asks for a fish, will instead of a
   fish give him a serpent; or if he asks for an egg, will give him a scor-
   pion? If you then, who are evil, know how to give good gifts to your
   children, by how much more will the heavenly Father give the Holy
   Spirit to those who ask him?"

---

155. At this point in the gospel of Luke, Jesus also provides a short version of the
Lord's Prayer. In this text that is consolidated with the longer version of the Prayer set
out in the Sermon on the Mount.*

119. INWARD AND OUTWARD VIRTUE
Luke 11:37–41, 53–54

1. One day, while Jesus was speaking, a Pharisee asked him to dine with him, so he went in and took his place at the table. The Pharisee was surprised to see that Jesus did not first ceremonially wash his hands before eating.

2. But the Lord said to him, "You Pharisees *are careful to* clean the outside of the cup and of the dish, but on the inside you are full of greed and wickedness. You fools! Did not the one who made the outside make the inside also?[156] But give *the foods* that are within the dish as alms to the poor, and behold, then everything will be clean to you."[157]

3. And as Jesus was leaving, the scribes and Pharisees began to press him hard on many subjects, trying to provoke him, watching to catch something out of his mouth that they might use against him.

120. THE RICH MAN PLANS BIGGER BARNS
Luke 12:13–21, 31–34

1. Someone in the crowd *outside* called to him, "Teacher, tell my brother to divide our father's inheritance with me."

2. But Jesus replied, "My friend, who appointed me a judge or arbitrator over you, *especially for that kind of question?*" And he cautioned them, "Take care, and beware of all forms of greed and covetousness; for a man's life does not consist in the abundance of his possessions."

3. And he told them this parable: "The lands of a certain rich man brought forth a plentiful crop. And the man thought to himself, 'What shall I do, for I have no place to store my harvest?' Then he said, 'I will do this: I will tear down my barns, and build bigger ones, and there

---

156. Luke describes Jesus' denunciation of the Pharisees ("Woe unto you, Pharisees!") at this point during the meal. In this text that is consolidated with Matthew's description of a very similar denunciation given later during Holy Week, in Chapter 171. A speech involving such pointed conflict with the religious authorities seems more likely to have come during the period of crisis in that final week.

157. It is not clear whether this sentence should be taken literally or ironically. Does the worthy act of giving alms show repentance and thus compensate for other shortcomings, or does the formalized act of almsgiving merely give the self-righteous Pharisees a reason for thinking of themselves as automatically purified?

I will store all my grain and my goods. And I will say to myself, My friend, you have ample goods laid up for many years. Now take your ease! Eat, drink, and be merry.'

4. "But God said to him, 'Thou fool! This very night thy life shall be demanded from you. And who then will take possession of the things you have prepared for yourself?'

5. "So it shall be with anyone who stores up riches for himself, and is not rich toward God. Rather, therefore, seek the kingdom of God, and all the needful things of the world shall be yours as well.

6. "Do not fear, little flock, for it is your Father's good pleasure to give you the kingdom. Sell all that you have and give to the poor. Provide yourselves with purses that will never wear out, with a treasure in heaven that will never fail, where no thief can come near and no moth destroy. For where your treasure is, there will your heart be also."

121. THE PARABLE OF THE WATCHFUL SERVANTS
Matthew 24:45–51; Luke 12:35–38, 41–48

1. "Keep your loins girded[158] and your lamps lit. Be like servants who are waiting for their master to come home from the marriage feast, so that they may open the door to him at once when he comes and knocks.

2. "Blessed are those servants whom the master finds watchful when he comes. Truly, I say to you, he will dress himself for serving, and have them sit at the table, and will come and serve them himself. If he comes late in the second or third watch of the night, and finds them alert, fortunate are those servants."

3. Peter asked, "Lord, are you telling this parable for us or for everyone?" And the Lord said, "Who is truly the faithful and wise steward, whom his master will set over his household, to give the people their allowance of food at the proper time? Fortunate is the servant whose master

158. The man who "girds up his loins" has made himself ready for strenuous work. Men at the time customarily wore long tunics, which came to the ankles and impeded movement. When they needed more freedom of action, they hitched up the tunic and held it in place by folding the extra material under the belt, which was called the girdle. An equivalent modern reference would be to the man who "rolls up his sleeves."

finds him at work when he comes. I tell you truly, he will put that one in charge of all his possessions.

4. "But instead suppose that servant is wicked and says to himself, 'My master is delayed in coming,' and he begins to beat the menservants and the maidservants, and to eat and drink with the drunkards. Then the master of that servant will come on a day when he does not expect him and at an hour he does not know, and will cut him in pieces and assign him to a place with the hypocrites and unbelievers, where there will be weeping and gnashing of teeth.

5. "The servant who knew his master's will, but did not prepare or act according to his will, shall be beaten with many lashes. But the one who did not know, and so did things worthy of punishment, shall be beaten with few lashes. For from him who has been given much, much shall be required; and from those to whom much has been entrusted, still more will be demanded."

122. WHO CAN SEE THE COMING FIRE?
Luke 12:49–57

1. "I have come to bring a fire upon the earth, and how I wish it were already kindled! But I have a baptism I must first undergo, and I will be under a heavy burden until that is accomplished![159]

2. "Do you think that I have come to bring peace on earth? No, I tell you, but rather division! From now on there will be five divided in one family, three against two and two against three. They will be divided, father against son and son against father, mother against daughter and daughter against her mother, mother-in-law against her daughter-in-law and daughter-in-law against her mother-in-law."

3. He also said to the people, "When you see a cloud forming in the west, you say at once, 'The rain is coming,' and so it does. And when you see a south wind blowing, you say, 'It will be a hot day,' and so it is. You hypocrites! You know how to interpret the appearance of the earth and sky; so why do you not know how to interpret the present times? And why do you not judge for yourselves what is right?"

---

159. The "baptism" here is the pain of his trial and crucifixion.

1 2 3. ALL MUST REPENT OR PERISH
Luke 13:1–9

1. Some of those present then told Jesus about the Galileans whose blood Pilate had mixed with *the blood of* their sacrifices.[160] And Jesus responded, "Do you think that those Galileans were worse sinners than all the other Galileans, because they suffered in that way? No, I tell you! Unless you repent you will all perish as well.

2. "Or those eighteen upon whom the tower in Siloam fell, and killed them. Do you think they were worse sinners than all others who lived in Jerusalem? No, I tell you! Unless you repent you will all perish as well."

3. And he told this parable: "A man had a fig tree planted in his vineyard, and he came to look for fruit on it and found none. So he said to the gardener, 'Lo, these three years now I have come seeking fruit on this fig tree, and I still find none. So cut it down; why should it cumber the ground?'

4. "But the gardener answered him, 'Let it alone, sir, for one more year, until I can dig around it and put down manure. If it bears fruit next year, well and good; but if not, then you may cut it down.'"

1 2 4. HEALING THE STOOPED WOMAN
Luke 13:10–17

1. One day Jesus was teaching in one of the synagogues on the sabbath. And a woman was there who had been crippled by an evil spirit for eighteen years. She was hunched over and could not by any effort straighten herself.

2. When Jesus saw her, he called her to him and said to her, "Woman, you are freed from your infirmity." He laid his hands upon her; and immediately she stood up straight, and she praised God.

3. But the leader of the synagogue was indignant because Jesus had healed on the sabbath, and he said to the people, "There are six days

---

160. This does not mean that the Galileans' blood was offered as a sacrifice, but rather that they had been killed in the temple while engaged in the pious act of offering some other sacrifice. Pontius Pilate had earned a reputation for harshness and insensitivity during his tenure as the Roman governor.*

on which work may be done; come on those days to be healed, and not on the sabbath day."

4. But the Lord answered him, "You hypocrites! On the sabbath do not each of you untie your ox or your ass from the stall, and lead it out to give it water? And so should not this woman, a daughter of Abraham whom Satan has bound for eighteen long years, be likewise loosed from her bond on the sabbath day?"

5. With these words all his opponents were put to shame; but all the people rejoiced at the splendid things that Jesus was doing.

125. JESUS ANNOUNCES THAT HE IS THE CHRIST
John 10:22–39

1. And then it was winter in Jerusalem, and time for Hanukkah, the Feast of Dedication.[161] Jesus was walking through Solomon's Colonnade in the temple courtyard. And a crowd gathered around him and demanded of him, "How long will you keep us in suspense? If you are the Messiah, tell us plainly."

2. Jesus answered them, "I have already told you, but you do not believe me.[162] The works that I do in my Father's name bear witness on my behalf; but you do not believe, because you do not belong to my flock. My sheep listen to my voice, and I know them, and they follow me; and I give them eternal life, and they shall never perish; and no one shall pluck them out of my hand. My Father, who has given them to me, is greater than all others, and no one can wrest anything from his hand. And I and my Father are one."

3. At this the crowd again took up stones to stone him. Jesus challenged them, "At my Father's direction I have done many good works among you; for which of these do you wish to stone me?" The crowd answered him, "We do not stone you for any good work, but for blasphemy; because you, although only a man, make yourself out to be God."

---

161. John refers to it simply as the Feast of Dedication.

162. This clearly implies an affirmative answer. Thus here and on other occasions Jesus stated that he was the Messiah or the Christ, even though he referred to himself more usually as the Son of Man. Jesus also declared that he was the Messiah to the Woman at the Well, see Chapter 36:8, and to Simon Peter when he gave him the keys to the kingdom, see Chapter 91:3–4.

4. Jesus answered them, "Is it not written in your scriptures *that God once said to the judges of Israel,* 'I say you are gods'?[163] But if he called them 'gods' to whom nothing more than the word of God came—and scripture cannot be disregarded—then what would you call the one whom the Father specially consecrated and sent into the world? Why do you charge, 'You are blaspheming,' because I said, 'I am the Son of God'?

5. "If I am not doing the works of my Father, then do not believe me; but if I do them, then even though you do not believe me, believe the works, so that you may know and believe that the Father is in me, and I am in the Father."

6. Again they tried to seize him, but he eluded their grasp.

126. WITHDRAWAL FROM JERUSALEM
John 10:40–42

1. Then Jesus withdrew again beyond the Jordan, to the place where John had been baptizing at first; and there he stayed for a time.

2. Many people went to Jesus, and they said, "John did no miracles, but all the things he spoke about this man were true." And many believed in Jesus there.

---

163. The reference is to Psalm 82:6.

"Flevit Super Illam" (detail), by Enrique Simonet
Photo: Album / Art Resource, NY

VIII. THE LAST ITINERANT MINISTRY

127. SETTING OFF ON THE CIRCUIT
Luke 13:22

1. After a while Jesus set out through the towns and villages, teaching as he went.

2. *This last journey would take him in a circle, north to Galilee, and then back south again with the Passover crowds,* always making his way toward Jerusalem.[164]

128. WHETHER MANY OR FEW WILL BE SAVED
Luke 13:23–30

1. One day someone asked Jesus, "Lord, will only a few be saved?" And Jesus replied, "Strive to get in through the narrow gate; for many, I tell you, will seek to enter and will not be able.

2. "When once the householder has gotten up and shut the door, you will be left to stand outside and knock, saying, 'Sir, open the door to us.' He will answer you, 'I do not know where you come from.' Then you will say, 'We have eaten and drunk with you, and you taught in our streets.'

---

164. This circuit took Jesus throughout most of the Jewish-inhabited lands. It is sometimes referred to as the "Perean ministry," because much of the travels were in the district of Perea, the territory on the east bank of the Jordan. Many Jews traveled between Galilee and Jerusalem by this route, which enabled them to bypass the unfriendly towns of Samaria on the west bank.*

But he will say, 'I tell you, I do not know where you come from; depart from me, all you evildoers!'

3. "Then there will be weeping there and gnashing of teeth, when you see Abraham and Isaac and Jacob and all the prophets at home in the kingdom of God, while you yourselves are thrust out. People will come from east and west, and from north and south, and take their place at the table in the kingdom of God. And behold, some who are last will be first, and some who are first will be last."

129. LAMENT OVER JERUSALEM
Matthew 23:37–39; Luke 13:31–35

1. On that same day some Pharisees came to Jesus and said, "Leave this place and go somewhere else, for Herod wishes to kill you." And Jesus said to them, "Go and tell that fox, 'Behold, I will be casting out demons and performing cures today and tomorrow, and on the third day I will complete my work. Nonetheless I must continue on my way steadily today and tomorrow and the day following, for it cannot be that a prophet should perish in any place but Jerusalem.'

2. "O Jerusalem, Jerusalem, you who kill the prophets and stone those who are sent to you! How often I have longed to gather your children together, even as a hen gathers her chickens under her wings; but you were not willing!

3. "Behold, your house is left to you desolate and forsaken! For I tell you, you will not see me again until the time comes when you say, 'Blessed is he who comes in the name of the Lord!'"

130. TAKING PLACES AT THE TABLE
Luke 14:1–24

1. One sabbath Jesus went to dine at the house of one of the chief Pharisees; and all of the dinner guests were watching him closely.

2. A man was there whose limbs were swollen from dropsy. Jesus spoke to the Pharisees and the specialists in religious law, asking, "Is it lawful to heal on the sabbath, or not?" But they were silent. So he took the man and healed him, and sent him away. Then he said to the guests,

"Which of you, having an ass or an ox that has fallen into a pit on a sabbath day, will not immediately pull him out?" And they could not reply to this.

3. When Jesus saw how the guests all sought to take the most prominent places at the table for themselves, he counseled them, saying, "When you are invited by any one to a marriage feast, do not sit down in a place of honor, for a person more distinguished than you may have been invited; and the host who invited both of you will come and say to you, 'Give your seat to this man,' and then you must move with shame to take the lowest place. Instead, when you are invited, first go and sit in the lowest place, so that when your host comes he may say to you, 'Friend, move up higher,' and then you will be honored in front of all the other guests. For every one who exalts himself will be humbled, and he who humbles himself will be exalted."

4. Then Jesus said to his host, "When you give a luncheon or a dinner, do not invite your friends or your brothers or your kinsmen or rich neighbors. For they will invite you in return, and you will be repaid. But when you give a banquet, invite the poor, the crippled, the lame, the blind, and you will be blessed, because they do not have anything to repay you. You will be repaid at the resurrection of the righteous."

5. When one of those at the table with Jesus heard this, he said to him, "Blessed is everyone who shall dine in the kingdom of God!"

6. But Jesus said to him, "A man once gave a great banquet, and invited many; and when the time came he sent his servant to tell those who had been invited, 'Come, for everything is now ready.'

7. "But then they all alike began to make excuses. The first said to him, 'I have just bought a field, and I must go inspect it; I pray you, allow me to be excused.' Another said, 'I have bought five yoke of oxen, and am on my way to try them out; I pray you, allow me to be excused.' And another said, 'I have just been married, and therefore I cannot come.'

8. "The servant came and reported this to his master. Then the master in anger said to his servant, 'Go out at once into the streets and alleys of the city, and bring in the poor and the lame and the halt and the blind.' And later the servant said, 'Sir, what you have commanded has been done, and there is still room.'

9. "The master said to the servant, 'Then go out to the highways and hedges, and prevail on *even the vagabonds* to come in, so that my

house may be filled. For I tell you, none of those who were invited shall taste my banquet.'"

131. RAISING LAZARUS FROM THE DEAD
John 11:1–44

1. Now a certain man named Lazarus was ill. He was from Bethany, the village of Mary and her sister Martha. This Mary, whose brother Lazarus now lay ill, was the one who anointed the Lord with ointment and wiped his feet with her hair.[165]

2. So the sisters sent word to Jesus, saying, "Lord, your good friend is very sick." But when Jesus heard this he said, "This sickness is not unto death, but for the glory of God, so that the Son of God might be glorified through it."

3. Now Jesus loved Martha and her sister and Lazarus. Yet when he heard that Lazarus was ill, he remained two days longer in the place where he was. Then after that he said to his disciples, "Let us go back into Judea."

4. The disciples said to him, "Rabbi, only a few days ago the people there were seeking to stone you, and now you are going there again?" Jesus answered, "Are there not twelve hours in the day? If any one walks in the day, he does not stumble, because he can see by the light of this world. But if any one walks in the night, he stumbles, because the light is not in him."[166]

5. Then Jesus said, "Our friend Lazarus has fallen asleep, but I am going there to awaken him." His disciples replied, "Lord, if he is sleeping, he will soon be well." In fact Jesus had been speaking of his death, but the disciples thought he meant only taking rest in sleep. So then Jesus told them plainly, "Lazarus is dead. And for your sakes I am glad I was not there, so that you can be given reason to believe. Now let us go to him."

165. The reference here might be to either of two anointings that fit this description. One is the anointing performed by this same Mary at a later time, about six days before Passover, when Jesus will return to Bethany. See Chapter 154:3. The other is the anointing that had previously been performed by the unnamed penitent woman in Chapter 61:2. Reasonable arguments have been made for each of these possibilities.*

166. The meaning of this passage is probably this: One can safely travel even until the last hour of daylight. Similarly, I may be getting near the end of my worldly mission, but the time for my death has not yet come. Therefore, I can safely go to Judea now, without fear, because my destiny lies elsewhere.

6. Then Thomas, called the Twin, said to his fellow disciples, "Let us also go *with Jesus*, so that we may die with him."

7. When Jesus arrived, he found that Lazarus had already been in the tomb four days. Bethany was near Jerusalem, about two miles away, and many of the people there had come to Martha and Mary to comfort them about their brother.

8. When Martha heard that Jesus was approaching, she went and met him, while Mary remained sitting in the house. Martha said to Jesus, "Lord, if you had been here, my brother would not have died. But I know that whatever you ask from God, even now, God will give you."

9. Jesus said to her, "Your brother will rise again." Martha answered, "I know that he will rise again in the resurrection at the last day." Jesus said to her, "I am the resurrection and the life; whoever believes in me, though he die, yet shall he live; and whosoever lives and believes in me shall never die. Do you believe this?" She said to him, "Yes, Lord; I believe that you are the Christ, the Son of God, the one who is to come into the world."

10. When Martha had said this, she went back and called her sister Mary aside, saying quietly, "The Teacher is here and is asking for you." And when Mary heard this, she rose quickly and went to him. For Jesus had not yet come into the village, but was still at the place where Martha had met him. When the mourners who were with her in the house, consoling her, saw Mary rise and leave so quickly, they followed her, supposing that she was going to the tomb to weep there.

11. When Mary came to the place where Jesus was and saw him, she fell at his feet, saying to him, "Lord, if you had been here, my brother would not have died." And as Jesus saw her weeping, and the mourners who had come with her also weeping, he was troubled in his spirit and moved by a deep anger,[167] and he asked, "Where have you laid him?" They said to him, "Lord, come and see." Jesus wept. So the mourners said, "See how much he loved him!" But some of them said, "Could not someone who opened the eyes of the blind man have also kept this man from dying?"

12. Then Jesus, once more deeply moved in spirit, came to the tomb. It was a cave, and a stone covered its entrance.

---

167. Jesus is usually described here as being "deeply moved in spirit," or as "groaning in the spirit." The underlying phrase, however, has the further connotation of indignation or rejection of the circumstances. Jesus was not just grieved by the presence of death, but resolved to do something about it.

13. Jesus said, "Take away the stone." Martha, the sister of the dead man, said to him, "Lord, by this time there will be an odor, for he has been dead four days." Jesus said to her, "Did I not tell you that if you had faith, you would see the glory of God?" So they took away the stone.

14. Then Jesus lifted up his eyes and said, "Father, I thank thee for hearing me. I know that you always hear me, but I have said this aloud for the sake of the people standing by, so that they may believe that you have sent me."

15. When he had said this, he shouted with a great voice, "Lazarus, come forth!" And the dead man came out, his hands and feet bound with linen strips, and his face wrapped in a headcloth. Jesus said to the people around, "Unbind him, and let him go."

132. THE HIGH COUNCIL BEGINS TO PLOT
John 11:45–54

1. Many of the Jews, who had come to visit Mary and had seen what Jesus did, believed in him; but some went to the Pharisees and told them what he had done.

2. So the chief priests and the Pharisees gathered the high council of the Sanhedrin and asked, "What are we to do? For this man performs many miracles. If we allow him to go on in this way, every one will believe in him, and then the Romans will come and destroy both our holy place and our nation."[168]

3. Then one of them, Caiaphas, who was high priest that year, said to them, "You know nothing at all! You do not understand that it is better for you that one man should die for the people, than that the whole nation should be destroyed." He did not speak these words of his own accord, but being high priest that year he was inspired to speak in prophecy, that Jesus would indeed die for the nation—but not for that nation only, but also for all the children of God who are scattered over the world, to bring them together into one body.[169]

---

168. In other words, if Jesus were accepted by the people as the Messiah, this would lead to a popular demand to confer on him the political title of king of Israel, which would be interpreted by the Romans as an act of rebellion, and would lead to severe reprisals against the entire Jewish nation.

169. Literally, "to collect into one the scattered children of God." In other words, because he was under divine inspiration, Caiaphas was able to prophesy accurately.

4. So from that day forth the council began to plot Jesus' death.[170]

5. Jesus therefore no longer walked openly among the Jews, but withdrew from Bethany to the country near the edge of the wilderness, to a town called Ephraim; and there he stayed with his disciples.

I 3 3. THE COST OF DISCIPLESHIP[171]
Luke 14:25–35

1. At this time great crowds were traveling with Jesus, and he turned and said to them, "If any one comes to me and is not prepared to forsake his own father and mother, and his wife and children, and his brothers and sisters—yes, and even his own life—he cannot be my disciple.[172] Whoever does not bear his own cross and follow me, cannot be my disciple.

2. "For which of you, wanting to build a tower, would not first sit down and calculate the cost, whether he has enough money to complete it? Otherwise, when he has laid a foundation, and is not able to finish, all who see it will mock him, saying, 'This man began to build, and was not able to finish.'

3. "Or what king, going out to meet another king in war, will not first sit down and consider whether he is able with ten thousand men to resist one who comes against him with twenty thousand? And if he cannot, then while the other is still a great way off, he will send a delegation to ask for terms of peace.

These correctly-forecast events unfolded in a way different from what Caiaphas and the Sanhedrin would have anticipated, however. Jesus did die for the people, but he died for all the people of the world, rather than for any one nation.*

170. Caiaphas and the chief priests were Sadducees, and this temple-based establishment sect, with its ties to the Roman authorities and its own concrete interests to defend, became Jesus's most formidable enemies from this point onward.

171. This is the title of a book by Dietrich Bonhoeffer, a Lutheran pastor in Germany during the Nazi years. He had managed to escape to the United States, but then returned home to encourage the maintenance of Christian values among the people. He was arrested in 1943 and hanged in April 1945, twenty-three days before the German surrender.

172. This passage is sometimes literally translated to say that the disciple must "hate" his parents and other family members. However, in this context the word is probably best read as comparative rather than absolute. The point is not that the parents are to be affirmatively disliked, but rather that they are to be subordinated to the work of discipleship.

4. "So likewise, whoever of you does not renounce everything that he has cannot be my disciple. Salt is good; but if salt has lost its taste, how can it be made salty again? Half-hearted salt is not useful either for conditioning the soil or for fertilizer; men throw it away. He who has ears to hear, let him hear."

134. PARABLE OF THE LOST SHEEP
Luke 15:1–7

1. Now tax-gatherers and other sinners often came to Jesus to hear him teach. But the Pharisees and the scribes *still* grumbled about this, saying, "This man welcomes sinners and even eats with them."

2. So Jesus told them this parable: "What man of you, having a hundred sheep, if he loses one of them, does not leave the ninety-nine on the hillsides,[173] and seek after the one which is lost, until he finds it? And when he finds it, he lays it on his shoulders, rejoicing. When he comes home, he calls together his friends and neighbors, saying to them, 'Rejoice with me, for I have found my sheep which was lost.'

3. "Likewise, I tell you, there will be more joy in heaven over one sinner who repents than over ninety-nine righteous persons who need no repentance."[174]

135. PARABLE OF THE LOST COIN
Luke 15:8–10

1. "Or consider a woman who has ten silver coins and loses one of them. Does she not light a lamp and sweep the house and seek carefully until she finds it? And when she has found it, she calls together her friends

---

173. The Greek word here, *eremos*, is often translated in this parable as "wilderness." The term can also refer, however, to territory that is unoccupied but supports some vegetation, and is used as common grazing land. That meaning seems more appropriate in this context, where the ninety-nine sheep might be left unattended to some degree, but are presumably not to be placed at the undue risk that leaving them in a true wilderness would imply.

174. This parable and the two that follow it all involve the theme of things that were lost, and then later found.

and neighbors, saying, 'Rejoice with me, for I have found the coin which I had lost.'

2. "Likewise, I tell you, there is joy among the angels of God over even one sinner who repents."

I 36. PARABLE OF THE PRODIGAL SON
Luke 15:11–32

1. And Jesus said, "There was a man who had two sons; and the younger of them said to his father, 'Father, let me have now the share of the property that will be coming to me.' And so the father divided his property between them.

2. "A few days later, the younger son gathered together all that he had, and journeyed to a distant country, and there he wasted his substance in riotous living.

3. "But after he had spent everything, a great famine arose in the land, and he began to be in want. So he went and hired himself to one of the citizens of that country, who sent him out into his fields to feed the swine. He would gladly have filled himself with the husks that the swine were eating; but no one gave him anything.

4. "When he finally came to his senses he said, 'How many of my father's hired servants have bread enough and to spare, while I perish here with hunger! I will rise and return to my father, and I will say to him, Father, I have sinned against heaven and against you; I am no longer worthy to be called your son; treat me as one of your hired servants.' And he arose and went to his father.

5. "But while he was still a long way off, his father saw him and was filled with love and pity for him, and ran and embraced him and kissed him. The son said to him, 'Father, I have sinned against heaven and against you; I am no longer worthy to be called your son.' But the father said to his servants, 'Make haste! Bring forth the best robe and put it on him, and put a ring on his hand, and sandals on his feet; and bring out the fatted calf and kill it, and let us eat and be merry; for this my son was dead, and is alive again; he was lost, and is found.' And they began to celebrate.

6. "Now the elder son had been working in the field, and as he came and drew near the house, he heard the music and dancing. He called one of

his servants and asked what this meant. And the servant said to him, 'Your brother has come home, and your father has killed the fatted calf, because he has received him back safe and sound.'

7. "But the elder brother was angry and refused to go into the house. His father came out and began to plead with him, but he answered his father, 'I have served you for, lo, these many years, and I never disobeyed your command; yet you never gave me so much as a young goat so that I might make merry with my friends. But when this son of yours comes home, who has squandered your property on harlots, for him you killed the fatted calf!'

8. "Then the father said to him, 'My son, you have always stood by me, and all that I have is yours.[175] But it was fitting that we should make merry and be glad, for this your brother was dead, and is alive; he was lost, and is found.'"

I 37. PARABLE OF THE DISHONEST MANAGER
Luke 16:1–15

1. Jesus also told this story to his disciples:[176] "There was a rich man who had a manager to handle his affairs; and a report was brought to him that the man was wasting his money. So he called in the manager and said to him, 'What is this that I hear about you? Prepare a final accounting of your work, for you can no longer be my manager.'

2. "And the manager said to himself, 'What shall I do now, since my master is taking the job away from me? I have not the strength to dig, and am ashamed to beg. But I do know what I can do to make sure that people will still receive me into their houses after I am put out of my position.'

3. "So calling in his master's debtors one by one, he asked the first, 'How much do you owe my master?' The debtor said, 'A hundred measures of olive oil.' And the manager said to him, 'Take your account, sit down quickly, and write fifty instead.'

---

175. This preserves justice for the elder brother as well.

176. This parable and the next make another set, both of them dealing with the proper and beneficial use of worldly wealth.

4. "Then he asked another, 'And how much do you owe?' The man said, 'A hundred measures of wheat.' The manager said to him, 'Take your account, and make it eighty.'

5. "In this the master had to acknowledge the practical shrewdness of the dishonest manager;[177] for the children of this world are wiser than the children of light in dealing with their own kind. And I tell you, *there is a lesson here for you as well*: if you possess the wealth of this world, even though that wealth is unrighteous in itself, you should use it to make friends and to do good, so that when your life is over you will be received into the eternal dwelling places.

6. "He who is faithful in little things is also faithful in large ones; and he who is dishonest in little things is also dishonest in large ones. So if you have not been faithful in the use of the unrighteous wealth of this world, who will entrust you with the true riches? And if you have not been faithful in the use of that which is another's, who will give you that which is your own?

7. "No servant can serve two masters; for either he will hate the one and love the other, or he will be devoted to the one and despise the other. You cannot serve both God and mammon."

8. The Pharisees, who were great lovers of money, heard all this, and they began to ridicule Jesus. But he said to them, "You like to present yourselves as righteous before men, but God knows your hearts; and what is highly esteemed among men is detestable in the sight of God."

138. THE RICH MAN AND LAZARUS
Luke 16:19–31

1. Jesus continued, "There was a certain rich man, who dressed in purple and fine linen and who feasted sumptuously every day. And at his gate lay a poor man named Lazarus,[178] full of sores, who hoped only to be

---

177. Literally, the master "praised" the dishonest manager. It is clear that this is not to be read literally, however. The master had already dismissed the man for just that kind of sharp practice. The better reading is therefore as a rueful acknowledgment of the manager's worldly cleverness.

178. This is not the same man that Jesus raised from the dead. The name "Lazarus" was fairly common at the time, and meant "God is my help." It is appropriate to the circumstances of the men in both stories.

fed with what fell from the rich man's table; and the dogs came and licked his sores.

2. "It came to pass that the poor man died, and was carried by the angels to the bosom of Abraham. The rich man also died and was buried; and in Hades, where he was in torment, he lifted up his eyes, and saw Abraham far away and Lazarus at his side.

3. "And he called out, 'Father Abraham, have pity on me, and send Lazarus to dip the tip of his finger in water and cool my tongue; for I am in anguish in these flames.' But Abraham said, 'My child, remember that in your lifetime you received your good things, and Lazarus in like manner received evil things; but now he is comforted here, and you are in torment.

4. "'And besides all this, between us and you a great chasm has been set, so that those who wish to pass from here to you will not be able, nor can anyone cross over from there to us.'

5. "The rich man said, 'Then I beg you, father, to send Lazarus to my father's house, where I have five brothers, so that he may warn them, and they will not also come to this place of torment.' Abraham replied, 'They have Moses and the prophets; let your brothers hear them.' The rich man said, 'No, father Abraham; but if some one comes to them from the dead, they will repent.' But Abraham said to him, 'If they do not listen to Moses and the prophets, neither will they be persuaded even if some one should rise from the dead.'"

I 39. TEACHINGS ABOUT SERVICE AND DUTY
Luke 17:7–10

1. And Jesus said, "Will any one, who has a servant plowing or keeping sheep, say to him when he has come in from the field, 'Come at once, sit down, and eat with me?' Will he not instead say to him, 'Prepare my meal, and put on your apron, and serve me while I eat and drink; and afterward you may eat and drink'? Does he thank the servant because he did as he was told? Of course not.

2. "So you too, when you have done all that is commanded of you, should say, 'There is no special merit in our service; we have only done our duty.'"

140. TEN LEPERS ARE HEALED, BUT ONLY ONE GIVES THANKS
Luke 17:11–19

1. One day, on his way *back* to Jerusalem, Jesus was traveling near the border between Samaria and Galilee. As he entered a village, he was met by ten lepers, who stood at a distance and raised their voices and called, "Jesus, Master, take pity on us!"

2. When Jesus saw them he said to them, "Go and show yourselves to the priests." And it came to pass that, as they were on their way, they were made clean.

3. One of the lepers, when he saw that he was healed, turned back, praising God with a loud voice; and he fell facedown at Jesus' feet, giving him thanks. And this man was a Samaritan.

4. Jesus asked, "Were not ten made clean? But where are the other nine? Do we find no one returning to praise God except this foreigner?" And he said to the healed man, "Rise and be on your way; your faith has made you well."

141. WHERE IS THE KINGDOM OF GOD?
Luke 17:20–25

1. One day Jesus was asked by the Pharisees when the kingdom of God would come. He replied, "The kingdom of God is not coming with outward signs for you to observe, nor will people be able to say, 'See, here it is!' or 'There it is!'

2. "*Instead I say to the righteous,* behold, the kingdom of God is already within you; *and I say to the unrighteous,* beware, the kingdom of God is already among you."[179]

---

179. This verse presents two possible translations of the same original phrase. The Greek word used here—*entos*—can mean either "within" or "among." Two interpretations of the passage are therefore possible. One would emphasize how the kingdom of God is coming without outward show, and will instead work its way through a change in the hearts of believers, because already "the kingdom of God is within you." This interpretation would be consistent with many teachings of Jesus, such as in the Sermon on the Mount, that emphasize the spiritual nature of the children of the light. A different interpretation is also possible, however. This would emphasize how the kingdom of God will come without the prior warning of outward signs, but with power and

3. And he explained to his disciples, "The time is coming when you will long to see one of the days when the Son of Man is with you, and you will not see it. And people will say to you, 'See, here he is!' or 'There he is!' Do not go; do not follow them. For the Son of Man in his coming will be like the lightning that blazes out and lights the sky from one end to the other. But first he must suffer many things and be rejected by this generation."

142. PARABLE OF THE UNRIGHTEOUS JUDGE
Luke 18:1–8

1. And Jesus told his disciples a parable, to show that they ought always to pray and not lose heart. He said, "In a certain city there was a judge who neither feared God nor cared what people thought; and there was a widow in that city who kept coming to him and pleading, 'Grant me justice; vindicate me against my adversary.'

2. "For a while the judge refused, but finally he said to himself, 'Though I do not fear God or regard man, yet because this widow keeps troubling me I will give her justice, or else she will wear me out by her continual pleas.'"

3. And Jesus continued, "Learn a lesson from this unrighteous judge. Will God not give justice to his own elect, when they cry out to him day and night? Will he delay forever over them? I tell you, he will see that they receive justice, and will do so quickly. Yet even so, when the Son of Man comes, will he find any faithful ones on the earth?"

---

probably drastic consequences, and that it may come soon because it is close at hand and indeed "is already among" the people. This interpretation can be part of a vision of impending apocalyptic judgment. In its tone it is consistent with the next verse of this chapter, and with the description of the Second Coming in Chapter 173:14. There is no way of knowing which interpretation was intended, and by now each has earned a recognized place in Christian thought. This account has therefore used the italicized words to present both possible interpretations.*

143. THE PHARISEE AND THE TAX GATHERER
Luke 18:9–14

1. He also told this parable to some who trusted in their own righteousness, and looked down on others. "Two men went up into the temple to pray, one a Pharisee and the other a tax gatherer.

2. "The Pharisee stood and prayed his way about himself: 'God, I thank thee that I am not as other men are—extortioners, evildoers, adulterers—or even as this tax gatherer is. I fast twice a week, and I give tithes of all that I get.'

3. "The tax gatherer, standing at a distance, would not so much as lift up his eyes to heaven, but beat his breast, saying, 'God, be merciful to me, a sinner!' But I tell you, this man, rather than the other, went back to his house justified before God; for every one who exalts himself will be humbled, but he who humbles himself will be exalted."

144. MARRIAGE, DIVORCE, AND CHASTITY
Matthew 19:1–12; Mark 10:1–12; Luke 16:18

1. When Jesus finished saying these things, he departed from Galilee and headed for the region of Judea, *going by way of the lands* beyond the Jordan. Large crowds followed him, and he healed them there, and, as was his custom, he taught them.

2. Some Pharisees came up to him and, in an effort to ensnare him, they asked, "Is it lawful for a man to divorce his wife for any reason he wishes?"

3. "What did Moses command you?," Jesus replied. They said, "Moses permitted a man to give his wife a certificate of divorce and send her away." Jesus said, "Moses allowed you to put away your wives because your hearts were hard. But in the beginning it was not this way.

4. "Have you not read that the Creator who made them at the beginning made them male and female, and said, 'For this reason a man shall leave his father and mother and be joined to his wife, and the two will become one flesh.' So they are no longer two, but one. Therefore what God has joined together, let no man put asunder."

5. When they were back in the house the disciples asked him again about this matter. And he said to them, "I tell you, whoever divorces his wife, except for unfaithfulness, and marries another, commits adultery against her; and if she divorces her husband and marries another, she commits adultery. And he who marries a woman divorced from her husband *likewise* commits adultery."

6. The disciples said to him, "If this is the situation of a man with his wife, then it is not good to marry." And he said to them, "Not all men can accept that conclusion, but only those to whom *the gift of chastity* is given. Some men have been eunuchs from birth, and some have been made eunuchs by men, and some have decided to live like eunuchs[180] for the sake of the kingdom of heaven. He who is able to follow this course, let him follow it."

145. BLESSING THE LITTLE CHILDREN
Matthew 19:13–15; Mark 10:13–16; Luke 18:15–17

1. Then some little children were brought to Jesus so that he might lay his hands on them and pray for them. People were bringing even infants so that he might touch them. And when his disciples saw this, they rebuked the parents.

2. But when Jesus saw what the disciples were doing he was angry with them. He called the children to him, saying, "Allow the little children to come to me, and do not hinder them; for the kingdom of God belongs to such as these. I tell you truly, whoever does not receive the kingdom of God like a little child will never enter it."

3. And he took the children in his arms and blessed them, laying his hands upon them; and then he went on his way.

---

180. Literally, "have made themselves eunuchs." This is generally understood as a metaphor for a man's decision to forego marriage. The suggestion is probably not to be followed literally, although some prominent early Christians, possibly including Origen, actually did so.*

146. THE EYE OF THE NEEDLE
Matthew 19:16-30; Mark 10:17-31; Luke 18:18-30

1. As Jesus was setting out *to continue* his journey, an influential *young* man ran up and knelt before him, and asked him, "Good teacher, what good thing must I do to inherit eternal life?"

2. Jesus said to him, "Why do you ask me about what is good? And why do you call me good? No one is good but God alone. But if you wish to enter into life, keep the commandments."

3. "Which ones?" the man asked. And Jesus said, "You know the commandments: 'Do not murder; do not commit adultery; do not steal; do not bear false witness; do not defraud; honor thy father and mother; and love thy neighbor as thyself.'"

4. The young man said to him "Teacher, all these commandments I have followed from my youth. What do I still lack?" And Jesus, looking upon him, loved him and said to him, "You lack one thing. If you would be perfect, go, sell all that you have, and give the money to the poor, and you will have treasure in heaven. Then come, and follow me."

5. When the man heard this his face fell, and he went away sorrowful, for he had great possessions.

6. Jesus looked at him and said to his disciples, "I tell you truly, it is hard for a rich man to enter the kingdom of heaven!" The disciples were amazed at his words. But Jesus said to them again, "Children, how hard it is to enter the kingdom of God. It is easier for a camel to pass through the eye of a needle than for a rich man to enter the kingdom of God."

7. When the disciples heard this they were greatly astonished, and they asked one another, "Who then can be saved?" Jesus looked at them and said, "With men alone it is impossible, but not with God; for with God all things are possible."

8. Then Peter said to him, "Remember, we have forsaken everything to follow you. What will we have for that?" Jesus said to them, "I tell you truly, in the new world, when the Son of Man shall sit upon his glorious throne, then you who have followed me will also sit on twelve thrones, judging the twelve tribes of Israel.[181] And I tell you truly, there

---

181. Israel had been organized through the twelve tribes in its early history, but that structure had long since been replaced by more centralized monarchies. By appealing

is no one who has left house or wife, or brothers or sisters, or mother or father, or children or lands, for my name's sake and for the gospel, and for the sake of the kingdom of God, who will fail to receive back many times as much. In this present age he will receive a hundred times as much—houses and brothers and sisters and mothers and children and lands —along with persecutions—and in the world to come he will receive eternal life.

9. "Thus many that are first shall be last, and many who are last shall be first."

147. PARABLE OF THE VINEYARD WORKERS
Matthew 20:1–16

1. *And Jesus explained,* "The kingdom of heaven is like the landowner who went out early in the morning to hire laborers for his vineyard. When he had agreed with the laborers on a denarius a day, he sent them into his vineyard.

2. "Then going out about the third hour of the day[182] he saw others standing idle in the marketplace; and he said to them, 'You go into the vineyard too, and I will pay you whatever is right.' And so they went. Going out again about the sixth hour and the ninth hour, he did the same thing. And about the eleventh hour[183] he went out and found still others standing, and he asked them, 'Why have you been standing here idle all day?' They said to him, 'Because no one has hired us.' So he said to them, 'You go and work in the vineyard as well.'

3. "When evening came, the owner of the vineyard said to his manager, 'Call in the laborers and pay them their wages, beginning with the last ones hired, up until the first.'

4. "When those hired about the eleventh hour came, each of them received a denarius. Then when the first came, they thought they would be given more; but each of them received a denarius as well. And upon receiving it they protested to the landowner, saying, 'These last men worked only one hour, but you have made them equal to us who have borne the burden and heat of the day.'

---

to the memory of the twelve tribes, Jesus was reminding the nation of its original roots.

182. Midmorning or 9:00 a.m., with the hours counted from dawn.

183. Five in the afternoon, an hour before the work day ended at six.

5. "But he replied to one of them, 'Friend, I am doing you no wrong. Did you not agree with me on a denarius a day? Take what is yours, and go. I wish to give to this last one as much as I give to you. Am I not allowed to do as I wish with my own things? Or do you resent my generosity to others?'

6. "So the last shall be first, and the first shall be last."

I48. JESUS PREDICTS HIS DEATH AND RESURRECTION A THIRD TIME
Matthew 20:17–19; Mark 10:32–34; Luke 18:31–34

1. They were now on the road, going up to Jerusalem, and Jesus was walking ahead of the group. The disciples were amazed *at his courage in going there*, and the people following behind were filled with dread.

2. Once more he took the twelve aside and told them what was going to happen to him. "Behold, we are going up to Jerusalem, and everything that has been written about the Son of Man by the prophets will be accomplished.

3. "For he will be delivered to the chief priests and the scribes. They will condemn him to death, and will hand him over to the foreigners to be mocked and insulted and spat upon. And after they have flogged him they will crucify him; but on the third day he will rise again."

4. But the disciples understood none of these things. Jesus' meaning was hidden from them, and they did not grasp what he said.

I49. CORRECTING TWO AMBITIOUS APOSTLES
Matthew 20:20–28; Mark 10:35–45

1. Later the mother of the sons of Zebedee came up to Jesus with her sons, James and John, and kneeling before him they asked him for a favor. "Teacher," they said, "we want you to do for us whatever we ask of you." And he said to them, "What do you want me to do for you?"

2. The mother said, "Grant that these two sons of mine may sit, one at your right hand and one at your left, in your kingdom." And James and John asked *the same*, to sit at his side in his glory.

3. But Jesus answered, "You do not know what you are asking. Are you able to drink the cup that I am to drink, or be baptized with the baptism with which I will be baptized?" And they said to him, "We are able."

4. Jesus replied to them, "You will indeed drink my cup; and with the baptism with which I am baptized, you will be baptized. But to sit at my right hand or at my left is not for me to grant. Those places are for those for whom they have been prepared by my Father."

5. When the *other* ten heard of this, they became indignant at James and John. So Jesus called them all to him and said to them, "You know that among the Gentiles, those who are recognized as rulers lord it over the people, and their great men dominate the others.

6. "But it shall not be so among you. Whoever would be great among you must be your servant; and whoever would be first among you must be the slave of all. For even the Son of Man came not to be served but to serve, and to give his life as a ransom for many."[184]

150. ZACCHAEUS CLIMBS A SYCAMORE TREE
Mark 10:46a; Luke 19:1–10

1. Then they came to Jericho.[185] Jesus entered the city and was passing through it. A man named Zacchaeus was there; he was a supervisor of the tax gatherers, and rich.

---

184. This is a statement of the plan of salvation. Jesus' death on the cross will be a voluntary sacrifice to save individuals from sin and death. The concept of "ransom" or "redemption" explains the terms of the exchange. There is considerable variation among churches in their understanding of the details, but the basic concept is that all humanity had come under a sentence of judgment as a result of the original sin of Adam and Eve, and the subsequent sins of individuals. Thereafter humanity owed God a certain debt, most notably that of mortality and death. Jesus, however, by offering himself as a sacrifice, will pay that debt or redeem humanity from its burdens, allowing believers to attain eternal life. His sacrifice will also provide a moral example, showing the power of love and right action.*

185. Jericho lies about five miles west of the Jordan river, so when Jesus reached it he was back in Judea proper.

2. Zacchaeus sought to see what Jesus looked like, but could not, on account of the crowd, because he was short of stature. So he ran on ahead, along the way where Jesus was to pass, and climbed up into a sycamore[186] tree to see him.

3. And when Jesus came to that place, he looked up and said to him, "Zacchaeus, make haste and come down; for I must be a guest in your home today." So Zacchaeus came down at once, and received Jesus into his house with joy.

4. When the crowd saw this they all began to grumble, "He has gone in to be the guest of a sinful man." But Zacchaeus stood and said to the Lord, "Behold, Lord, I will give half of my possessions to the poor. And if I have wrongly exacted anything from any man, I will restore it fourfold."

5. Jesus said to him, "Today salvation has come to this house, because this man too is a son of Abraham. And the Son of Man has come to seek for and to save that which was lost."

151. THE PARABLE OF THE INVESTMENTS
Luke 19:11–28

1. As the people were listening to these things, Jesus went on to tell them a parable, because he was close to Jerusalem, and because they thought that the kingdom of God was about to appear very soon.

2. So he said, "A nobleman was called away to a distant country to be invested with kingly powers and then return. Calling ten of his servants, he divided among them ten pounds of silver and said to them, 'Manage this money for me until I come back.'

3. "But his citizens hated him and sent a delegation after him to say, 'We do not want this man to rule over us.'

4. "When he returned, having received the kingly power *nonetheless*, he called for the servants, to whom he had given the money, so that he might learn what they had gained by trading with it. The first one came before him and said, 'Lord, your pound has made ten pounds more.' And the king said to him, 'Well done, good servant! Because you have

---

186. This was not the familiar northern sycamore, but a species of fig or mulberry tree, with low branches.

been trustworthy in a very small matter, you shall have authority over ten cities.'

5. "The second came and said, 'Lord, your pound has made five pounds more.' And the king said to him, 'Then you are to rule over five cities.'

6. "Then another came, saying, 'Lord, here is your pound, which I kept stored away safely, wrapped up in a cloth. I was afraid of you, because you are a harsh man; you take out what you did not deposit, and reap what you did not sow.' And the king said to him, 'I will condemn you with your own words, you wicked servant! You knew that I was a harsh man, taking out what I did not deposit and reaping what I did not sow? They why did you not place my money with the moneychangers, so that at my return I could have collected it with interest?'

7. "And the king said to the people who were standing by, 'Take the pound from him, and give it to the man who has the ten pounds.' The people said to him, 'Lord, he already has ten pounds!' But the king replied, 'I tell you, that to every one who has, more will be given; but from him who has not, even what he does have will be taken away. And as for these enemies of mine, who did not want me to rule over them, bring them here and slaughter them in front of me.'"[187]

8. And when Jesus had finished this story, he went on ahead, going up[188] to Jerusalem.

152. THE BLIND BEGGAR BARTIMAEUS
Matthew 20:29-34; Mark 10:46b-52; Luke 18:35-43

1. As Jesus was leaving[189] Jericho, with his disciples and a great crowd following him, two blind men were sitting by the roadside. *One of these men*, Bartimaeus, the son of Timaeus, was begging there.

187. Jesus based this parable on events from local history. Judea had been a client kingdom of the Roman Empire until about twenty years before. As a result, Archelaus, the son of Herod the Great, like the king in this parable, had to travel to the distant country of Rome and obtain the approval of Augustus Caesar before he could formally begin his reign. Thereafter he ruled with great cruelty, at one point killing nearly three thousand pilgrims to Jerusalem for alleged sedition, and so alarming Joseph and Mary that on their return from Egypt they decided to settle in Galilee instead. See Chapter 16:2.

188. Jericho is near the Dead Sea, below sea level, while Jerusalem is about four thousand feet higher. The eighteen miles to Jerusalem is therefore perceptibly uphill.

189. Matthew and Mark report that these events happened as Jesus was leaving

2. Hearing the crowd going by, Bartimaeus asked what this was. They told him, "Jesus of Nazareth is passing by." And when he heard this, he began to shout, "Lord Jesus, Son of David, have mercy on me!"

3. Those who were leading the procession rebuked him, telling him to be silent, but he cried out all the louder, "Son of David, have mercy on me!"

4. Then Jesus stopped, and ordered the man to be brought to him. So they called Bartimaeus, saying to him, "Take heart! Rise; he is summoning you!" And throwing aside his cloak he sprang up and went to Jesus. When he came near, Jesus asked him, "What do you want me to do for you?"

5. He said, "Lord, I want to see." Jesus had compassion on him and touched his eyes, and said to him, "Receive your sight. Go; your faith has made you well."

6. Immediately Bartimaeus received his sight, *as did the other man*, and then they followed Jesus along the road, praising God. And when they saw this, all the people also gave praise to God.

I53. THE PASSOVER CROWDS LOOK FOR JESUS
John 11:55-57

1. Now it was almost time for the Jewish celebration of the Passover. Many people had gone up to Jerusalem from the country, to purify themselves before the feast. They were looking for Jesus and asking one another as they stood in the temple courtyards, "What do you think? Surely he will not come to the festival, will he?"

2. For the chief priests and the Pharisees had both given orders that if any one knew where Jesus was, he should report it, so that they might arrest him.[190]

Jericho. Luke reports that they occurred as Jesus approached Jericho. This text follows the majority position of Matthew and Mark. The apparent difference among the gospels might be reconciled on the assumption that they are describing different cities. Matthew and Mark may be reporting that Jesus was leaving the long established city of old Jericho, while Luke may be saying that Jesus was approaching the recently developed complex of new Jericho, which had been built by Herod the Great as a winter palace and administrative center about two miles further along in the direction of Jerusalem.*

190. All males were required to observe Passover, preferably in Jerusalem, but an

I 54. MARY ANOINTS JESUS AT BETHANY
Matthew 26:6–13; Mark 14:3–9; John 12:1–8

1. Six day before the Passover,[191] Jesus arrived at Bethany, *just outside of Jerusalem,*[192] the home town of Lazarus, whom Jesus had raised from the dead.

2. There a dinner was given for Jesus at the house of Simon the Leper. Martha served, and Lazarus was one of those who reclined at the table with him.[193]

3. Mary came in with an alabaster jar containing a pound of very precious ointment, made of pure nard.[194] She broke open the jar and poured the ointment over Jesus' head and feet, and wiped his feet with her hair; and the house was filled with the fragrance of the perfume.

4. When the disciples saw this, they were indignant, saying to one another, "To what purpose was this waste?" One of the disciples, Judas Iscariot, who would later betray Jesus, reproached her, saying, "Why was this ointment not sold, and the money given to the poor? It could have brought more than a year's wages." This he said, not because he cared about the poor, but because he was a thief; and having charge of the moneybag he used to steal from what was put into it.

5. But Jesus, aware of this talk, said to them, "Leave her alone. Why do you trouble this woman? She has done a beautiful thing for me. She has kept this ointment against the day of my burial. For you have the poor always with you, and you may do them good whenever you wish; but you will not always have me.

---

appearance at a predictable time and place made Jesus more vulnerable to arrest.

191. John reports that this dinner took place when Jesus first arrived in Bethany, six days before Passover. Matthew and Mark report that the dinner occurred later, two days before Passover. The earlier date seems somewhat more likely, because the appearance of Lazarus at this dinner would help to explain the enthusiastic reception that Jesus received on his entry into Jerusalem the next day.*

192. Bethany is about two miles from Jerusalem, on the southeastern slope of the Mount of Olives. This was a particularly suitable place for Jesus' last stop before reaching Jerusalem. The town was on the route used by Jews from Galilee who wished to travel on the east bank of the Jordan while bypassing Samaria; it evidently included a substantial population of people of Galilean origin; and several of Jesus' friends lived there.*

193. The anniversary of this visit is remembered in some churches as "Lazarus Saturday," the day before Palm Sunday.

194. The spikenard, from which this perfume is made, is a plant with aromatic roots.

6. "She has done what she could. In pouring this perfume on my body, she has anointed it beforehand to prepare me for burial. And I tell you truly, wherever the gospel is preached in the whole world, what she has done will be told in memory of her."

155. MURDER IS IN THE AIR
John 12:9–11

1. In the meantime a great crowd had learned that Jesus was there; and they came, not only on account of him, but also to see Lazarus, whom he had raised from the dead.

2. So the chief priests made plans to kill Lazarus as well, because he was the reason why many of the Jews were falling away from them and believing in Jesus.

Triumphal Entry, by Liz Lemon Swindle

© 2015, Liz Lemon Swindle, licensed by Foundation Arts (www.foundationarts.com)

IX. HOLY WEEK

PALM SUNDAY

156. THE TRIUMPHAL ENTRY INTO JERUSALEM
Matthew 21:1–11; Mark 11:1–11; Luke 19:29–44; John 12:12–19

1. The next day, a great crowd of people who had come for the festival heard that Jesus was coming to Jerusalem. So they took fronds of palm trees and went out to greet him.

2. When Jesus and his disciples drew near Jerusalem, and came to Bethphage at the hill called the Mount of Olives, he sent two disciples on ahead, saying to them, "Go into the village ahead of you, and as soon as you enter it you will find a donkey tied there, and with her a colt which no one has ever ridden.[195] Untie them and bring them here. If anyone asks you, 'Why are you doing this?' say, 'The Lord has need of them and will send them back shortly.' And he will let you have them at once."

3. So the messengers went away, and found things as Jesus had told them. They found the colt in the open street, tied up at a doorway. And as they were untying it, its owners and some bystanders said to them, "What are you doing, untying the colt?" They answered with the words Jesus had said, "The Lord has need of it;" and the owners let them go.

---

195. A colt is a young donkey. It was significant that no one had ever ridden this particular colt. Jewish law stipulated that an animal was not acceptable for sacred purposes—such as bearing the Messiah—if it had previously been put to domestic or utilitarian work.*

4. The disciples brought the donkey and the colt to Jesus; and they threw their cloaks on the colt, and Jesus sat upon it. All this took place to fulfill what had been spoken by the prophet, who said,

> Tell the daughter of Zion, Fear not!
> Behold, thy king is coming to you,
> humble, and mounted on a donkey—
> upon a colt, the foal of a beast of burden.

His disciples did not understand this prophecy at first; but after Jesus was glorified, then they remembered that they had done these things for him, and realized that this had been written about him.

5. As Jesus rode along, many people in the great crowd spread their cloaks on the road, and others spread leafy branches which they had cut from the trees in the fields.

6. And as Jesus approached the place where the road starts down the Mount of Olives, the whole multitude of the disciples began to rejoice and praise God with a loud voice for all the miracles that they had seen, saying, "Blessed be the King who comes in the name of the Lord! Peace in heaven and glory in the highest!"

7. And the crowds that went before him and that followed after him shouted out, "Hosanna! Blessed is he who comes in the name of the Lord! Blessed is the King of Israel! Hosanna to the Son of David![196] Blessed is the coming kingdom of our father David! Hosanna in the highest!"

8. Now the people that had been with Jesus when he called Lazarus out of the tomb and raised him from the dead had continued to tell others about it. For this reason also the crowd went out to meet him, because they heard he had performed this miracle. The Pharisees then said to one another, "You see that we can do nothing about this; look, the whole world has gone after him."

9. And some of the Pharisees in the crowd said to Jesus, "Teacher, rebuke your disciples." He answered, "I tell you, even if these disciples were to keep silent, then the very stones would cry out in celebration."[197]

---

196. Hosanna simply means "Save us!" The full implications of the word are suggested, however, by Psalm 118:25–26, which indicates that it could be appropriately used in connection with the Messiah. The greeting here was therefore a statement that the crowd recognized Jesus and saluted him as the promised savior—the savior, perhaps, who would deliver them from Roman rule.*

197. Literally, the stones "would cry out." Alternatively, the stones might be crying out to condemn the Pharisees' attempts to dampen the joy of the people.

10. But as Jesus drew closer to Jerusalem and saw the city he began to weep over it, saying, "How I wish that you, of all places, could recognize on this day the things that would bring you peace! But they are hidden from your eyes. So the days shall come upon you, when your enemies will build up a barricade around you, and surround you, and hem you in on every side; and they will level you to the ground—you and all your children within your walls. They will not leave one stone upon another, because you did not recognize the time when God came to offer you his care."[198]

11. And when Jesus entered Jerusalem, and went into the temple, all the city was in a commotion, saying, "Who is this?" And the crowds answered, "This is Jesus, the prophet from Nazareth in Galilee."

12. By the time Jesus had looked around at everything it had become late, and so he went *back* out to Bethany with the twelve.

FIG MONDAY

157. CURSING THE UNFRUITFUL FIG TREE
Matthew 21:18–19; Mark 11:12–14

1. In the morning of the following day, as they left Bethany and were returning to the city, Jesus was hungry. Seeing a fig tree in the distance, in leaf by the roadside, he went to see if he could find anything on it. But when he came to it he found nothing but leaves, for it was not the season for figs.

2. And he said to it, "May no one ever eat fruit from you again." His disciples heard him say this. And the fig tree began to wither at once.[199]

---

198. Jerusalem was in fact besieged and sacked in just this way about 35 years after Jesus' death, by Roman legions under Titus, the son of the emperor Vespasian, near the end of the Jewish Revolt. This happened in the summer of A.D. 70. Josephus says that over 90 percent of the population perished. The gospels were composed around this time, with most of the estimated dates falling between the years 60 and 95. At least some of the gospel writers would have been familiar with these events.

199. Literally, "withered." The account of the final withering the next day makes it clear that the process was only beginning at this time.

158. CLEANSING THE TEMPLE
Matthew 21:12–16; Mark 11:15–18; Luke 19:45–48;
John 2:14–22

1. After that they came to Jerusalem. Jesus entered the temple of God, and there he found those who were selling cattle and sheep and doves, and the moneychangers at their business.[200]

2. Making a whip of small cords, he drove all who were buying and selling there out of the temple, along with the sheep and cattle. He poured out the coins of the moneychangers, and overturned their tables. He overturned the seats of those who sold doves, and he told them, "Take these things away; you shall not make my Father's house a house of trade." And he taught them all, saying to them, "Is it not written, 'My house shall be called a house of prayer for all nations'? But you have made it a den of thieves." And he would not allow any one to carry merchandise through the temple courtyards.

3. His disciples remembered that it was written, "Zeal for thy house will consume me."

4. The leaders of the temple responded by demanding of him, "What can you show us as your authority for doing these things?" Jesus answered them, "Destroy this temple, and in three days I will raise it up again." The temple leaders then said, "It has taken forty-six years to build this temple, and you will raise it up in three days?" But Jesus was speaking about the temple of his own body. When he was raised from the dead, his disciples remembered that he had said this; and they believed the scripture and the words which Jesus had spoken.

5. After this he began to teach daily in the temple. And the blind and the lame came to him there, and he healed them.

6. But when the chief priests and the scribes saw the amazing things that he did, and heard the children calling out in the temple, "Hosanna to the Son of David!" they were sorely displeased, and they said to him,

---

200. Having these enterprises at the temple was not quite as surprising then as it may appear now. Jewish practice at that time called for animal sacrifices, and, in fact, doves had been sacrificed on Jesus' behalf at his birth. See Chapter 13:1. Some provision had to be made for worshipers to acquire these animals, and further provision for handling payment from travelers who may have brought a variety of foreign currencies that had to be exchanged for the Jewish money used at the temple. These activities were confined to the outer courtyard of the temple. They did not need to be actually within the temple precincts at all, however.

"Do you hear what these children are saying?" And Jesus said to them, "Yes; have you never read,

> Out of the mouth of babes and sucklings
> Thou has brought perfect praise?"

7. When the chief priests and the scribes and the principal men of the people heard this they sought a way to destroy Jesus; for they feared him, because the entire crowd was astonished at his teaching. But they could not find anything they could do, because the people hung on his words.

159. WHAT JESUS' DEATH WILL ACCOMPLISH
John 12:20–36a

1. Among those who had gone up to worship at the feast were some Greeks. These came to Philip, who was from Bethsaida in Galilee, and said to him, "Sir, we wish to meet Jesus." Philip went and told Andrew; and Andrew and Philip went together to tell Jesus.

2. And Jesus answered them, "Now the time has come for the Son of Man to be glorified. I tell you truly, unless a grain of wheat falls into the earth and dies, it remains only a single seed; but if it dies in this way, it will bring forth much new fruit. He who loves his life will lose it, but he who cares nothing for his life in this world will keep it to live for all eternity. Whoever serves me, must follow me; and wherever I am, there my servant will also be; and if any one serves me, the Father will honor him.

3. "Now my soul is troubled. But what shall I say *about that*? 'Father, save me from this hour'? No; it was for this very purpose that I have come to this hour. *Instead,* 'Father, bring glory to thy name.'" Then a voice came from heaven, "I have already glorified it, and will glorify it again."[201]

4. When the crowd there heard this voice, some said that it was thunder. Others said, "An angel has spoken to him." Jesus said, "This voice did not speak for my sake, but for yours. The time for judgment on the world has now come, and now *Satan,* the ruler of this world, shall be

---

201. The glorification of the Father is brought about through the deeds and activities of Jesus. These bring glory to God the Father by carrying out his plan for Jesus' mission, even as they also bring glory to the Son.

cast out.[202] And I, when I am lifted up from the earth, will draw all people to me." He said this to show by what kind of death he was going to die.

5. But the crowd said to him, "We have learned from the scriptures that the Christ will remain forever. How then can you say that the Son of Man must be lifted up? Who is this Son of Man?" Jesus answered them, "The light will be with you just a little while longer. Walk while you have the light, lest the darkness overtake you; for those who walk in darkness do not know where they are going. While you have the light, put your trust in the light, so that you may become children of the light."

160. MOST STILL REJECT JESUS
Matthew 21:17; Mark 11:19; John 12:36b–50

1. After Jesus had said this, he departed and hid himself from the crowd. Although he had done so many miracles before them, still they did not believe in him. This was so that the word spoken by the prophet Isaiah might be fulfilled: "Lord, who has believed our message, and to whom has the power of the Lord been revealed?" Therefore they could not believe. And Isaiah had foretold that as well:

> He has blinded their eyes and hardened their hearts,
> lest they should see with their eyes,
> and understand with their hearts,
> and turn, and I would heal them.

Isaiah said these things because he foresaw Jesus' glory and spoke of him.

2. Nevertheless many people, even among the leaders of the Jews, did believe in him, but because of the Pharisees they did not confess it, out of fear that they would be expelled from the synagogue; for they loved the approval of men more than the approval of God.

3. Then Jesus said in a loud voice, "He who believes in me, does not believe in me only, but also in the one who sent me. And he who sees me is also seeing the one who sent me. I have come as a light into the world, so that whoever believes in me shall not remain in darkness. If

---

202. Satan will not be finally defeated at this time, but through Christ's death and resurrection mankind will now be better able to resist him.*

any one hears my words and does not follow them, I do not judge him; for I did not come to judge the world, but to save the world. He who rejects me and rejects my teachings will nonetheless have a judge; he will be judged on the last day in accordance with the words that I have spoken. For I have not spoken on my own authority; the Father who sent me has himself told me what I should say and how I should say it. And I know that his commandments lead to eternal life. What I say, therefore, I say just as the Father has bidden me."

4. And when evening came, Jesus left them and went out of the city to Bethany, and he lodged there for the night.

HOLY TUESDAY

I6I. THE FIG TREE IS COMPLETELY WITHERED
Matthew 21:20–22; Mark 11:20–26

1. As Jesus and his disciples passed by in the morning, they saw the fig tree withered away to its roots. Peter remembered and said to Jesus, "Master, look! The fig tree that you cursed has *completely* withered."

2. When the disciples saw this they marveled, asking, "How did the fig tree wither so quickly?" And Jesus answered them, "Have faith in God. I tell you truly, if you have faith, you will not only be able to do what has been done to the fig tree, but you can even say to this mountain, 'Be uprooted and cast into the sea.' If you do not doubt in your heart, but believe that what you say will come to pass, it will be done for you.

3. "Therefore, I tell you, whatever you ask for in prayer, believe that you have already received it, and it will be yours.

4. "And whenever you stand praying, if you have anything against any one, first forgive them; so that your Father in heaven may forgive you your own transgressions. For if you do not forgive, neither will your Father in heaven forgive your transgressions."

162. THE TEMPLE LEADERS CHALLENGE JESUS' AUTHORITY
Matthew 21:23–27; Mark 11:27–33; Luke 20:1–8

1. Then they came again to Jerusalem and entered the temple. As Jesus was walking in the temple courtyards, teaching the people and preaching the gospel, the chief priests, scribes and elders[203] came up and asked, "By what authority are you doing these things? And who gave you that authority?"

2. Jesus answered them, "I in turn will ask you one question; and if you give me the answer, then I will tell you by what authority I do these things. So tell me! John's authority to perform baptisms[204]—where did that come from? From heaven or from men?

3. The delegation took council among themselves. "If we say, 'From heaven,' he will say to us, 'Why then did you not believe him?'[205] But if we say, 'From men,' then the people will stone us, for they are all convinced that John was a true prophet."

4. So they answered Jesus, "We do not know where it was from." And Jesus said to them, "Then neither will I tell you by what authority I do these things."

163. PARABLE OF THE TWO SONS
Matthew 21:28–32; Mark 12:1a; Luke 20:9a

1. Jesus then began to speak to the people in parables, *reproaching them for their failure to recognize the Messiah.*[206]

2. "What would you think about this? A man had two sons, and he went to the first and said, 'Son, go and work in the vineyard today.' And the son answered, 'I will not;' but afterward he repented and went. Then

---

203. Representatives from these three groups made up the Sanhedrin, the Jewish ruling council. The people questioning Jesus here may have been carrying a cautionary challenge from the council.*

204. Literally, "the baptism of John." The underlying question here is where John got the authority to introduce his new doctrines about the practice—repentance and a one-time public baptism that would wash away substantive sins as well as ritual impurity.*

205. Believe John, that is, when he identified Jesus as the Messiah.

206. The next three parables address this topic.

the man went to the second son and said the same thing; and this son answered, 'I will go, sir,' but did not go.

3. "Now, which of the two obeyed the will of his father?" "The first," they said.

4. Jesus said to them, "I tell you truly, the tax gatherers and harlots will get into the kingdom of God before you. For John came to you and showed you the path of righteousness, and you did not believe him, but the tax gatherers and the harlots did believe him. And even after you saw this happening, you still did not repent and believe him."[207]

164. PARABLE OF THE WICKED TENANTS
Matthew 21:33–44; Mark 12:1b–11; Luke 20:9b–18

1. "Listen to another parable. There was a householder who planted a vineyard. He set a wall around it, and dug a pit for the wine press, and built a watchtower. Then he leased it out to tenants, and went on a long journey to another country.

2. "When the harvest time came, he sent a servant to the tenants, to collect his share of the fruits of the vineyard. But the tenants took the servant and beat him, and sent him away empty-handed. Then the man sent another servant to them, and they beat him on the head, and treated him shamefully, and sent him away empty-handed as well. And he sent yet a third; this one they stoned and threw out of the vineyard. And he sent another, and that one they killed. And so later with many others, some they beat and some they killed.

3. "The owner of the vineyard said to himself, 'What shall I do?' But he still had one more, a son whom he loved. Last of all he sent that one to the tenants, thinking, 'Surely they will respect my son.' But when the tenants saw him, they said to each other, 'This is the heir; come, let us kill him, and then his inheritance will be ours.' So they seized him, took him out of the vineyard, and killed him.

4. "Now when the owner of the vineyard returns, what will he do to those tenants?" The people replied, "He will see that those horrible men are put to a horrible death." "*Even more*," said Jesus. "He will destroy those

---

207. The point of this parable is that the actions of the two sons spoke louder than their words, and, by analogy, that too few people have taken concrete actions to show their faith.

tenants and then lease out the vineyard to other tenants, who will give him his share of the crop at the proper seasons."

5. When the people heard this, they said, "God forbid!" But Jesus looked straight at them and said, "What then is the meaning of this scripture:

> The very stone that the builders rejected
> has now become the cornerstone;
> This is the Lord's doing,
> and it is marvelous in our eyes.

Whoever falls on this stone will be broken to pieces, and whomever it falls on will be crushed to powder. Therefore I tell you that the kingdom of God will be taken away from you and given to a people who will bring forth the proper fruit."

165. PARABLE OF THE WEDDING GARMENT
Matthew 21:45—22:14; Mark 12:12; Luke 20:19

1. Jesus spoke still another parable, saying, "The kingdom of heaven may be likened to a king who gave a wedding feast for his son; and he sent his servants to call those who were invited to the feast, but they refused to come.

2. "So he sent other servants, saying to them, 'Tell those who are invited, Behold, I have prepared the dinner; my oxen and my fattened cattle have been butchered, and everything is ready. Come to the wedding feast!' But they made light of it and went off, one to his farm and another to his business. The rest seized his servants, treated them dishonorably, and then killed them. The king was enraged; he sent his soldiers and destroyed those murderers and burned their city.

3. "Then he said to his servants, 'The wedding feast is ready, but those who were invited were not worthy. Therefore go out to the town gates and invite to the feast as many people as you find.' And the servants went out into the streets and gathered all whom they found, the bad as well as the good; and so the wedding hall was filled with guests.

4. "But when the king came in to greet the guests, he noticed a man who was not wearing a wedding garment; and he said to him, 'Friend, how did you get in here without a wedding garment?' The man had no response to that. Then the king said to his attendants, 'Bind him hand and foot, and cast him into the outer darkness, where there shall

be weeping and gnashing of teeth.' For many are called, but few are chosen."[208]

6. When the scribes and the chief priests and the Pharisees heard Jesus' parables, they realized that he was speaking against them. They wanted to arrest him at once, but they were afraid of the crowd, because the people held Jesus to be a prophet; so they left him alone and went away.

166. RENDERING UNTO CAESAR
Matthew 22:15–22; Mark 12:13–17; Luke 20:20–26

1. Then the Pharisees took counsel on how they might ensnare Jesus in his talk. So they watched him, and sent some of their disciples to him, along with some agents of Herod, who pretended to be righteous men. They hoped to catch Jesus in some remark so that they could deliver him up to the power and authority of the governor.

2. These spies came and said to him, "Teacher, we know that you are a man of integrity, and show no partiality; for you do not pay heed to the status of men, but speak and teach what is right, and truly teach the way of God.

3. "Tell us, then, what you think. Is it right for us to pay taxes to Caesar, or not? Should we pay them, or should we not?"

4. But Jesus, aware of their guile, said, "Why are you trying to trap me, you hypocrites?[209] Bring me a coin used for paying the tax, and let me look at it." So they brought a denarius. Jesus asked them, "Whose likeness is this on it, and whose name?" "Caesar's," they replied. Then Jesus said to them, "Therefore render unto Caesar the things that are Caesar's, and unto God the things that are God's."

5. And so they were not able to catch Jesus by what he said before the people. When they heard his answer they marveled, and were silent; and they left him and went away.

---

208. That is, the invitation is given to many, but few are willing to take the steps needed to fully accept it, such as finding a wedding garment, and only those few are then chosen.

209. Their question had been intended to put Jesus in a dilemma. If he said it was wrong to pay the tax, he could be denounced as a political agitator. If he said it was proper, he would lose influence among the people who hated the Roman occupation and its exactions.

167. HUMAN NATURE AFTER THE RESURRECTION
Matthew 22:23–33; Mark 12:18–27; Luke 20:27–39

1. That same day, *in a further effort to catch Jesus in his words,* some Sadducees, who say there is no resurrection, came to him and asked him a question. "Teacher, Moses wrote for us that if a man's brother dies, and leaves a wife, but leaves no child, then the man must marry the widow, and have children with her to carry on his brother's line.

2. "Now imagine there were seven brothers among us. The first married, and died, and having no children he left his wife to his brother. The second brother took her, and then died, leaving no children. And the third likewise, and on down to the seventh; and indeed, none of the seven left any children. Last of all the woman died as well. In the resurrection, then, whose wife will she be? For all seven had married her."

3. Jesus answered them, "You going astray here because you do not understand the scriptures or the power of God. The children of this world marry and are given in marriage. But those who are considered worthy to reach the next world, when they rise from the dead, will neither marry nor be given in marriage, for they can never more die, but will be like angels in heaven. They are the children of God, being children of the resurrection.

4. "And as for the fact of the resurrection, have you not read in the book of Moses, in the passage about the bush,[210] how Moses himself showed you that the dead are raised? For there God said to him, 'I am the God of Abraham, and the God of Isaac, and the God of Jacob.' He is not a God of the dead, but of the living, for the people of all generations are alive in his sight. So you are greatly mistaken."

5. When the crowd heard this, they were astonished at his teaching. And some of the scribes answered, "Teacher, that was well said."

---

210. The reference is to the time that God spoke to Moses out of the burning bush. See Exodus 3:4–6.

168. A QUESTION ABOUT THE GREATEST COMMANDMENT
Matthew 22:34–40; Mark 12:28–34a

1. When the Pharisees heard that Jesus had silenced the Sadducees, they gathered together themselves. One of them, a specialist in religious law, went over *in time to* hear them disputing with one another; and recognizing that Jesus answered them well, asked him a question to test him. "Teacher, what is the greatest commandment in the law?"

2. Jesus answered, "The first is, 'Hear, O Israel: The Lord our God, the Lord is one; and thou shalt love the Lord your God with all your heart, and with all your soul, and with all your mind, and with all your strength.' This is the first and greatest commandment.

3. "And the second is like unto it: 'Thou shalt love thy neighbor as thyself.' On these two commandments hang all of the law and the prophets. There is no other commandment greater than these."

4. And the legal scholar said to him, "You are right, Teacher; you have spoken the truth that he is one, and there is no other but he. And to love him with all the heart, and with all the understanding, and with all the strength; and to love one's neighbor as oneself, is much more important than all the burnt offerings and sacrifices."

5. When Jesus saw that the scholar answered wisely, he said to him, "You are not far from the kingdom of God."

169. JESUS ESTABLISHES HIS ROUTINE
Luke 21:37–38

1. *By this time Jesus had established a daily practice.*

2. Every day he would teach at the temple, and all the people would assemble there early in the morning to hear him. And each evening he went out of the city to spend the night on the hill called the Mount of Olives.[211]

---

211. The town of Bethany is on the far slope of the Mount of Olives, so it would be consistent with this description for Jesus to spend some nights there.

HOLY WEDNESDAY

170. ANCESTRY OF THE CHRIST
Matthew 22:41–46; Mark 12:34b–37; Luke 20:40–44

1. *The next morning,* as Jesus taught in the temple courtyards, and the Pharisees were gathered together, he asked them a question, saying, "How can the scribes say that the Christ is the son of David?[212] What do you think about the Christ? Whose son is he?"

2. "The son of David," they said to him.

3. Jesus replied, "Then how is it that David, guided by the Holy Spirit, calls him 'my Lord'? For David himself says in the Book of Psalms,

> The Lord said to my Lord,
> Sit thou at my right hand,
> until I make thy enemies
> A footstool beneath thy feet.

If David himself thus calls the Christ 'my Lord,' how can the Christ be his son?"[213]

4. The great throng listened to Jesus with delight. No one was able to say a word in answer to this, nor from that day on did any one dare to ask him any more questions.

171. "WOE UNTO YOU, PHARISEES!"[214]
Matthew 23:1–36; Mark 12:38–40; Luke 11:42–52, 12:1–3, 20:45–47

1. Then with all the crowd listening, Jesus turned to his disciples and said, "Beware of the scribes! They and the Pharisees sit in Moses' seat;

---

212. Not meaning a direct son, but a lineal descendant.

213. Jesus does not deny that he is the son of David. Rather, his point is that he is not merely the human heir to David's line; he is also the son of God.*

214. The account of this denunciation in Matthew is sometimes called the Seven Woes, and the one in Luke the Six Woes. Because the two do not entirely overlap, the combined version in this chapter lists a total of nine woes.

so understand and follow all the rules that they teach you. But do not follow their example, for they do not practice what they preach.[215]

2. "They do all their deeds only to be seen by others; and so they make their prayer boxes large and the fringe on their garments long.[216] They like to walk about in long robes, and they love having the places of honor at banquets and the best seats in the synagogues, and respectful greetings in the market places, and being called 'Teacher' by men. But they devour widows' houses, even while they make long prayers for pretense. Such people will receive a special damnation.

3. "You, however, are not to let anyone call you teacher, for you all have only one teacher, and you are all brothers together. And call no man on earth your father, for you have only one Father, who is in heaven. Nor yet be called leaders, for you have only one leader, the Christ. The one who is greatest among you shall be your servant; for whoever exalts himself will be humbled, and whoever humbles himself will be exalted."

4. One of the experts in religious law answered him, "Teacher, in saying these things you insult us as well."

5. And Jesus said, "Woe unto you lawyers! For you bundle up heavy burdens, hard to bear, and lay them on men's shoulders; but you yourselves will not lift a finger to help move them.

6. "Woe unto you, lawyers and scribes and Pharisees, hypocrites! For you have taken away the key of knowledge. You shut the door to the kingdom of heaven in people's faces. You do not enter in yourselves, and you prevent others from entering.

7. "Woe to you, scribes and Pharisees, hypocrites! You cross land and sea to make a single convert, and when he becomes a convert, you make him twice as much a child of hell as yourselves.

---

215. Jesus' speech on this theme is a memorable denunciation, and also one that made important enemies. When Jesus entered Jerusalem on Palm Sunday, he received the accolades due to a king, something that would have given the Romans grounds for concern about a possible uprising. The next morning Jesus unambiguously challenged the Jewish Sadducees, when he drove the moneychangers from the temple that they controlled. In the present remarks Jesus similarly castigates the scribes and the Pharisees. By the end of this denunciation, Jesus is in open opposition to all the important elements of the Jerusalem establishment.

216. Both of these items are conspicuous accoutrements of Jewish religious wear. Prayer boxes (Greek, *phylacteries*) are small boxes containing passages from the Old Testament, which are bound to the forehead and arm with leather strips.

8. "Woe to you, blind guides, who say, 'If any one swears by the temple, it means nothing; but if any one swears by the gold of the temple, he is bound by that oath.' You blind fools! For which is greater, the gold, or the temple that has made the gold sacred? And you say, 'If any one swears by the altar, it means nothing; but if any one swears by the gift that is on the altar, he is bound by that oath.' You blind men! Which is greater, the gift, or the altar that makes the gift sacred? So whoever swears by the altar, swears by it and by everything on it; and whoever swears by the temple, swears by it and by him who dwells within it; and whoever swears by heaven, swears by the throne of God and by the one who sits upon it.

9. "Woe to you, scribes and Pharisees, hypocrites! You pay the tithe on *even* your mint and rue and dill and cumin, and every little herb, but have neglected the weightier matters of the law—justice and mercy and the love of God. You ought to have paid the tithes without neglecting these other things. You blind guides! You strain out a gnat *from your drinking water*, but swallow a camel!

10. "Woe to you Pharisees! For you love to have places of honor in the synagogues and greetings in the market places!

11. "Woe to you, scribes and Pharisees, hypocrites! You clean the outside of the cup and the bowl, while inside they remain full of greed and self-indulgence. You blind Pharisee! First clean the inside of the cup and of the bowl, and then the outside can become clean as well.

12. "Woe to you, scribes and Pharisees, hypocrites! For you are like white-washed sepulchres, which outwardly appear beautiful, but within are full of dead men's bones and all uncleanness. So you outwardly appear righteous to men, but within you are full of hypocrisy and wickedness. And you are like unmarked graves which are not seen, and men walk over them unawares.

13. "Woe unto you, scribes and Pharisees, hypocrites! For you build tombs for the prophets and decorate the graves of the righteous, saying, 'If we had lived in the days of our fathers, we would not have joined with them in shedding the blood of the prophets.' But in saying that you are witnesses against yourselves, that you are the descendants of those who murdered the prophets, and that you consent to their deeds; for they killed them, and you build their tombs. And now you can go on to complete their works of wickedness. You serpents, you brood of vipers, how can you escape being condemned to hell? For God in his wisdom has said, 'I will send them *more* prophets and wise men and

teachers, some of whom they will kill and crucify, and some of whom they will scourge in their synagogues and persecute from town to town.' Then upon you will fall the guilt for all the righteous blood shed from the foundation of the world—from the blood of innocent Abel to the blood of Zechariah the son of Barachiah, whom you murdered in the temple between the sanctuary and the altar. I tell you truly, the judgment for all these things shall fall upon this generation."

14. While Jesus was speaking a crowd of many thousands had gathered, so closely pressed that they were stepping on one another. Jesus turned to his disciples and warned them first of all, "Be on your guard against the leaven of the Pharisees, which is hypocrisy. There is nothing covered up that will not be revealed, or hidden that will not be known. Whatever you have said in the dark shall be heard in the light, and what you have whispered in private rooms shall be shouted from the housetops."

172. THE WIDOW'S MITE
Mark 12:41–44; Luke 21:1–4

1. Then Jesus sat down opposite the temple treasury, and watched people putting money and gifts into the collection boxes. Many rich people put in large sums; and then a poor widow came, and dropped in two mites, the smallest of copper coins, which together make a penny.[217]

2. Jesus called his disciples to him and said, "I tell you truly, this poor widow has put more into the treasury than all the others; for they all gave what they could spare out of their abundance, but she out of her poverty has given everything she had, all that she had to live on."

---

217. The Greek refers to obscure coinage, of very small value. The King James Version translated the concept into Renaissance English coins: "two mites, which make a farthing."

173. TEACHINGS ABOUT THE SECOND COMING

Matthew 24:1–44, 25:1–46; Mark 13:1–37; Luke 12:39–40, 17:26–37, 21:5–36

The destruction of Jerusalem
Matthew 24:1–2; Mark 13:1–2; Luke 21:5–6

1. Jesus then left the temple, and was walking away when his disciples came to him and pointed out how it was adorned with beautiful stonework and offerings to God. "Look, Teacher, what massive stones and splendid buildings!" But Jesus responded, "Do you see all these things? I tell you truly, one day there will not be one stone left upon another; every one of them will be thrown down."[218]

Jesus' followers must stand firm
Matthew 24:3–14; Mark 13:3–13; Luke 21:7–19

2. Later, as Jesus sat on the Mount of Olives across the valley from the temple, Peter and James and John and Andrew came to him privately and asked him, "Teacher, tell us, when will all these things happen, and what will show that they are about to take place? What sign will signal your coming and the end of the age?"[219]

3. And Jesus answered them, "Take care that no one deceives you. For many will come in my name, saying, 'I am the Christ,' and 'The time is at hand!' and they will lead many astray. Do not follow them.

4. "You will hear of wars, and rumors of wars, and upheavals among the people, but see that you are not frightened; these things must happen first, but the end will not come at once. Nation will rise against nation, and kingdom against kingdom; there will be famines, pestilences, and great earthquakes in various places; and there will be terrible sights and great portents from heaven. But all this is only the beginning of the travails.

---

218. The temple itself is completely gone today, but a part of one of the outer walls of the temple complex still survives as the Western Wall. Although this is best known as the "Wailing Wall" and a pilgrimage site for Jews, it also has significance for Christians as a remnant of the temple where Jesus spent much of Holy Week.

219. Because of the setting of this conversation on the Mount of Olives, these teachings are sometimes referred to as the Olivet Discourse.

5. "So take heed to yourselves. Before all this they will lay their hands on you and persecute you. They will deliver you up to the councils *of the Jews,* and you will be beaten in synagogues and prisons; and you will be brought before the governors and kings *of the Romans.* Then they will hand you over for confinement and execution, because you are my followers.

6. "But this will be an opportunity for you to bear testimony before them. When they arrest you and deliver you up for trial, settle it in your minds not to worry beforehand about how to defend yourselves. Say whatever is given to you at that time, for it is not you who will be speaking, but the Holy Spirit. And I will give you words and wisdom, which none of your enemies will be able to resist or prove wrong.

7. "You will be hated by all nations for my name's sake. And then many will fall away, and betray one another, and hate one another. Brother will betray brother to death, and the father his child, and children will rise up against parents and have them put to death. You will be betrayed even by parents and kinsmen and friends and brothers, and some of you they will put to death. Many false prophets will arise and lead people astray. And because lawlessness will increase, most men's love will grow cold.

8. "But not a hair of your head will perish. By your endurance you will protect your lives; and he who stands firm to the end will be saved.

9. "This gospel about the kingdom must first be preached throughout the whole world, as a testimony to all the nations; and then the end will come.

Signs of the second coming
Matthew 24:15-27, 24:29-31; Mark 13:14-27; Luke 17:31-33, 21:20-28

10. "When you see Jerusalem surrounded by armies, then know that the time of its destruction is near. And when you see 'the abomination that causes desolation,' spoken of by the prophet Daniel, set up where it ought not to be, standing in the holy place[220]—let the reader understand!—then let those who are in Judea flee to the mountains, and let those who are inside the city depart, and let those who are out in the country not enter it.

---

220. Jesus is probably referring to the Roman armies that will come and occupy Jerusalem in A.D. 70, and set up their standards and idols in the temple.

11. "On that day, let no one who is on the rooftop, with his possessions inside the house, go down and enter it to take anything out; and let no one who is in the field turn back to fetch his cloak. For these are the days of vengeance, so that all things which are written may be fulfilled. Remember Lot's wife![221]

12. "Whoever tries to save his life will lose it, but whoever loses his life will preserve it.

13. "Alas for the pregnant women and the nursing mothers in those days! For there will be great distress upon the land and wrath against this people; they will fall by the edge of the sword, and be led away captive into all the nations; and Jerusalem will be trodden underfoot by the Gentiles, until the span of time appointed to the Gentiles has been completed.

14. "Pray that your flight will not be in winter or on the sabbath. For then there will be such tribulation as has not been seen, from the beginning of the creation which God created until now, and never will be seen again. And if the Lord had not *resolved to* cut short the days, no human flesh would survive; but for the sake of the elect, whom he has chosen, those days will be shortened.

15. "And at that time if anyone says to you, 'Look, here is the Christ!' or 'Look, there he is!' do not believe it. False Christs and false prophets will appear and perform great signs and miracles, so as to deceive, if possible, even the elect. So be on your guard. Behold, I have told you all things beforehand.

16. "If they say to you, 'Lo, he is out in the desert,' do not go out; if they say, 'Lo, he is hidden in the inner rooms,' do not believe it. Just as the lightning comes out of the east and blazes as far as the west, so will be the coming of the Son of Man.

17. "Immediately after the tribulation of those days, there will be signs in the sun and moon and stars:

> The sun will be darkened,
> and the moon will not give its light;
> The stars will fall from the sky,
> and the powers of heaven will be shaken.

---

221. Lot's wife turned back to look at the destruction of Sodom and Gomorrah, and was turned into a pillar of salt.

And upon the earth, the nations will be in distress, disoriented at the roaring of the sea and the waves, men's hearts failing them with fear and with foreboding of what is to come upon the world.

18. "And then the sign of the Son of Man[222] will appear in the sky, and all the nations of the earth will lament, and they will see the Son of Man coming on the clouds of heaven with great power and glory. And he will send out his angels with a mighty blast on the trumpet, and they will gather his chosen ones from the four winds, from the ends of the earth to the ends of the sky.

19. "Now when these things begin to take place, straighten up and lift your heads, because your redemption is drawing near."

Watch and pray!
Matthew 24:28, 24:32–42; Mark 13:28–33; Luke 17:26–30, 17:34–37, 21:29–36

20. And he told them this parable. "Now learn a lesson from the fig tree, and all the trees. As soon as its twigs become tender and its leaves come out, you can see that and know for yourselves that summer is near. So too, when you see these things happening, you will know that the kingdom of God is near, at the very gates. I tell you truly, this generation will not pass away until all these things take place. Heaven and earth will pass away, but my words will not pass away.

21. "But no one knows when that day and hour will come, not even the angels in heaven, nor the Son, but only the Father.

22. "As it was in the days of Noah, so it will be at the coming of the Son of Man. In the days before the flood, the people ate, they drank, they married, they were given in marriage, up until the day when Noah entered the ark; and they knew nothing of what would happen until the flood came and swept them all away. So too shall be the coming of the Son of Man. And it will be as it was in the days of Lot. People ate, they drank, they bought, they sold, they planted, they built; but on the day when Lot went out from Sodom, fire and brimstone rained down

---

222. Jesus refers to himself as the "Son of Man" throughout the gospels, but this particular use of the term connects him directly with the prophets of the Old Testament. Daniel 7:13–14 had given this prediction: "I saw visions in the night, and behold, with the clouds of heaven there came one like a son of man, and he approached the Ancient of Days and was led into his presence. And to him was given dominion and glory and kingdom, so that people of every nation and language should serve him; his dominion is an everlasting dominion, which shall not pass away, and his kingdom is one that shall never be destroyed."

from heaven and destroyed them all. Thus it shall be on the day when the Son of Man is revealed.

23. "I tell you, on that night there will be two people in the same bed; the one shall be taken and the other left behind. There will be two women grinding grain at the mill; one shall be taken and the other left behind. Two men will be in the field; one shall be taken and the other left.

24. "Take heed, watch, and pray! Be on guard, lest your hearts be weighed down with carousing and drunkenness and the cares of this life, and that day close upon you suddenly like a snare; for it will come upon all those who dwell upon the face of the whole earth. So watch at all times, praying that you may be found worthy to escape all these things that are about to happen, and to stand before the Son of Man. Watch, for you do not know on what day your Lord will come."

25. His disciples asked him, "Where will this happen, Lord?" And he said to them, "Wherever there is a dead body, there the vultures will gather.[223]

Unpredictable as a thief in the night
Matthew 24:43-44; Mark 13:34-37; Luke 12:39-40

26. "It is like a man going on a journey. He leaves his home and puts his servants in charge, each with his assigned tasks, and commands the doorkeeper to be on the watch.

27. "So you too must be watchful, for you do not know when the master of the house will come—in the evening, or at midnight, or at cockcrow, or in the morning—lest he come suddenly and find you sleeping.

28. "And be certain of this, that if the owner of the house had known at what hour of the night the thief was coming, he would have been awake, and would not have let his house be broken into. Therefore you too must always be ready; for the Son of Man will come at an hour when you do not expect him. What I say to you I say to all: Watch.

---

223. The underlying Greek word—*aetos*—means "bird of prey." Some older bibles render this as "eagles" here. "Vultures" seems to suit this particular context better, however. The idea is that the day of judgment will seek out sinners wherever they are.

Parable of the wise and foolish virgins
Matthew 25:1–13

29. "Or the *coming of the* kingdom of heaven may be likened to ten virgins who took their lamps and went forth to meet the bridegroom.[224] Five of them were foolish, and five were wise. When the ones that were foolish took their lamps, they took no oil with them; but the wise took flasks of oil along with their lamps.

30. "When the bridegroom was long in coming, they all slumbered and slept. But at midnight there was a cry, 'Behold, the bridegroom comes! Come out to meet him!'

31. "Then all the virgins rose and trimmed their lamps. And the foolish ones said to the wise, 'Give us some of your oil, for our lamps are going out.' But the wise replied, 'No; there may not be enough for us and for you; go instead to the dealers and buy oil for yourselves.' And while they were away buying it, the bridegroom came, and those who were ready went in with him to the wedding feast; and the door was shut.

32. "Later the other virgins also came, saying, 'Lord, Lord, open the door for us.' But he replied, 'I tell you truly, I do not know you.' Watch therefore, for you know neither the day nor the hour when the Son of Man will come.

Parable of the silver talents
Matthew 25:14–30

33. "Or it will be like a man going on a journey, who called his servants and entrusted his property to them; to one he gave five talent-weights *of silver*, to another two, and to another one, to each according to his ability. Then he set off.[225]

34. "The one who had received the five talents went out immediately and began to trade with them; and he made five talents more. Likewise, the one who had received the two talents put them to work and made two talents more. But the one who had received the single talent went and dug a hole in the ground, and hid his master's money.

35. "After a long time the master of those servants returned and called them for an accounting. The one who had received the five talents

---

224. The virgins here are friends and attendants of the bride, not brides themselves.

225. This parable has many similarities with the other story of investments in Chapter 151. There are enough differences, however, such as in the number of talents involved, to show that Jesus told this story twice, in different forms.

came forward, bringing five talents more, saying, 'Master, you delivered to me five talents; and see, I have made five talents more.' His
master said to him, 'Well done, thou good and faithful servant; you
have been faithful over small things, so I will put you in charge of large
ones; come and share the joy of your master.' Likewise, the one who
had the two talents came forward, saying, 'Master, you delivered to me
two talents; and see, I have made two talents more.' His master said to
him, 'Well done, good and faithful servant; you have been faithful over
small things, so I will set you over large ones; come and share the joy
of your master.'

36. "And then the one who had received the single talent came forward,
saying, 'Master, I knew you to be a hard man, reaping where you did
not sow, and gathering where you did not scatter any seed; so I was
afraid, and I went and hid your talent in the ground. Now see, you have
what is yours.'

37. "But his master answered him, 'You wicked and slothful servant! You
knew that I reap where I have not sown, and gather where I have not
scattered seed? Then you should have invested my money with the
moneychangers, so that at my coming I should have received back my
property with interest. Take the talent from him, and give it to the one
who has the ten talents! For to every one who has, more will be given,
and he shall have an abundance; but from those who have nothing,
even what they have will be taken away. Now cast this useless servant
into the outer darkness, where there will be weeping and gnashing of
teeth.'

The last judgment
Matthew 25:31–46

38. "When the Son of Man comes in his glory, and all the angels with him,
then he will sit on his glorious throne. All the nations will be gathered
before him, and he will separate the people one from another, as a
shepherd separates the sheep from the goats; and he will put the sheep
on his right hand, but the goats on the left.[226]

39. "Then the King will say to those on his right hand, 'Come, you who are
blessed by my Father, inherit the kingdom prepared for you from the
foundation of the world. For I was hungry and you gave me food, I was

---

226. A last judgment is also described in Revelation 20:11–12. Churches differ in
their views on the relationship between these two passages. The passages may describe
two different judgments, applied to two separate groups of people, such as the living and
the dead, or they may be describing the same event from two different perspectives.*

thirsty and you gave me drink, I was a stranger and you took me in, I was naked and you clothed me, I was sick and you cared for me, I was in prison and you came to visit me.'

40. "And the righteous will answer him, 'Lord, when did we ever see thee hungry and feed thee, or thirsty and give thee drink? And when did we see thee a stranger and take thee in, or naked and clothe thee? Or when did we see thee sick or in prison and visit thee?' And the King will answer them, 'I tell you truly, whatever you did for one of the least of these brothers and sisters of mine, you did for me.'

41. "Then he will say to those on his left hand, 'Depart from me, you accursed ones, into the eternal fire prepared for the devil and his angels. For I was hungry and you gave me no food, I was thirsty and you gave me no drink, I was a stranger and you did not take me in, naked and you did not clothe me, sick and in prison and you did not visit me.'

42. "And they too will answer, 'Lord, when did we see thee hungry or thirsty or a stranger or naked or sick or in prison, and did not minister to thee?' Then he will answer them, saying, 'I tell you truly, whatever you did not do for one of the least of these, you did not do for me.' Then these will go away into eternal punishment, but the righteous into eternal life."

174. THE FINAL CRISIS DRAWS CLOSER
Matthew 26:1–5; Mark 14:1–2; Luke 22:1–2

1. When Jesus had finished saying all these things, he said to his disciples, "You know that the Feast of Unleavened Bread, which is called the Passover, is coming in two days—and the Son of Man will be handed over to be crucified."

2. At the same time, the chief priests and the scribes and the elders of the people gathered in the palace of the high priest, whose name was Caiaphas, and took counsel together, as to how they might arrest Jesus through some deceit and put him to death. "But not during the feast," they said, "so that there will not be a riot among the people;" for they feared the people.[227]

---

227. As many as a hundred thousand pilgrims crowded into Jerusalem for the Passover, so there was always the potential for political demands and trouble.

175. JUDAS AGREES TO A BETRAYAL
Matthew 26:14–16; Mark 14:10–11; Luke 22:3–6

1. Then Satan entered into Judas, called Iscariot, who was one of the twelve; and he went to the chief priests and the officers of the temple guard and discussed how he might betray Jesus to them.

2. When they heard this offer they were greatly pleased, and they covenanted with him for money. "How much will you give me if I deliver him to you?" Judas asked. They counted out for him thirty pieces of silver.[228] And Judas consented.

3. And from then on Judas watched for an opportunity to betray Jesus to them when no crowd was present.

MAUNDY THURSDAY[229]

176. PREPARATIONS FOR THE LAST SUPPER
Matthew 26:17–20; Mark 14:12–17; Luke 22:7–16; John 13:1–2a

1. Then came the first day of the Feast of Unleavened Bread, on which the Passover lamb is sacrificed.[230] Jesus sent Peter and John ahead, saying, "Go and make preparations for us to eat the Passover meal." And they asked him, "Where would you have us prepare it?"

2. He replied, "As you go into the city, a man carrying a jar of water will meet you; follow him into the house which he enters, and tell the owner of the house, 'The Teacher says, My appointed time is near. Where is the guest room, where I will keep the Passover with my disciples?'

---

228. This was the standard value for a slave as set in Mosaic law. See Exodus 21:32. The priests may have fixed on this particular valuation as a way of expressing their disdain for Jesus.

229. Also known as "Holy Thursday," this is the day on which the Last Supper was held. The name "Maundy" is probably derived from the Latin phrase, "Mandatum novum do vobis"—"I am giving you a new commandment"—which comes from Jesus' instructions at the end of the first Eucharist, that his followers should love one another.*

230. Each household would kill a lamb in preparation for its Passover meal. This utilitarian task also had a public memorial function, however. It was an offering to remember the lambs' blood used to mark the doorposts of Jewish houses and tell the angel of death to "pass over" them while killing the firstborn sons elsewhere.

And he will show you to a large upper room, furnished and prepared; make everything ready for us there."

3. The disciples set out and went to the city, and found things as Jesus had told them. So they did as he had directed, and they prepared the Passover meal.[231]

4. And when it was evening, Jesus arrived with the twelve. It was just before the feast of the Passover. Jesus knew that the time had come for him to leave this world and go to the Father. But having loved his own who were in the world, he loved them to the end.

5. So Jesus and his apostles reclined together at the table. And he said to them, "I have earnestly desired to eat this Passover with you before I suffer; for I tell you, I shall not eat another one until its meaning has been fulfilled in the kingdom of God." And *then* the supper was served.

177. WASHING THE DISCIPLES' FEET
Luke 22:24–30; John 13:2b–19

1. Now the devil had already put it into the heart of Judas Iscariot, Simon's son, to betray Jesus. And a dispute also arose among the apostles, as to which of them should be considered the foremost.

2. Jesus knew that the Father had put all matters into his hands, and that he had come from God and would return to God. So he rose from supper, laid aside his outer garments, and took a towel and tied it around his waist. Then he poured water into a basin, and began to wash the disciples' feet, and to dry them with the towel that was tied around him.

---

231. The meal that they prepared would become the Last Supper. This meal was clearly related in some way to the observance of Passover, but it is not clear whether it was formally a Passover seder—the important meal taken on the first night of Passover. The gospel accounts point in different directions on this. The passage here suggests that the meal was a seder, while John's more explicit chronology, noted below, suggests that the seder was actually held the following night. The question is a difficult one. For two reasons, however, the usual conclusion is that the Last Supper was held a day before Passover. First, it seems unlikely that the Jewish religious establishment would have condoned a capital trial and execution on as important a holiday as Passover. And second, if Jesus already knew of his coming fate, he could well have wished to ensure one last formal meal with his friends by holding one a day earlier.*

3. He came to Simon Peter; and Peter said to him, "Lord, are you going to wash my feet?" Jesus replied, "You do not realize now what I am doing, but later on you will understand." Peter said to him, "No; you shall never wash my feet!" Jesus answered him, "Unless I wash you, you can have no part in me."

4. Simon Peter said to him, "Lord, then wash not only my feet, but also my hands and my head." Jesus said to him, "He who has bathed does not need to wash again, except for his feet, and then he is clean all over. And you are clean, but not all of you." For he knew who was going to betray him; and that was why he said, "Not all of you are clean."

5. When he had finished washing the disciples' feet, he put his garments back on and resumed his place. "Do you understand what I have done for you?," he asked them. "You call me Master[232] and Lord; and rightly so, for that is what I am. But if I, your Lord and Master, have washed your feet, then you should also wash one another's feet. For I have given you an example, so that you should do as I have done for you.

6. "I tell you truly, a servant is not greater than his master; nor is a messenger greater than the one who sent him. The kings of the Gentiles lord it over them; and those in authority over them call themselves 'benefactors.' But let it not be so with you. Rather, the greatest among you should become like the youngest, and the one who leads should become like the one who serves.

7. "Now that you understand these things, blessed are you if you do them. For who is greater, the one who sits at the table, or the one who serves? Is it not the one who sits at the table? But I am among you as one who serves.

8. "You are the ones who have stood by me in my trials; and just as my Father has granted me a kingdom, so I grant to you that you may eat and drink at my table in my kingdom, and sit on thrones judging the twelve tribes of Israel.

9. "I am not speaking about all of you; I well know those whom I have chosen. But this is to fulfill the scripture, 'He who ate my bread has lifted up his heel against me.' I am telling you this now, before it takes place, so that when it does take place you will believe that I am the one."

---

232. Meaning, in this context, "Teacher."

178. JUDAS DECLINES A FINAL CHANCE TO REPENT

Matthew 26:21–25; Mark 14:18–21; Luke 22:21–23; John 13:21–30

1. When Jesus had said these things, and as they were reclining at the table eating, he became troubled in spirit, and he declared to them, "I tell you truly, one of you will betray me, one who is eating with me. The hand of him who betrays me is with mine on the table."

2. The disciples looked at one another, wondering of whom he spoke. They were deeply distressed, and they questioned one another, asking which of them would do such a thing. And they began to say to him, one after another, "Surely not I, Lord?"

3. He answered, "It is one of the twelve, someone who is dipping bread in the same bowl with me, who will betray me. The Son of Man will die, just as it is written of him; but woe to that man by whom the Son of Man is betrayed! It would be better for him if he had never been born."

4. One of his disciples, the one whom Jesus loved,[233] was reclining at the table next to him. Simon Peter gestured to this disciple to ask Jesus of whom he was speaking. So leaning back against Jesus's chest,[234] he asked him *quietly*, "Lord, who is it?" Jesus answered, "It is the one to whom I will give this piece of bread when I have dipped it in the bowl." Then, taking the bread and dipping it, he gave it to Judas, the son of Simon Iscariot.

5. Judas, the one who would betray him, said, "I am the one, Teacher?" Jesus replied, "You have said it yourself."

---

233. This is thought to be John, the writer of the fourth gospel. He evidently thought it would be immodest to refer to himself by name in his own composition. To modern ears it might seem equally forward to refer to himself as the disciple whom Jesus loved, but the term may have had different connotations at the time.

234. The physical closeness during this exchange was probably due to the arrangements for a dinner in the classical period. Jesus and the disciples were eating in the Roman style, lying on couches or perhaps seated on cushions around a central table. They would have been lying on their left sides, propped up on their left elbows, so as to keep the right hands free for eating. If the house were modest, and the couches wide, two or three people might share a single couch. A favored friend would be at the right-hand side of the host, where the host could easily see him. In such a case, if the friend wants to say something to the host quietly and in confidence, he can roll to his left so as to speak at a very short distance. From the fact that the others that the table did not hear the exchange, as is made clear two verses later, it seems that such a *sotto voce* exchange was involved here.*

6. When Judas had eaten the bread, Satan *again* entered into him. Jesus said to him, "What you are going to do, do quickly." No one at the table knew why Jesus said this. Some thought that, because Judas had charge of the moneybag, Jesus was telling him, "Buy the things we need for the feast;" or that he should give something to the poor. So, after receiving the piece of bread, Judas immediately went out; and it was night.

179. INSTITUTION OF THE LORD'S SUPPER
Matthew 26:26–29; Mark 14:22–25; Luke 22:17–20; John 13:31–35; 1 Corinthians 11:24–25

1. After Judas had gone out,[235] Jesus said, "Now the time has come when the Son of Man is glorified, and God will be glorified through him. And as God is glorified through the Son, God himself will also glorify the Son, and he will do so quickly."

2. As they were eating, Jesus took bread, and gave thanks, and blessed it and broke it, and gave it to the disciples, saying, "Take this and eat. This is my body, which is given for you. Do this in remembrance of me."

3. And after supper he took a cup in the same way, and when he had given thanks he gave it to them, saying, "Drink of it, all of you," and they all drank of it. "This is my blood of the new covenant, which is shed for you and for many for the forgiveness of sins. Whenever you drink it, do this in remembrance of me."[236]

4. And he said to them, "I tell you truly, I shall not drink again of the fruit of the vine until that day when I drink it new with you in my Father's kingdom."

---

235. Luke describes Judas as remaining through the Eucharist. The other accounts, however, point to his earlier exit at this time. This seems to fit better with the purposeful mood of the Last Supper. The main feature of the Last Supper is the institution of the ceremonies that will ensure that Jesus' life and teachings are remembered. And it is only after Judas has gone out that the remaining members of the company can naturally turn to that forward-looking and communal purpose.

236. Luke describes these remarks as made in connection with drinking two separate cups of wine.

5. Then Jesus said to them, "My children, I will be with you only a little longer. You will seek me; but as I said to the priests and the Pharisees, so now I say to you, 'Where I am going you cannot come.'

6. "So I am giving you a new commandment: that you love one another. Just as I have loved you, so too you should love one another. By this all people will know that you are my disciples, if you have love among yourselves."

180. JESUS PREDICTS THAT PETER WILL DISAVOW HIM
Matthew 26:31–35; Mark 14:27–31; Luke 22:31–38; John 13:36–38

1. Simon Peter asked him, "Lord, where are you going?" Jesus answered, "Where I am going you cannot follow now; but you shall follow me later." Peter said to him, "Lord, why cannot I follow you now? I will lay down my life for you."

2. Jesus answered, "You will lay down your life for me? This night you will all fall away because of what will happen to me; for it is written, 'I will strike the shepherd, and the sheep of the flock will be scattered.' But after I am risen, I will go ahead of you to Galilee."

3. Peter declared to him, "Even if all others desert you because of what will happen to you, I will not desert you." "Simon, Simon," Jesus answered, "understand this, that Satan has asked to have all of you handed over to him, so that he might sift you like wheat.[237] But I have prayed for you, that your faith may not fail; and when you have turned back to yourself and to me, then strengthen your brethren." And Peter said to him, "Lord, I am ready to go with you, both into prison and to death."

4. Jesus said to him, "I tell you truly, Peter, this very night, before the cock crows tomorrow morning,[238] you will deny three times that you even know me."

---

237. That is, so that he might shake the apostles and test their faith. Satan asked for and received a similar freedom of action in trying the faith of Job.*

238. Three of the gospels refer to a single cockcrow, but Mark says that Peter's denials will take place before the cock crows twice. This text deals with the discrepancy by describing the first of Mark's bird calls as something ambiguous, which might have left observers uncertain as to whether it was a separate cockcrow. See Chapter 190:2.

5. But Peter said emphatically, "Even if it means I must die with you, I will never deny you." And so said all the disciples.

6. Then Jesus asked them, "When I sent you out without a wallet or traveling bag or walking shoes, did you lack anything?" "Nothing," they said. He said to them, "But now, let him who has a wallet take it with him, and likewise a traveling bag. And let him who has no sword sell his cloak and buy one. For I tell you that this scripture must be fulfilled in me, 'And he was numbered with the transgressors;' for that which is written about me will now come to pass."

7. They said, "See, Lord, here are two swords." And he said to them, "That is enough."[239]

181. "I AM THE WAY"
John 14:1–15

1. *Then Jesus relaxed and said,* "But do not let your hearts be troubled. Believe in God; and believe also in me. In my Father's house there are rooms *for all his people.*[240] If this were not so, would I have told you that I am going to prepare a place for you? And when I have gone and made a place ready for you, I will come again and take you to myself, so that where I am, there you may also be. And you know the way to the place where I am going."

2. Thomas said to him, "Lord, we do not know where you are going; so how can we know the way?" Jesus said to him, "I am the way, and the truth, and the life. No one comes to the Father except through me.

3. "If you had truly known me, you would already know my Father as well; but from now on you do know him and have seen him." Philip said to him, "Lord, show us the Father, and that will be enough for us." Jesus said to him, "Can I have been with you for such a long time, Philip, and still you do not know me? Whoever has seen me has seen

---

239. It is not clear what Jesus meant when he said, "That is enough." The statement may mean that two swords are a sufficient response to the command that the apostles arm themselves; or it may mean that the apostles did not understand the message of nonviolence, and that too much had already been said about weapons; or it may mean that two swords were enough to define the group as traitors and rebels, thus numbering Jesus among the transgressors in a respect that could lead to a sentence of death.

240. Literally, "many rooms," or "many dwelling places."

the Father. So how can you say, 'Show us the Father'? Do you not believe that I am in the Father and the Father is in me?

4. "The words that I say to you I do not speak on my own authority. Rather, it is the Father, living in me, who does the works *you have seen.*
Believe me that I am in the Father and the Father is in me; or at least
believe me on the evidence of the works themselves.

5. "I tell you truly, he who believes in me will also do the works that I
have been doing; and he will do even greater works than these, because
I am going to the Father.[241] Whatever you may ask in my name, that I
shall do, so that the Father may be glorified through the Son. If you ask
for anything in my name, I will do it.

6. "And if you love me, you will keep my commandments."

I 8 2. THE PROMISE TO SEND THE HOLY SPIRIT
John 14:16–31

1. "And I will ask the Father, and he will send you another Counselor, to
be with you forever—the Spirit of Truth.[242] The world cannot accept
this spirit, because it neither sees him nor knows him; but you know
him, for he already lives with you, and shall remain in you.

2. "I will not leave you comfortless; I will come back to you. Just a little
while longer, and the world will see me no more; but you will see me.
And because I live, you will live also. On that day you will know that
I am in my Father, and you are in me, and I in you. Whoever knows
my commandments and keeps them, that is one who loves me; and he
who loves me will be loved by my Father, and I will love him and will
show myself to him."[243]

3. The other Judas—not Judas Iscariot—said to him, "Why is it, Lord,
that you will show yourself to us, and not to the whole world?" Jesus
answered him, "If a man loves me, he will follow my teachings, and

---

241. The miracles to be done by the followers of Jesus might be "greater" in either
of two senses. They might be greater in the sense of demonstrating still greater powers,
or greater in the sense that they will be carried out by more numerous messengers of
the faith.

242. Thus all three persons of the Trinity are named in this verse.

243. The act of showing himself may involve a physical appearance to the eyesight,
but on most occasions it is likely to involve something that speaks to the heart and
results in an inner awareness of Jesus' presence.

my Father will love him, and we will come to him and make our home with him. But he who does not love me will not follow my teachings. This judgment which you hear is not mine, but it is from the Father who sent me.

4. "I have told you these things now, while I am still with you. But the Counselor, the Holy Spirit, whom the Father will send in my name— he will teach you all things, and bring to your remembrance all that I have said to you.

5. "Peace I leave with you; my peace I give to you. I do not give this to you as the world gives. So do not let your hearts be troubled, nor let them be afraid. You heard me say to you, 'I am going away, and I will come back to you.' If you loved me, you would rejoice that I am going to the Father, for the Father is greater than I.[244] I have told you this now, before it takes place, so that when it does take place you will believe.

6. "I will not speak with you much longer, for the ruler of this world is coming.[245] He has no power over me; but I will do as the Father has commanded me, so that the world may know that I love the Father.

7. "Come now, let us be on our way."

183. FAREWELL DISCOURSE ON THE WAY TO GETHSEMANE
Matthew 26:30; Mark 14:26; Luke 22:39; John 15:1—16:33

1. And when they had sung a hymn, Jesus left for the Mount of Olives, as was his custom; and the disciples went with him.[246] *And as they walked he spoke to them.*

---

244. This apparently simple line bears on the relationship between the Father and the Son, and has been the source of immense doctrinal dispute over the years.*

245. This is probably a reference to Satan, although it might also refer to the power of the Roman Empire.

246. The gospels disagree as to the exact point in the evening's conversation when the group left the upper room and began the walk toward the Mount of Olives. The statement in John at this point, "Come now, let us be on our way," most strongly suggests a departure here. This is also a likely transition point because it permits both a dinner conversation and also a talk on the way to Gethsemane.

Parable of the vine

2. "I am the true vine, and my Father is the gardener. He cuts off every branch of me that bears no fruit; and every branch that does bear fruit he prunes, so that it may bear still more fruit. You are already pruned clean by the teachings I have given you. Abide with me, and I will abide with you. Just as the branch cannot bear fruit by itself, unless it remains in the vine, neither can you bear fruit unless you remain in me.

3. "I am the vine, and you are the branches. If a man abides in me, and I in him, then he will bear much fruit; for without me you can do nothing. If a man does not abide in me, he is thrown away like a cut-off branch and withers; such branches are gathered, thrown into the fire, and burned. But if you remain in me, and my words remain in you, then you may ask for whatever you wish, and it shall be done for you. In this way my Father is glorified, when you bear much fruit, and so prove yourselves to be my disciples.

The commandment to love one another

4. "As the Father has loved me, so I have loved you; continue in my love. If you keep my commandments, you will abide in my love, just as I have kept my Father's commandments and abide in his love. I have told you these things so that my joy may be in you, and your joy may be complete.

5. "This is my commandment, that you love one another as I have loved you. Greater love has no man than this, that he lay down his life for his friends. You are my friends if you do what I command you. I no longer call you servants, for the servant is not informed of his master's business; but I have called you friends, because I have made known to you everything that I have heard from my Father.

6. "You did not choose me, but I chose you; and I appointed you to go and bear fruit, and that your fruit should endure. Then whatever you ask of the Father in my name, he will give it to you. And this I command you, to love one another.

Warning of trials to come

7. "If the world hates you, know that it hated me before you. If you were of the world, the world would love you as its own; but because you are not of the world, and I have chosen you out of the world, therefore the world hates you.

8. "Remember what I said to you, 'A servant is not greater than his master.' If they persecuted me, they will also persecute you. If they had followed my teaching, they would also follow yours. But they will do all these things to you on account of me, because they do not know the one who sent me.

9. "If I had not come and taught them, they would not be guilty of sin; but now they have no excuse for their sin. Whoever hates me hates my Father as well. If I had not done among them such works as no other man ever did, they would not be guilty of sin; but now they have seen the works and yet still hate both me and my Father. This is to fulfill what is written in their law, 'They hated me without cause.'

10. "But when the Counselor comes, whom I shall send to you from the Father—the Spirit of Truth, who proceeds from the Father[247]—he will declare the truth about me; and you too shall bear witness, because you have been with me from the beginning.

11. "I have told you these things so that your faith will not be shaken. They will expel you from the synagogues; indeed, the time is coming when whoever kills you will think he is doing good service to God. They will do this to you because they have not known the Father, or me. But I am telling you these things now, so that when they come to pass, you will remember that I told you of them.

Preparing the disciples for his departure

12. "I did not say these things to you at the beginning, because I was still with you. Now I am going away to the one who sent me; and yet none of you has asked me, 'Where are you going?' Instead, because of what I have told you, sorrow has filled your hearts.

13. "But I tell you this truth: it is better for you that I am going away. If I do not go away, the Counselor will not come to you; but if I do go, I will send him to you.

14. "And when the Counselor comes, he will show the world its errors concerning sin, and righteousness, and the coming judgment. Its errors concerning sin, because men have not believed in me; concerning

---

247. The great schism between the Catholic and Orthodox churches, dating to the year 1054, while having many underlying causes, formally turned on the use of a single word involved in this passage. Does the Holy Spirit proceed solely from the Father (the Orthodox view), or from the Father "and the Son" (in the Latin, "filioque")? Possible compromise formulations, along the lines of procession "from the Father at the request of the Son," have not yet healed the breach.

righteousness, because I am going to the Father and you will see me no more; and concerning the coming judgment, because the ruler of this world has already been judged.

15. "I have many more things to say to you, but you cannot bear them now. When the Spirit of Truth comes, he will guide you into all the truth. He will not speak on his own authority, but he will speak everything he hears, and he will disclose to you the things that are to come. He will bring glory to me, for he will take all the things that I teach and am, and make them known to you. All things whatsoever that pertain to the Father pertain to me as well; therefore I said that the Spirit will take of what is mine and make it known to you.

16. "A little while, and you will see me no more; then a little while longer and you will see me again, because I am going to the Father."

17. Some of his disciples asked one another, "What is this that he is saying to us, 'A little while, and you will not see me; and a little while longer, and you will see me;' and 'because I am going to the Father'?" They asked, "What does he mean by 'a little while'? We do not understand."

18. Jesus realized that they wanted to ask him about this; so he said to them, "Are you asking yourselves what I meant by saying, 'A little while, and you will see me no more; and a little while longer, and you will see me again'? I tell you truly, you will weep and mourn, even while the world rejoices. You will be sorrowful, but your sorrow will turn to joy. When a woman is in labor she feels sorrow, because her hour has come; but when she is delivered of the child, she no longer remembers the anguish, for joy that a child has been born into the world. So too with you. You feel sorrow now, but I will see you again and your hearts will rejoice, and no one will take that joy away from you. On that day you will ask nothing more of me.

19. "I tell you truly, if you ask anything of the Father in my name, he will give it to you. Until now you have not asked for anything in my name. Now ask, and you shall receive, so that your joy may be made complete.

20. "I have spoken with you about these matters in figures of speech; but the time is coming when I shall no longer speak to you in figurative language but will tell you plainly about the Father. On that day you will ask in my name. I need not undertake to ask the Father on your behalf; for the Father himself already loves you, because you have loved me and have believed that I came from God. I came forth from the Father and have entered the world; now I am leaving the world and going back to the Father."

21. His disciples said, "At last you are speaking plainly, not in figures of speech or parables! Now we are sure that you know all things, and need not even wait for the question to be asked. From this we believe that you came from God."[248]

22. "You believe at last!" Jesus replied. "But remember that the time is coming, indeed it is already here, when you will be scattered, each one to his own way, and you will leave me alone. Yet I am not all alone, for the Father is with me.

23. "I have told you these things, so that through me you may have peace. In this world you will have tribulation. But be of good heart; I have overcome the world."

184. PRAYER FOR HIS FOLLOWERS
John 17:1–26

1. When Jesus had spoken these words, he lifted up his eyes to heaven and prayed.

2. "Father, the hour has come. Glorify thy Son, so that the Son may glorify thee. Just as you have given him authority over all humanity, he will give eternal life to all those people that you have granted to him. And this is *their way to* eternal life: that they know you, the only true God, and Jesus Christ, whom thou hast sent. I have glorified thee on earth, by accomplishing the work which thou hast given me to do; and now, Father, glorify me in heaven by bringing me back into the glory I shared with you before the world was made.

3. "I have made your name known to the people that you have given to me out of the world.[249] They were yours; and you gave them to me; and they have kept thy word. Now they understand that everything you have given me truly comes from thee; for I have passed on to them the words which you gave to me, and they have accepted this message, and know in truth that I came from thee; and they believe that you did send me.

---

248. The disciples had asked themselves the question in verse 17 above, and Jesus has now given them an explanation even without having been explicitly asked about it. The disciples saw in this a supernatural ability to read their hearts.

249. The reference is to the apostles.

4. "My prayer is for them. My prayer is not for the world, but for those whom you have given me, for they are yours. All my things are thine, and thine are mine; and I am glorified through them. Now I am staying in the world no longer, but they are still in the world, and I am coming to thee.

5. "Holy Father, protect them by thy name—the name which you have given me—so that they may be one, even as we are one. While I was with them in the world, I guarded them by the power of thy name. Those that thou gave me I have kept, and not one of them is lost, except only the son of perdition, and that only so that the scripture might be fulfilled. But now I am coming to thee; and so I say these things while I am still in the world, so that they might be filled with the same joy that I have.

6. "I have given them thy word; and the world has hated them because they are not of the world, even as I am not of the world. I do not pray that you take them out of the world, but that you keep them safe from evil. For they are not of the world, even as I am not of the world.

7. "Sanctify them through the truth; thy word is truth. Even as you sent me into the world, so I have sent them into the world. And for their sakes I consecrate myself,[250] so that they too may be made holy through the truth.

8. "My prayer is not for these only, but also for those who will come to believe in me through their teaching, so that they all may be one. Even as you, Father, are in me, and I in thee, let them be in us, so that the world may believe that thou hast sent me. The glory which you gave me I have given to them, so that they may be one even as we are one, I in them and thou in me. May they become perfectly united, so that the world will know that you have sent me, and have loved them even as you have loved me.

9. "Father, I desire that they also, whom you have given me, may be with me where I am.[251] Then they may see the glory which you gave me because you loved me before the foundation of the world. O righteous Father, the world has not known thee, but I have known thee; and these disciples know that you have sent me. I have made your name known to them, and will continue to make it known, so that the love you have for me will be in them, and I will be in them."

---

250. The implication here may be, "I make myself a holy sacrifice."
251. That is, in heaven.

185. THE AGONY IN THE GARDEN
Matthew 26:36–46; Mark 14:32–42; Luke 22:40–46; John 18:1

1. When Jesus had finished this prayer, he continued across the Kidron
    Valley, to a garden called Gethsemane,[252] which he and the disciples
    entered.

2. Jesus said to his disciples, "Sit here, while I go over there and pray."
    He took Peter and the two sons of Zebedee, James and John, along
    with him; and when he came to the place he began to be grieved and
    troubled. "My soul is overwhelmed with sorrows, even unto death," he
    said to them. "Remain here and keep watch with me. And pray that
    you do not fall into temptation."

3. Going a little farther, about a stone's throw beyond them, Jesus knelt
    down, and then fell face down on the ground, and he prayed that if it
    were possible, the hour *of his suffering* might pass him by. And he said,
    "Abba, Father, all things are possible for thee. If you are willing, let this
    cup pass from me. Nevertheless, not my will, but thine, be done." Then
    an angel from heaven appeared to him, strengthening him. And in his
    anguish he prayed still more earnestly; and his sweat became like great
    drops of blood falling down upon the earth.

4. When he rose from prayer, he went back to the disciples and found
    them asleep, overcome with sorrow, and he said to Peter, "Simon, are
    you asleep? Could you not keep watch with me for one hour? And why
    are all of you sleeping? Rise, and watch, and pray, so that you will not
    fall into temptation. For indeed the spirit is willing, but the flesh is
    weak."

5. Then for a second time he went away and prayed, saying the same
    words as before. "My Father, if this cup cannot be taken away unless
    I drink it, then thy will be done." And again he returned and found
    the disciples sleeping, for their eyes were very heavy; and they did not
    know what to say to him.

6. So, leaving them once more, he went away and prayed for a third time,
    saying the same words. Then he came back the third time and said
    to the disciples, "Are you still sleeping and taking your rest? Enough
    of that! Behold, the time has come, and the Son of Man is betrayed

---

252. At the foot of the Mount of Olives. The name "Gethsemane" is derived from
Aramaic words meaning "oil press." The garden was likely to have consisted primarily
of a grove of olive trees, rather than flowers.

into the hands of sinners. Rise, let us be going; see, my betrayer approaches!"

Ecce homo (detail), by Antonio Ciseri
Photo: Scala / Art Resource, NY

X. TRIAL AND CRUCIFIXION

GOOD FRIDAY

186. BETRAYAL AND ARREST

Matthew 26:47–56; Mark 14:43–52; Luke 22:47–54a;
John 18:2–12

1. The man called Judas, one of the twelve, who betrayed him, also knew the place, for Jesus often met there with his disciples. So, while Jesus was still speaking, Judas arrived, leading a great crowd, including a band of soldiers and some temple guards, sent from the chief priests, the scribes, the elders and the Pharisees. They were carrying lanterns and torches, and were armed with swords and clubs.

2. The betrayer had arranged a signal with them, saying, "The one that I kiss is the man you want; arrest him and take him away under guard." Judas therefore approached Jesus to kiss him; but Jesus said to him, "Judas, would you betray the Son of Man with a kiss?" Then Judas went at once to Jesus and said, "Greetings, Master!"[253] and kissed him affectionately. And Jesus said to him, "My friend, do what you came to do."

3. Then Jesus, knowing all the things that were coming upon him, stepped forward and said to the crowd, "Whom do you seek?" They answered him, "Jesus of Nazareth." Jesus said to them, "I am he." Judas, who betrayed him, was *once more* standing with the crowd. When Jesus said to them, "I am he," they backed away and fell to the ground.[254]

---

253. Literally, "Greetings, Rabbi!"

254. Literally, Jesus responded by saying, "I am"—a term that was also used as the

4. Therefore he asked them again, "Whom do you seek?" And they said, "Jesus of Nazareth." Jesus answered, "I told you that I am he. So, if you are looking for me, let these other men go." He said this to fulfill the words that he had spoken, "Of those whom you gave me I have lost not one."

5. Then men from the crowd came up, and laid hands on Jesus and held him.

6. When the disciples who were around him saw what was about to happen, they said, "Lord, should we fight them with our swords?" Simon Peter, who had a sword, reached for it, drew it out, and struck the servant of the high priest, cutting off his right ear. The servant's name was Malchus. But Jesus said to Peter, "No more of this!" And he touched the servant's ear and healed him.

7. "Put your sword back into its sheath," Jesus said to Peter, "for all those who live by the sword shall die by the sword. Do you think that I could not call upon my Father, and he would not at once send me more than a dozen legions of angels? But how then would the scriptures be fulfilled, which say that it must be so? Shall I not drink the cup which the Father has given me?"

8. Then Jesus said to the chief priests and the officers of the temple guard and the elders, who had come for him, "Am I some dangerous insurrectionist,[255] that you have come out with swords and clubs to capture me? I sat with you every day, teaching in the temple courtyards, and you did not lay a hand on me. Now this is your hour, when the power of darkness rules. But all this has taken place so that the writings of the prophets might be fulfilled."

9. Then the band of soldiers and their commanding officer and the temple guards of the Jews arrested Jesus and bound him, and led him away.

10. At that point all the disciples deserted Jesus and fled. One young man followed behind Jesus, with a linen cloth cast about his bare body. They laid hold of him, but he slipped out of the covering and ran away naked.

---

name of God, see Chapter 114:13, and could have been recognized as an assertion of divine status. This is probably what accounts for the action of the crowd in backing away.

255. Literally a "robber" or a "bandit," with an implication of one operating as part of a larger organized gang.

187. THE INITIAL EXAMINATION BEFORE ANNAS

Matthew 26:57a; Mark 14:53a; John 18:13-14, 19-24

1. Those who had arrested Jesus took him first to Annas; for he was *a former high priest and* the father-in-law of Caiaphas, who was the high priest that year.[256] It was Caiaphas who had advised the Jews that it would be expedient for one man to die for the sake of the people.

2. The *former* high priest *Annas* then questioned Jesus about his disciples and his teaching. Jesus answered him, "I have spoken openly to the world; I have always taught in synagogues and in the temple, where Jews have always come together; I have said nothing in secret.[257] And why are you asking me about these things? Ask my listeners what I said to them. They know what I said."

3. When he had said this, one of the guards standing nearby slapped Jesus with the palm of his hand, saying, "Is this the way you answer the high priest?" Jesus replied, "If I have spoken wrongly, explain what is wrong; but if I have spoken rightly, why did you strike me?"

4. Annas then sent Jesus, still bound, to Caiaphas the high priest, and his captors took him into the high priest's house.

188. TWO DISCIPLES FOLLOW TO THE HIGH PRIEST'S HOUSE

Matthew 26:58; Mark 14:54; Luke 22:54b-55; John 18:15-16, 18

1. Simon Peter had followed Jesus at a distance, and so had another disciple, all the way to the courtyard of the high priest.[258]

---

256. Annas had been the high priest at the time that John the Baptist began preaching. See Chapter 20:1. The historian Josephus reports that Annas not only held the priesthood himself, but was succeeded in that office by five of his sons. The views of such an influential and senior person would have been helpful to the temple authorities in assessing Jesus' case.*

257. Jesus' answer suggests that the question had been designed to establish that he and his disciples were a secret society of some kind, perhaps with political or revolutionary goals.

258. John reports some of the details in a different sequence, with the disciples' trip to the high priest's courtyard being described before we are told that Annas sent Jesus to Caiaphas' house. The simplest explanation is probably that John's account is not in rigorously chronological order.*

2. Because this other disciple was known to the high priest, he went with Jesus into the courtyard, while Peter stood outside at the gate. Then the other disciple, who was known to the high priest, went out and spoke to the servant girl who kept the gate, and brought Peter inside.

3. It was cold, and the servants and guards had kindled a charcoal fire in the middle of the courtyard, where they stood and warmed themselves. Peter stood with them, and when they had sat down together, Peter sat down among them to see what would happen, also warming himself at the fire.

189. INFORMAL TRIAL BEFORE THE HIGH PRIEST
Matthew 26:57b, 59–68; Mark 14:53b, 55–65; Luke 22:63–65

1. *Inside the house of the high priest,* all the chief priests, scribes and elders had gathered.

2. The chief priests and the whole council sought for evidence against Jesus, so that they might put him to death; but they found none. Though many came forward and bore false witness, their testimony did not agree. Finally two came forward and swore falsely against Jesus, saying, "We heard this man say, 'I will destroy the temple of God, which is made with hands, and in three days I will build another, not made with hands.'" Yet even on this their testimony did not agree.

3. The high priest stood up before the gathering and asked Jesus, "Have you no answer? What of the testimony these men are giving against you?" But Jesus was silent and gave no answer.

4. Then the high priest asked him, "Are you the Christ, the Son of the Blessed One? I charge you under oath in the name of the living God, tell us if you are the Christ, the Son of God." And Jesus said to him, "I am; it is just as you say.[259] And I tell you, before long you will see the Son of Man seated at the right hand of the Almighty, and coming on the clouds of heaven."

---

259. Literally, "you have said it." The expression is idiomatic. It is not an indirect denial, as a literal rendering might suggest, along the lines of, "that's what you say." It is instead an indirect affirmation, meaning, "yes, it is as you say." Earlier Jesus had used this same expression to Judas, and in that context he was clearly meaning to confirm that Judas had spoken accurately of his own guilt. See Chapter 178:5. Jesus will use the phrase several more times during his interrogations.

5. At this the high priest rent his garments and said, "Blasphemy! What more witnesses do we need? Now you have heard his blasphemy yourselves. What is your judgment?" And they all answered, "He deserves death."

6. Then the guards who were holding Jesus began to mock him and hit him with their fists. Some began to spit in his face. And some blindfolded him and slapped him, saying, "Prophesy to us, you 'Messiah'! Who was it that just hit you?" And they said many other blasphemous things to him.

190. PETER DENIES JESUS THREE TIMES
Matthew 26:69–75; Mark 14:66–72; Luke 22:56–62; John 18:17, 25–27

1. Meanwhile Peter was outside, sitting below in the courtyard. One of the servant girls of the high priest, the one who kept the gate, saw Peter as he sat in the firelight warming himself, and came up to him. She looked closely at him and said, "This man also was with the Galilean, Jesus of Nazareth." And she challenged Peter, "Are you not also one of that man's disciples?" But he denied it before them all, saying, "Woman, I am not; I do not know him. I do not even know what you are talking about."

2. A little later Peter went out into the gateway. *In the darkness outside a bird called.*[260] When the servant girl saw him there, she again said to the bystanders, "This man is one of them." And another maid saw him, and she accused Peter, "*Yes,* you too are one of them." And she repeated to the bystanders, "This fellow was with Jesus of Nazareth." At that Simon Peter *moved back to the fire and began to* stand and warm himself. But the bystanders pressed him, "Are you not also one of his disciples?" Again Peter denied it with an oath, saying, "My friend, I am not. I do not know the man."

3. After an interval of about an hour, the bystanders came up to Peter again, and one of them insisted, "Certainly you are also one of them,

---

260. In three of the gospels, Jesus tells Peter that he will deny him three times before the cock crows—presumably, before the cock crows once. Mark, however, says that this will happen before the cock crows twice. Some manuscripts of Mark therefore report at this point, "and the cock crowed." This volume preserves the ambiguity that exists among the gospels, postulating here a bird call of uncertain origin, to be followed later, after the third denial, by a single unambiguous cock-crow.

for you are a Galilean. Your accent gives you away." And one of the
servants of the high priest, a kinsman of the man whose ear Peter had
cut off, asked, "Did I not see you in the garden with him?" Peter once
more denied it, and he began to curse and he swore an oath, "Friend,
I do not understand what you are saying. I do not know this man you
are talking about."

4. And immediately, while he was still speaking, the cock crowed. *Just
at that time Jesus was being taken across the courtyard on the way to
his formal judgment.*[261] The Lord turned and looked straight at Peter.
And Peter remembered the word of the Lord, how he had said to him,
"Before the cock crows today, you will deny me three times." And he
went out and wept bitterly.

191. FORMAL CONDEMNATION
Matthew 27:1–2; Mark 15:1; Luke 22:66—23:1; John 18:28a

1. As soon as it was morning,[262] the formal council of the Sanhedrin assembled—the chief priests, the elders, and the scribes—and the whole
group reached the decision to put Jesus to death.

2. Jesus was brought before them, and they asked him, "If you are the
Messiah, tell us." But he said to them, "If I tell you, you will not believe
me; and if I ask you a question, you will not answer. But from now on
the Son of Man will be seated at the right hand of the Almighty God."

3. They all asked, "Are you then the Son of God?" And he said to them, "It
is just as you say." And they said, "What further evidence do we need?
We have heard it ourselves from his own mouth."

4. Then the whole company of them rose and bound Jesus, and led him
from Caiaphas to the palace of *Pontius* Pilate, the Roman governor.[263]

---

261. The gospels do not report what Jesus was doing at the time. The sentence in
italics, however, is a reasonable supposition that explains how Jesus could have been in
a position to look at Peter.*

262. Under Jewish law the council of the Sanhedrin was not permitted to meet at
night. Only this session, which convened as soon as the sunrise allowed it, had the
official power to condemn Jesus.

263. At this time Judea was a province of the Roman Empire, and the Roman-
appointed governor (or "prefect") was the ultimate political authority. This was a recent
development. During Jesus' youth, Judea had been a client but nominally independent
kingdom under the rule of Herod the Great and later his son Archelaus. However,
Archelaus' harsh rule caused his subjects to complain to the emperor Augustus, who

192. SUICIDE OF JUDAS
Matthew 27:3–10; Acts 1:18–19

1. When Judas, his betrayer, saw that Jesus was condemned, he felt remorse[264] and brought the thirty pieces of silver back to the chief priests and the elders, saying, "I have sinned, for I have betrayed innocent blood."

2. "What is that to us?," they replied. "Deal with it yourself."

3. Judas flung the pieces of silver into the temple sanctuary and departed. Then he went and hanged himself. *When he was cut down,* he fell headlong and his body burst open in the middle, and all his bowels spilled out.[265]

4. The chief priests took up the pieces of silver, but said, "It is not lawful to put them into the temple treasury, since they are blood money." So they took counsel among themselves and used the coins to buy the potter's field, *where Judas had hanged himself,* as a place to bury strangers. This story became known to all who were living in Jerusalem; so that to this day the field is called in their language Akeldama, that is, the Field of Blood.

5. *In this way, through the agency of the priests,* Judas acquired a field with the reward he got for his wickedness.[266] And thus the words spoken by the prophet Jeremiah were fulfilled: "They took the thirty pieces of silver, the price that had been set upon him by the sons of Israel, and they gave them to buy the potter's field, as the Lord directed."

deposed him, banished him to Vienne in Gaul, and instituted direct rule. This happened when Jesus was about twelve years old.*

264 Judas felt "remorse," but he did not "repent" in the sense of adopting a new mode of thought for the future.

265. Matthew reports that Judas hanged himself, while Acts reports that he fell and his body burst open. The words in italics are a reasonable way of linking these two events. The exact linkage is not specified, however, and other explanations are also possible.*

266. Matthew reports that it was the priests who bought the field, while Acts says that Judas acquired it with the money he received for his wickedness.*

193. APPEARANCE BEFORE PONTIUS PILATE
Matthew 27:11–14; Mark 15:2–5; Luke 23:2–7; John 18:28b–38

1. By now it was early morning. The men holding Jesus did not enter the governor's palace; they wanted to avoid ceremonial uncleanness,[267] so that they would be able to take the Passover meal. Pilate therefore went out to them.[268] Jesus stood before the governor, and Pilate asked, "What accusation are you bringing against this man?"

2. They answered him, "If this man were not a criminal, we would not have brought him before you." Pilate said to them, "Take him yourselves and judge him by your own law." But they said to him, "We do not have the authority to put anyone to death." This happened to fulfill the words Jesus had spoken, when he revealed the kind of death he was going to die.

3. Then the chief priests and elders began to accuse Jesus of many things, saying, "We found this man subverting our nation, and forbidding us to pay taxes to Caesar, and saying that he himself is Christ, a king."

4. So Pilate asked Jesus, "Are you the King of the Jews?" And Jesus answered him, "Yes; just as you say."

5. But to the accusations made by the chief priests and elders, Jesus gave no reply. Then Pilate asked him, "Have you no answer to make? Do you not hear how many charges they are bringing against you?" But Jesus said never a word, not even to answer a single charge, so that the governor was greatly astonished.

6. Pilate went back into the palace and summoned Jesus to him, and asked him *again*, "Are you the King of the Jews?" Jesus answered, "Is this your own question, or did others say this to you about me?" Pilate answered, "Am I a Jew? Your own nation and the chief priests have handed you over to me. What have you done?"

7. Jesus answered, "My kingdom is not of this world. If my kingdom were of this world, my people would fight, so that I might not be handed over to the high priest and the council; but in fact my kingdom is not an earthly kingdom."

---

267. Many Jews of the time believed that entering the house of a gentile could make them impure for ceremonial purposes, particularly if they did so during a holy period.

268. We know surprisingly little about Pilate personally, considering his importance in the gospel accounts. He was evidently born to a military family of proud tradition but modest means, of the tribe of the Pontii, from the hill region of Samnium south of Rome.*

8. Pilate said to him, "So you are a king then?" Jesus answered, "Yes, just as you say; I am a king. *But in this sense:* I was born and have come into the world to bear witness to the truth. Everyone who is on the side of truth listens to my voice." And Pilate said to him, "Truth. What is truth?"[269]

9. After he had said this, Pilate went out to the chief priests and the crowd again, and said to all of them, "I do not find that this man has done any crime." But they were insistent, saying, "He stirs up the people, teaching throughout all the lands of the Jews, beginning from Galilee even to here."

10. When Pilate heard Galilee spoken of, he asked whether the man was a Galilean. And when he learned that Jesus came under Herod's jurisdiction, he sent him over to Herod, who was also in Jerusalem at that time.

194. APPEARANCE BEFORE HEROD
Luke 23:8–12

1. Herod was greatly pleased to see Jesus. He had long desired to meet him, because he had heard about him and had been hoping to see Jesus perform a miracle.

2. So Herod questioned him at great length; but Jesus gave him no answer at all. Meanwhile the chief priests and the scribes stood nearby, vehemently accusing him.

3. Then Herod and his soldiers treated Jesus with contempt and began to ridicule him. Finally, Herod put a magnificent robe on Jesus and sent him back to Pilate. And on that day Herod and Pilate became friends, although before this there had been tension between them.[270]

---

269. In John, Pilate says only "What is truth?" In this translation the word "truth" is given twice, to better convey the sense that Pilate spoke in cynicism and worldliness, rather than in an actual inquiry about truth. This is made clear in the next verse, when Pilate leaves without waiting for an answer.

270. There would have been tension because Herod had unsuccessfully petitioned Rome to be reinvested with the title of king, an enhancement of local rule that would have diminished the prefect's power.

195. RETURN TO PILATE
Matthew 27:19; Luke 23:13–16

1. Pilate then called together the chief priests, the other leaders, and the people, and he said to them, "You brought me this man as one who was subverting the people; but after examining him in your presence, I have not found him guilty of any of your charges against him. And neither did Herod, for he sent him back to us.

2. "As you can see, he has done nothing that deserves death; I will therefore have him whipped and then release him."

3. And while Pilate was sitting in judgment on the case, his wife sent word to him, "Do nothing against that innocent man, for I have suffered much today because of a dream I had about him."

196. THE CROWD CHOOSES BARABBAS
Matthew 27:15–18, 20–23; Mark 15:6–14; Luke 23:17–23; John 18:39–40

1. Now it was the governor's custom at the Passover feast to release any one prisoner that the crowd desired.

2. At that time they had a notorious prisoner, called Barabbas, a bandit who was jailed among the rebels who had committed murder during an insurrection that had taken place in the city.[271] And the crowd came up and asked Pilate to follow his usual custom with them.

3. So Pilate asked them, "Whom do you want me to release to you, Barabbas or Jesus who is called the Christ? Do you want me to release the 'King of the Jews' for you?" For he knew that it was out of envy that the chief priests had handed Jesus over to him. But the chief priests and the elders stirred up the crowd to have Pilate release Barabbas instead, and to destroy Jesus. So when the governor asked them, "Which of the two do you want me to release for you?" they cried out together, "Barabbas! Not this man! Away with him, and give us Barabbas!"

---

271. Barabbas may have been a political rebel himself. Most probably, insurrectionists were called "robbers" or "bandits" by the authorities in an effort to undermine their legitimacy. Josephus favors these terms whenever he describes revolutionaries.*

5. Wanting to release Jesus, Pilate spoke to them again. "What shall I do then with Jesus, called Christ, whom you call the King of the Jews?" They all cried out, "Let him be crucified."

6. A third time Pilate said to them, "Why, what evil has he done? I have found in this man no crime deserving death; I will therefore chastise him and release him." But the crowd was insistent, and they shouted all the more, "Let him be crucified! Crucify him!" And their voices prevailed.

197. PILATE WASHES HIS HANDS
Matthew 27:24–26; Mark 15:15; Luke 23:24–25a; John 19:1

1. When Pilate saw that he was getting nowhere, but rather that a riot was beginning, he announced that it would be as they demanded. He took water and washed his hands before the crowd, saying, "I am innocent of this man's blood; anything after this is your responsibility."[272] And all the people answered, "His blood be on us, and on our children!"[273]

2. Then Pilate, wishing to satisfy the crowd, released Barabbas, the man who had been cast into prison for insurrection and murder, the one they asked for. And after having Jesus scourged, he handed him over to be crucified.

198. THE SOLDIERS MOCK JESUS
Matthew 27:27–30; Mark 15:16–19; John 19:2–3

1. So the governor's soldiers took Jesus into the palace, known as the Praetorium, and they assembled all the soldiers of the guard around him.

---

272. Literally, "See to it yourselves," or "See ye to it."

273. This last line has caused many problems in history, but it need not have done so. Christians do not need to recognize this kind of continuing collective responsibility, or accept the offer of it. In 1965 the Second Vatican Council issued a declaration stating that, although some Jewish authorities and their followers had called for Jesus' execution, the guilt for this act did not extend to all the Jews of that time, or to any of the Jews of our own time.*

2. The soldiers stripped Jesus, and they clothed him in a scarlet cloak, and put a purple robe upon him.[274] They plaited together a crown of thorns and put it on his head, and they put a reed staff in his right hand. Then they knelt down before him *as if* in homage and mocked him, saying, "Hail, King of the Jews!"

3. Then they took the reed and began to strike him on the head with it; and they spat upon him; and they slapped him in the face.

199. FINAL APPEAL AND THE DEATH SENTENCE
Matthew 27:31; Mark 15:20; Luke 23:25b; John 19:4–16

1. *But then Pilate had second thoughts.* He went out once more, and said to the crowd, "Behold, I am bringing him out to you, so that you may see that I cannot find any grounds for a charge against him." Then Jesus came out, wearing the crown of thorns and the purple robe. And Pilate said to them, "Look at the man!"[275]

2. But when the chief priests and their officials saw him, they cried out, "Crucify, crucify him!" Pilate said to them, "Take him yourselves and crucify him, for I find no crime in him." They answered him, "We have a law, and by that law he ought to die, because he has called himself the Son of God."

3. When Pilate heard these words, he became all the more afraid. He went back into the palace and asked Jesus, "Where are you from?" But Jesus gave no answer. Pilate therefore said to him, "You will not speak to me? Do you not understand that I have the power to release you, and the power to crucify you?"

4. Jesus answered him, "You would have no power over me at all unless it had been given to you from above; therefore the one who handed me over to you bears an even greater sin *than yours*."

---

274. The cloak was probably a short military cloak, of the type commonly worn by Roman soldiers; the robe was a longer, richer outer garment. Like the crown of thorns and the reed staff, these were put on Jesus by the soldiers in order to mock any claim of kingly authority.

275. Traditionally, "Behold the man!" or, in Latin, "Ecce homo!" Pilate evidently hoped that Jesus' battered appearance, bearing the signs of mockery and physical abuse, would convince the crowd that he had already been stringently interrogated and sufficiently punished.

5. From then on Pilate tried to set Jesus free, but the crowd cried out loudly, "If you release this man, you are no friend of Caesar; every one who calls himself a king is speaking against Caesar."

6. When Pilate heard these words he brought Jesus out, and he sat down in the judgment seat at the place called The Stone Pavement, or in Hebrew, Gabbatha. It was the day of preparation for the Passover, in the morning.[276]

7. Pilate said to the crowd, "Here is your king." They cried out, "Away with him, away with him, crucify him!" Pilate asked them, "Shall I crucify your king?" The chief priests answered, "We have no king but Caesar."

8. Then Pilate delivered Jesus up to their will. After the soldiers had finished mocking him, they stripped him of the purple robe and put his own clothes back on him. Then they led him away to crucify him.

200. THE ROAD TO CALVARY
Matthew 27:32; Mark 15:21; Luke 23:26–32; John 19:17a

1. So Jesus went out, bearing his own cross.

2. As the soldiers were taking him out, they came upon a passer-by, one Simon of Cyrene, the father of Alexander and Rufus, who was coming in from the country. They seized him and laid the cross on him, and compelled him to carry it behind Jesus.

3. And there followed behind Jesus a great multitude of the people, and of women who mourned and wailed for him. But Jesus turned to them and said, "Daughters of Jerusalem, do not weep for me, but weep for yourselves and your children. For the days are coming when you will say, 'Blessed are the barren, and the wombs that never bore, and the breasts that never nursed!' Then people will say to the mountains, 'Fall

---

276. Literally, "about the sixth hour." John's reference to this particular hour raises a number of questions. If he was using the standard Jewish time of the era, counting the hours from dawn, then the time would be noon—too late for Mark's statement in a later chapter that Jesus was crucified at 9:00 a.m. See Chapter 201:2. On the other hand, if John was using Roman time, counting the hours from midnight, then it would be six o'clock in the morning—too early for all the other events of the morning to have already taken place. Perhaps the best resolution lies in John's statement that it was "about" the sixth hour, implying only that the time was broadly some point in the early morning.

on us,' and to the hills, 'Cover us.' For if men will do these things when the tree is green, what will happen when it is dry?"[277]

4. And two other men, who were criminals, were also led out to be put to death with him.

201. THE CRUCIFIXION
Matthew 27:33–34, 37–38; Mark 15:22–24a, 25–28; Luke 23:33–34a, 38; John 19:17b–22

1. They brought Jesus to the place called Calvary or Golgotha, which in Hebrew means The Place of the Skull.[278] And they offered him wine to drink, mixed with gall and myrrh;[279] but when he tasted it, he would not drink it.

2. There they crucified him, and with him the two bandits,[280] one on his right and one on his left, and Jesus between them. And so the scripture was fulfilled which says, "He was numbered with the transgressors." It was nine o'clock when they crucified him.

3. Jesus said, "Father, forgive them; for they know not what they do."

4. Pilate had a notice prepared of the charges against Jesus, and they put it on the cross over his head. It read, "This is Jesus of Nazareth, the King of the Jews."[281] Many of the Jews read this, for the place where Jesus was crucified was near the city; and the notice was written in Hebrew, in Latin, and in Greek. The chief priests then said to Pilate, "Do not write, 'The King of the Jews,' but rather, 'This man said, I am King of the Jews.'" Pilate answered, "What I have written, I have written."

---

277. This was a proverbial expression, asking what worse things are to come.

278. "Calvary" is the familiar Latin version of the other two names, which are the ones that are given in the gospels.

279 This drink would have been bitter and mildly intoxicating.

280. Matthew and Mark specify that the two criminals were "bandits." It is likely that the term is used here, as it evidently was in the case of Barabbas, to designate insurrectionists.

281. The Latin version of this notice would have read, "Iesus Nazarenus Rex Iudaeorum." The initials of this phrase—INRI—are a frequent detail in images of the crucifixion.

202. INSULTS ON THE CROSS
Matthew 27:35–36, 39–44; Mark 15:24b, 29–32; Luke 23:34b–37, 39–43; John 19:23–24

1. When the soldiers had crucified Jesus they took his garments and divided them into four shares, one for each soldier, casting lots to decide what each should take. They also took his inner tunic. Now the tunic was without seam, woven in one piece from top to bottom; so they said to one another, "Let us not tear it, but cast lots *for it as well*, to see whose it shall be."

2. This was to fulfill the scripture, "They divided my garments among them, and for my clothing they cast lots." So the soldiers did this; and then they sat down and kept guard over him.

3. The people stood by, watching; but their leaders scoffed at Jesus. The ones who passed by called out insults at him, wagging their heads and saying, "Aha! You who were going to destroy the temple and build it in three days, save yourself! If you are the Son of God, come down from the cross."

4. The chief priests, scribes and elders mocked him in the same way among themselves. "He saved others; himself he cannot save. Let him do that, if he is the Messiah of God, his Chosen One! He is the King of Israel! Then let this Messiah, the King of Israel, come down now from the cross, and we will see and believe in him. He trusts in God; let God deliver him now, if he will have him; for this man said, 'I am the Son of God.'"

5. The soldiers also mocked him, coming up and offering him vinegar, and saying, "If you are the King of the Jews, save yourself!"

6. And the bandits who were crucified with Jesus taunted him in the same way. One of the criminals hanging there railed at him, saying, "Are you in truth the Christ? Then save yourself and us!" But the other rebuked him, saying, "Do you not fear God, since you are condemned in the same way that he is? But indeed we are condemned justly; for we are receiving the due reward for our deeds; but this man has done nothing wrong."

7. And he said, "Lord, remember me when you come into your kingdom." And Jesus said to him, "I tell you truly, today you shall be with me in Paradise."

203. LAST HOURS
Matthew 27:45–56; Mark 15:33–41; Luke 23:44–49; John 19:25–37

1. Standing near the cross of Jesus were his mother, his mother's sister, Mary the wife of Clopas, and Mary Magdalene.[282] When Jesus saw his mother there, and the disciple whom he loved standing nearby, he said to his mother, "Good woman, this is now your son!" Then he said to the disciple, "This is your mother!" And from that hour the disciple took Jesus' mother into his own home.[283]

2. It was now about noon, and there was darkness over all the land until three o'clock, for the sun's light failed.

3. And at three o'clock Jesus cried out with a loud voice, "Eloi, Eloi lema sabachthani?," which is to say, "My God, My God, why hast thou forsaken me?" Upon hearing this, some of the bystanders said, "Behold, he is calling for Elijah."[284]

4. After this, knowing that all things were now completed, and so that the scripture would be fulfilled, Jesus said, "I am thirsty." A bowl full of sour wine[285] stood there, so one of the men at once ran and soaked a sponge in it, put the sponge on a stalk of the hyssop plant, lifted it to Jesus' mouth, and offered it to him to drink. But the others said, "Wait, let us see whether Elijah will come to save him."

5. When Jesus had received the wine, he said, "It is finished." Then he called out with a loud voice, "Father, into thy hands I commend my spirit!" And having said this he bowed his head, breathed his last, and gave up the ghost.[286]

6. At that moment the veil of the temple[287] was torn in two, from top to bottom; and the earth shook, and the rocks were rent; and the graves

282. It is not clear from this description whether the sister of Jesus' mother, and Mary the wife of Clopas, were one person or two. It is clear, however, that there were three Marys at the foot of the cross.

283. Jesus had thus provided for his mother's welfare, instructing the disciple to care for her as if she were his own mother.

284. Evidently some listeners in the crowd confused the names "Eloi" and "Elijah."

285. This was the rough, inexpensive wine favored by soldiers; its taste was similar to vinegar.

286. Or, "yielded up his spirit." The time here, three in the afternoon, is the hour at which the lambs were being sacrificed for that evening's Passover observance.

287. This was a curtain of heavy cloth which separated the main part of the temple

were opened; and the bodies of many godly people who had died were raised to life, and after Jesus' resurrection they came out of the tombs and went into the holy city and appeared to many.

7. When the centurion and his companions, who were standing in front of Jesus, keeping guard over him, saw the earthquake and all else that took place, and heard his cry and saw the way he died, they were filled with fear, and the centurion praised God and said, "Certainly this was a righteous man; and truly this was the Son of God."

8. When the crowds who had gathered for this spectacle saw what had taken place, they returned home beating their breasts. But all those who knew Jesus, including the women who had followed him in Galilee and ministered to him, stood at a distance and watched things *to the end*. Among them were Mary Magdalene, and Mary the mother of James the younger[288] and of Joses, and Salome the mother of Zebedee's sons.[289] And many other women who had come up with him to Jerusalem were also there.

9. It was the day of preparation, and the sabbath the next day was to be a special high day.[290] So that the bodies would not remain on the crosses on the sabbath, the Jews asked Pilate that the men's legs be broken, and that they then be taken down. So the soldiers came and broke the legs of the first man, and then of the other who had been crucified with Jesus; but when they came to Jesus and saw that he was already dead, they did not break his legs. But one of the soldiers pierced his side with a spear, and at once there came out a flow of blood and water.

10. The man who saw this has borne witness so that you too may believe. His testimony is true, and he knows that he tells the truth. For these things took place so that the scripture might be fulfilled, "Not one of his bones shall be broken." And as another scripture says, "They shall look upon the one whom they have pierced."

from the innermost Holy of Holies. Only the high priest was permitted to go behind this curtain, and only on one day a year.*

288. This is probably James the son of Alphaeus, one of the twelve apostles. He is sometimes called James the Less, to distinguish him from the more influential figure of James the son of Zebedee, who is known as James the Greater.

289. This is a different woman from the Salome who had asked for the head of John the Baptist.

290. Because it was also in the Passover week.

204. THE BURIAL OF JESUS
Matthew 27:57–61; Mark 15:42–47; Luke 23:50–56a; John 19:38–42

1. It was the day of preparation, that is, the day before the sabbath. As evening approached, there came a rich man named Joseph, from Arimathea, a city of Judea. He was a distinguished member of the council, a good man and a just one, who had not consented to the council's purpose and actions, and he was waiting for the kingdom of God.

2. Now this Joseph of Arimathea had himself become a disciple of Jesus, but secretly, for fear of his colleagues. He gathered his courage and went in to Pilate, and asked for the body of Jesus.

3. Pilate was surprised to hear that Jesus had already died; and summoning the centurion, he asked him whether Jesus was truly dead. And when the centurion confirmed it, Pilate ordered that the body be given to Joseph.

4. So Joseph bought some linen cloth, and took down the body of Jesus, and took it away. With him was Nicodemus, who had once come to Jesus by night. Nicodemus brought a mixture of myrrh and aloes, about seventy-five pounds in weight.

5. They took the body of Jesus and wrapped it in the clean linen cloths,[291] along with the spices, which is the burial custom of the Jews.

6. Now near the place where Jesus was crucified there was a garden, and in the garden was Joseph's own new tomb, which he had hewn in the rock, and where no one had ever yet been laid. Because it was the Jewish day of preparation, and the sabbath was about to begin, and as the tomb was close at hand, they laid Jesus there. Then Joseph rolled a great stone in front of the entrance to the tomb and departed.

7. The women who had come with Jesus from Galilee had followed Joseph and were sitting there, facing the tomb. *Among them were* Mary Magdalene and the other Mary the mother of Joses. They saw the tomb, and how Jesus' body was laid in it. And then they returned home.

---

291. Different gospel accounts, and different translations, have referred to the grave cloths here as a "shroud" or as "strips of linen." This text has favored the more neutral and central term, "linen cloths."

HOLY SATURDAY

205. THE TOMB IS SEALED
Matthew 27:62–66

1. The next day, that is, the day after the day of preparation, the chief priests and the Pharisees gathered before Pilate and said, "Sir, we remember how that deceiver said, while he was still alive, 'After three days I will rise again.' Therefore give orders that the tomb be made secure until the third day; otherwise his disciples may come and steal the body away, and tell the people, 'He has been raised from the dead;' and that last deception will be worse than the first."

2. Pilate said to them, "Take a guard of soldiers; go, make the tomb as secure as you know how." So they went and secured the tomb by putting a seal on the entrance stone and setting a guard.

206. THE WOMEN PREPARE TO ANOINT THE BODY
Mark 16:1; Luke 23:56b—24:1a

1. On the sabbath the women rested according to the commandment.

2. But *on Saturday evening,* when the sabbath was past,[292] Mary Magdalene, and Mary the mother of James,[293] and Salome went and bought aromatic herbs, and prepared spices and ointments, so that they might go and anoint Jesus' body.

---

292. That is, after sunset on Saturday.

293. Mary was the mother of both James and Joses, see Chapter 203:8, so this Mary is the same woman who witnessed the closing of the tomb in Chapter 204:7.

The Empty Tomb

XI. THE RESURRECTION

EASTER SUNDAY

207. THE EMPTY TOMB
Matthew 28:1–8; Mark 16:2–8; Luke 24:1b–8, 10; John 20:1–2

1. After the sabbath,[294] very early on the first day of the week, while it was still dark, Mary Magdalene went to see the sepulchre, taking the spices which the women had prepared. *With her were* the other Mary the mother of James, Joanna, Salome, and the other women.

2. *About the time they were setting out* there was a great earthquake; for an angel of the Lord descended from heaven and came and rolled back the stone, and sat upon it. His face shone like lightning, and his garments were as white as snow. And for fear of him the guards shook and became like dead men.

3. *As they walked toward the sepulchre,* the women asked each other, "Who will roll away the stone for us from the entrance to the tomb?" They reached the tomb when the sun had just risen. And looking up, they saw that the stone, which was very large, had already been rolled away.

4. But when they went in they did not find the body of the Lord Jesus. While they were perplexed about this, suddenly two angels stood near them, *in the form of* men[295] in dazzling apparel. The women were frightened and bowed their faces to the ground.

---

294. That is, on Sunday morning, after the Jewish Sabbath, which is observed on Saturday.

295. Matthew and John explicitly designate these figures as angels, while Mark and Luke describe them as men dressed in clothing of unearthly brightness.

5. *One* angel said to the women, "Do not be afraid; for I know that you seek Jesus of Nazareth who was crucified. Why do you seek the living among the dead? He is not here; for he is risen, just as he said. Come, see the place where they laid him. Remember how he told you, while he was still in Galilee, that the Son of Man must be delivered into the hands of sinful men, and be crucified, and on the third day rise again." And then they remembered his words.

6. Entering the tomb they saw *the second angel, like* a young man, sitting on the right side, dressed in a white robe. And he said to them, "Then go quickly and tell his disciples and Peter that he has risen from the dead.[296] And behold, he is going before you into Galilee; there you will see him, as he said. That is my message for you." So the women departed quickly from the tomb with fear and great joy, and ran to tell his disciples.

7. But as they fled from the tomb, trembling and astonishment came upon *most of* the women, and they said nothing to any one, for they were afraid.

8. *But* Mary Magdalene ran on,[297] and went to Simon Peter and the other disciple, the one whom Jesus loved, and said to them, "They have taken the Lord out of the tomb, and we do not know where they have laid him."

---

296. Luke says that two men (that is, two angels) both spoke; Matthew attributes the lines to just the one angel who rolled away the stone and is still outside; while Mark attributes similar lines to a single angel who is sitting inside the tomb. These accounts can be best understood on the assumption that there were two angels; that both angels spoke; but that they were sometimes described as a single speaker because they took turns speaking and they sometimes spoke just to Mary Magdalene as the leader of the women.

297. This is a particularly difficult point. The different accounts highlight different aspects of the way in which this message was carried to the apostles. Luke reports that all the women delivered the message before the first of the apostles ran to the tomb; Matthew reports that they delivered the message only after they had met the risen Jesus; Mark reports that all of the women except for Mary Magdalene turned aside and said nothing; and John names only Mary Magdalene as discovering the empty tomb in the first place. A perfect harmony is not possible on the known accounts. The best understanding seems to be, however, that all the women set out to deliver the message, but only Mary Magdalene initially succeeded. Then at a later time all of the women arrived and provided additional details.

208. TWO APOSTLES VISIT THE TOMB
Luke 24:12; John 20:3–10

1. Peter then rose and went out, along with the other disciple, and they hurried together toward the tomb. Both men ran, but the other disciple outran Peter and reached the tomb first. Stooping down to look in, he saw the linen cloths lying there; but he did not go in.

2. Then Simon Peter came up, following him, and went into the tomb. He saw the linen cloths lying there, and the burial cloth, which had been around Jesus' head, not lying with the linen cloths but rolled up in a place by itself. Then the other disciple, who had reached the tomb first, also went in. They saw and believed *that something extraordinary had taken place, but* they still did not understand the scripture, that Jesus must rise from the dead.

3. So the disciples went back home wondering at what had happened.

209. APPEARANCE TO MARY MAGDALENE AND THE WOMEN
Matthew 28:9–10; Mark 16:9–11; Luke 24:9, 11; John 20:11–18

1. When Jesus rose early on that first day of the week, he appeared first to Mary Magdalene, from whom he had cast out seven demons.

2. *Mary had followed the two apostles to the tomb, and now was left alone there.* Mary stood weeping outside the tomb, and as she wept she stooped to look into the tomb; and she *again* saw *the* two angels in white, sitting where the body of Jesus had lain, one at the head and one at the feet. They said to her, "Woman, why are you weeping?" She said to them, "Because they have taken away my Lord, and I do not know where they have put him."

3. After she had said this, she turned around and saw Jesus standing there, but she did not realize that it was Jesus. He said to her, "Good woman, why are you weeping? Whom do you seek?" Thinking he was the gardener, she said to him, "Sir, if you have carried him away, tell me where you have laid him, and I will go and get him."

4. Jesus said to her, "Mary." She turned and cried out in Hebrew, "Rabboni!," which means Teacher. Jesus said to her, "Do not hold on to me, for I have not yet ascended to the Father; but go to my brethren and

say to them, I am ascending to my Father and your Father, to my God and your God."

5. Mary went back to tell those who had been with him. *Along the way she met the women who had been with her earlier.*[298] Then behold, Jesus met them and said, "All hail!" The women came and clasped his feet and worshiped him. And Jesus said to them, "Do not be afraid; go and tell my brethren to go to Galilee, and there they will see me."

6. The women went to the disciples, who were mourning and weeping. Mary Magdalene said to them, "I have seen the Lord;" and she told them the things that he had said to her. But when they heard that he was alive and that she had seen him, they would not believe it. *Then* all the women recounted the events to the eleven and to all the rest, but the words seemed to them an idle tale, and they *still* did not believe them.

210. THE GUARDS' PACT WITH THE CHIEF PRIESTS
Matthew 28:11–15

1. While the women were going to the apostles, some of the guard went into the city and told the chief priests all that had happened. And when the priests had met with the elders and taken counsel, they gave a large sum of money to the soldiers and said, "Tell people, 'His disciples came by night and stole him away while we were sleeping.' And if this

---

298. The gospels do not expressly state that Mary Magdalene met the other women at this time, but it is a logical inference that eliminates what would otherwise be some difficulties in the accounts. We saw in the earlier chapter that the other women departed from Mary Magdalene and did not go with her to the apostles to report the empty tomb. It is clear that Mary remained alone through the time of her initial meeting with the risen Jesus. Mark is explicit that Jesus appeared first to Mary. John similarly describes a meeting between just Jesus and Mary. Yet it is also clear that the other women were back with Mary at some point before she returned to the apostles with the second piece of news that Jesus had actually shown himself. Matthew has Jesus meeting all the women on the road with the greeting "All hail!" And Luke reports that all the women together eventually conveyed a message to the apostles. So the most logical reading is that Mary met the group of women along the road; the group was then met by Jesus; and after that the group carried the news to the apostles. This reading seems consistent with human nature as well as with the texts. After the startling events of the early morning, it seems quite natural that the women would be up and on the streets seeking news, rather than back home.*

comes to the governor's ears, we will intercede with him and keep you safe."

2. So the soldiers took the money and did as they were instructed; and this story is widely told among the Jewish people to this day.[299]

211. ON THE ROAD TO EMMAUS
Mark 16:12–13; Luke 24:13–35

1. After this, Jesus appeared in another form to two of his followers, as they were walking into the country.

2. That same day the two of them were going to a village called Emmaus, about seven miles from Jerusalem, and talking with each other about all that had happened. While they were talking and discussing matters, Jesus himself approached and began to walk with them. But their eyes were prevented from recognizing him.

3. He asked them, "What is it that you are talking about as you walk along?" They stopped, looking downcast. Then one of them, named Cleopas, answered him, "Are you the only visitor to Jerusalem who has not heard of the things that have just happened there?" "What things?" Jesus asked. And they said, "The things concerning Jesus of Nazareth. He was a prophet mighty in deed and word before God and all the people. Our chief priests and leaders delivered him over to be condemned to death, and they crucified him, but we had been hoping that he was the one who would redeem Israel.

4. "What is more, this is the third day since these things happened. And now some women of our company have amazed us. They were at the tomb early this morning, but they did not find his body. They came back saying that they had instead seen a vision of angels, who said that he was alive. Some of our companions went to the tomb, and found it just as the women had said; but him they did not see."

5. Then Jesus said to them, "How foolish you are, and how slow of heart to believe all that the prophets have spoken! Was it not necessary for the Christ to suffer these things before entering into his glory?" And

---

299. The accounts of Jesus' life, death, and resurrection naturally affected individual members of the Jewish community in different ways. The first-century Jewish historian Flavius Josephus included a paragraph about Jesus that illustrates many of those contemporary tensions.*

beginning with Moses and all the prophets, he explained to them what was said in all the scriptures about himself.

6. So they drew near to the village where they were going. Jesus seemed to be planning to continue further, but they prevailed on him not to, saying, "Stay with us, for it is almost evening and the day is now far spent." So he went in to stay with them.

7. When he was at dinner with them, he took the bread, and blessed and broke it, and began to give it to them. At that moment their eyes were opened and they recognized him; and then he vanished out of their sight.

8. They said to each other, "Did not our hearts burn within us while he talked on the road, while he explained the scriptures to us?" Within the hour they arose and started back to Jerusalem. There they found the eleven apostles, together with those others who had gathered with them, who said, "The Lord is risen indeed, and has appeared to Simon!" Then the two walkers told what had happened on the road, and how they recognized Jesus at the breaking of the bread, but *some of* the disciples did not believe them.[300]

212. APPEARANCE TO THE DISCIPLES
Mark 16:14; Luke 24:36–43; John 20:19–23

1. But then Jesus himself appeared as the eleven were still discussing this. On the evening of that day, the first day of the week, while the doors were locked where the disciples were assembled, for fear of the temple authorities, Jesus himself came and stood among them as they sat at their meal. "Peace be with you," he said.

2. The disciples were startled and frightened, and supposed that they were seeing a ghost. So he said to them, "Why are you troubled, and why do doubts arise in your hearts? Look at my hands and my feet; see that it is I myself. Touch me and see, for a ghost does not have flesh and bones as you see that I have." And when he had said this he showed them his hands and his feet and his side.

---

300. There was apparently a division of opinion among the disciples. Luke suggests that they accepted the account that the walkers to Emmaus had given them. Mark reports that they did not. We are given no further details about the appearance to Simon Peter. Evidently some disciples were convinced of the resurrection as a result of Simon Peter's report, while others had not yet heard that news, or had doubts for other reasons.

3. While they still could hardly believe it for joy and amazement, he said to them, "Have you anything here to eat?" They gave him a piece of broiled fish, and he took it and ate it before them. And he rebuked them for their unbelief and hardness of heart, because they had not believed those who saw him after he had risen. Then the disciples were overjoyed as they looked upon the Lord.

4. Jesus said to them once more, "Peace be with you. As the Father has sent me, even so I am sending you." When he had said this, he breathed on them, and said to them, "Receive the Holy Spirit. If you forgive the sins of any, they are forgiven; and if you do not forgive them, they are not forgiven."

LATER EVENTS

213. FORTY DAYS IN THE WORLD
Acts 1:3; 1 Corinthians 15:6a, 7

1. Later Jesus showed his apostles by many convincing proofs that he was alive after his passion. He appeared to them over a period of forty days, and spoke of things pertaining to the kingdom of God.

2. He appeared to more than five hundred of the brothers and sisters at one time. Then he was seen by James,[301] and after that by all the apostles.[302]

214. DOUBTING THOMAS
John 20:24–29

1. Now Thomas, one of the twelve, called the Twin, was not with them when Jesus came *that first evening*. So the other disciples told him, "We have seen the Lord." But he said to them, "Unless I see the marks of the nails in his hands, and place my finger in the wounds from the nails, and put my hand into his side, I will not believe."

---

301. This is probably James the Just, the brother of Jesus.*

302. This probably refers to the second group of seventy or seventy-two apostles that were eventually appointed; Jesus had already appeared to the original twelve.

2. Eight days later, his disciples were again in the house, and Thomas was with them. Even though the doors were locked, Jesus appeared and stood among them, and said, "Peace be with you." Then he said to Thomas, "Put your finger here, and see my hands; and reach out your hand, and place it in my side. Do not doubt, but believe." Thomas answered him, "My Lord and my God!"

3. Jesus said to him, "You believe because you have seen me. Blessed are those who have not seen, and yet still believe."

215. REUNION IN GALILEE
Matthew 28:16a; John 21:1–14

1. After this the eleven disciples went to Galilee, and Jesus revealed himself again to them by the Sea of Tiberias.[303] It happened in this way:

2. Simon Peter, Thomas called the Twin, Nathanael from Cana in Galilee, the sons of Zebedee, and two others of his disciples were all together. Simon Peter said to them, "I am going out to fish." They said to him, "We will go with you." They went out and got into the boat; but all that night they caught nothing.

3. Just as dawn was breaking, Jesus stood on the shore; yet the disciples did not realize that it was Jesus. He called to them, "Children, you do not have any fish, do you?" They answered him, "No." He said to them, "Cast the net on the right-hand side of the boat, and you will find some." So they cast it there, and now they were not able to haul it in, because of the multitude of fish.

4. Then the disciple whom Jesus loved exclaimed to Peter, "It is the Lord!" When Simon Peter heard that it was the Lord, he put on his tunic, for he was stripped for work, and jumped into the water. The other disciples came behind with the boat, towing the net full of fish, for they were not far from the shore, but only about a hundred yards off.

5. When they got out on land, they found a fire of burning coals, with fish lying on it, and bread. Jesus said to them, "Bring some of the fish you have just caught." So Simon Peter climbed into the boat and pulled the net ashore, full of large fish, a hundred and fifty-three of them; and even though there were so many, the net was not torn.

---

303. Another name for the Sea of Galilee.

6. Jesus said to them, "Come and have breakfast." None of the disciples dared ask him, "Who are you?," for they knew it was the Lord. Jesus came and took the bread and gave it to them, and did the same with the fish. This was now the third time that Jesus had appeared to the disciples after he was raised from the dead.

216. THE CHARGE TO PETER
John 21:15–23

1. When they had finished breakfast, Jesus said to Simon Peter, "Simon, son of John, do you love me more than these others do?" He replied, "Yes, Lord; you know that I love you." Jesus said to him, "Feed my lambs."

2. A second time Jesus asked him, "Simon, son of John, do you love me?" He said to him, "Yes, Lord; you know that I love you." Jesus said to him, "Tend my sheep."

3. Then he asked him a third time, "Simon, son of John, do you love me?" Peter was distressed because Jesus had now asked him three times, "Do you love me?" He said to him, "Lord, you know all things; you know that I love you." And Jesus said to him, "Feed my sheep."[304]

4. "I tell you truly, when you were young, you used to fasten your own belt and went wherever you wished; but when you are old, you will stretch out your hands, and someone else will fasten a belt around you and take you where you do not wish to go." Jesus said this to show by what kind of death Peter would glorify God.[305] And after this he said to him, "Follow me."

5. Peter turned and saw that the disciple whom Jesus loved was following them. This was the one who had reclined next to Jesus at the supper and had said, "Lord, who is it that is going to betray you?" When Peter saw him, he asked Jesus, "Lord, what about this man?" Jesus said to him, "If I wish him to remain alive until I return, what is that to you? You must follow me!" So a rumor spread among the brethren that this

---

304. By making these three avowals of love, Simon Peter has in some ways made up for his earlier three denials of Jesus. Evidently chastened by his prior experience, however, Peter now passes up the invitation to claim that he has more love than the other disciples do.

305. Peter was crucified at Rome in his old age.

disciple was not to die; yet Jesus did not say that he would not die, but only, "If I wish him to remain alive until I return, what is that to you?"

217. THE GREAT COMMISSION
Matthew 28:16b–20a; Mark 16:15–18; Luke 24:44–48

1. Then the disciples went to the mountain to which Jesus had directed them.[306] And when they saw him they worshiped him; but some *still* doubted.

2. And Jesus came to them and said, "*Remember* the words which I spoke to you while I was still with you—that everything written about me in the law of Moses and the prophets and the psalms must be fulfilled." Then he opened their minds so they might understand the scriptures, and he said to them, "Thus it is written, that the Christ should suffer and on the third day rise from the dead, and that repentance and forgiveness of sins should be proclaimed in his name to all nations, beginning from Jerusalem. You are witnesses of these things.

3. "All authority in heaven and earth has been given to me. Go therefore into all the world and preach the good news of the gospel to the whole creation. Make disciples of all nations, baptizing them in the name of the Father and of the Son and of the Holy Spirit, and teaching them to observe everything that I have commanded you. Whoever believes and is baptized will be saved; but he who does not believe will be condemned.

4. "And these signs will accompany those who believe: in my name they will cast out demons; they will speak in new tongues; with their hands they will pick up serpents, and if they drink any deadly thing, it will not hurt them; and they will lay their hands on the sick, and the sick will recover."[307]

---

306. The gospels differ on the site of the Great Commission. Mark and Luke report that the charge was given in the upper room in Jerusalem; Matthew says it was delivered on the mountaintop in Galilee; and John does not discuss the commission itself but does report that the disciples were in Galilee. This text presents a composite version, with the core of the commission being delivered on the mountaintop, but the final instructions being delivered back in Jerusalem. The first part of this construction is supported by the repeated instructions from the risen Jesus and the angels that his disciples should meet him in Galilee, while the second part is consistent with the report that some instructions were given in the upper room.

307. The most reliable early manuscripts do not include the material in Mark

218. FINAL WORDS TO HIS FOLLOWERS
Matthew 28:20b; Luke 24:49–50; Acts 1:4–8

1. *Back in Jerusalem,* the Lord Jesus and his apostles assembled *for his final words:* "I am going to send you what my Father promised, which you have heard of from me. For John baptized with water, but before many days pass you shall be baptized with the Holy Spirit. So remain here in the city until you are clothed with power from on high."

2. Then after he had spoken to them, he led them out in the direction of Bethany. When they were gathered together, they asked him, "Lord, is this the time when you will restore the sovereignty and kingship to Israel?" He said to them, "It is not for you to know the times or the seasons, which the Father has set by his own authority.

3. "But you shall receive power when the Holy Spirit comes upon you; and you shall be my witnesses in Jerusalem and in all Judea and Samaria, and to the ends of the earth. And lo, I am with you always, even unto the end of the world." Then he lifted up his hands and blessed them.

219. THE ASCENSION
Mark 16:19; Luke 24:51–53; Acts 1:9–12

1. And it came to pass that when the Lord Jesus had said this, while he was blessing them, and as they were looking on, he parted from them and was taken up into heaven, and a cloud received him and took him out of their sight, and he sat down at the right hand of God.

2. While the apostles were staring intently into heaven after Jesus, suddenly two men in white robes stood by them and said, "Men of Galilee, why do you stand here looking at the sky? This Jesus, who has been taken up from you into heaven, will return from heaven in the same way that you saw him going up."

16:9–20, which is sometimes referred to as the "long ending" of Mark. Those manuscripts end instead at Chapter 207:7, the moment when the women fled without speaking to anyone. The present verse comes from Mark 16:17–18, and is therefore a part of the long ending. Notwithstanding these complications, however, the long ending is accepted by most churches as authoritative.*

3. And the apostles worshiped him; and then they returned to Jerusalem with great joy from the Mount of Olives, which is close by the city, a sabbath day's journey away;[308] and they were continuously in the temple praising God.

220. THE FOUNDATION OF THE CHURCH
Mark 16:20a; Acts 2:1–4a

1. *Ten days later,* when the day of Pentecost had come, the disciples were all assembled in one place. Suddenly there came a sound from heaven like a rushing mighty wind, and it filled all the house where they were sitting. What seemed to be flames or divided tongues of fire appeared among them, and a tongue settled upon each of them. And they were all filled with the Holy Spirit.

2. And they went forth and proclaimed *the good news of the gospel* everywhere, while the Lord worked with them and confirmed their message by the miraculous signs that accompanied it.[309]

221. THE EPILOGUES OF JOHN AND MARK
Mark 16:20b; John 20:30–31; 21:24–25

1. Now Jesus did many other miracles in the presence of the disciples, which are not recorded in this book. Were every one of them to be recorded, I suppose that the world itself could not contain all the books that would be written.

2. But these are written that you may believe that Jesus is the Christ, the Son of God, and that by believing you may have life in his name. It is the disciple whom Jesus loved who is bearing witness to these things,

---

308. A sabbath day's journey is the distance permissible for travel on the Sabbath—somewhat under a mile. This is the distance from Jerusalem to the crest of the Mount of Olives. Bethany is about a mile further. Jesus evidently took his followers to a point within sight of Bethany, but still on the Mount of Olives. The ascension therefore took place near the same spot where Jesus had begun his triumphal entry on Palm Sunday.*

309. Pentecost is the Sunday that comes fifty days (Greek, *pentekonta*) after Easter, and ten days after Ascension Thursday. Because the arrival of the Holy Spirit was so important in enabling the apostles to spread the new faith, the feast of Pentecost is sometimes described as the birthday of the Church. In England it is also known as Whit Sunday or Whitsun.

and who has written these things down; and we know that his testimony is true.

3. Amen.

Appendix 1
MAPS

GALILEE

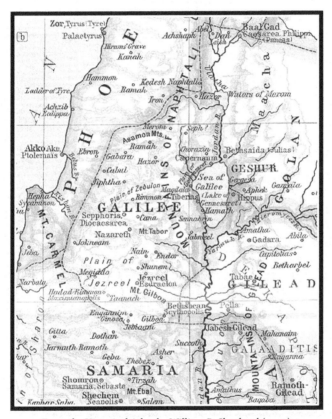

From the Historical Atlas, by William R. Shepherd (1911)

JUDEA

From the Historical Atlas, by William R. Shepherd (1911)

Appendix 2

PRINCIPLES OF COMPOSITION

This note will explain the general methodology that was used in assembling the text of this volume. Two sets of issues had to be considered during the writing process. One task was to find the best way of meshing the four gospels so as to create the most readable and illuminating single narrative. This was the work of *harmonizing*, and it was to some degree a technical matter of understanding the substance and the sequencing of the original texts. The second task was finding the best form of words to express this harmonized text. This was the task of *translating*, and it proved to be more an art than a science. It called for continuing efforts to maintain the right tone of language, and also to preserve particular phrases from older translations that have become a familiar part of Christian literature.

The discussion below will explain how I have approached these two tasks. This discussion will begin with first the general and then the specific issue of harmonization; and afterwards it will turn to the general and specific issues involved in the translation.

The general approach to harmonizing

The process of rearranging material, which is at the heart of this harmony, has taken three broad forms.

The first, and simplest, involves sequencing entire chapters of the gospels. Some incidents are recounted by one and only one of the gospel writers. For example, Luke describes Christ's birth at Bethlehem, and the announcement of that event to the shepherds in the nearby fields. Matthew describes the gifts of the Magi, the anger of King Herod, and the flight into Egypt. These varied incidents can be arranged into chronological order without any further internal editing.

In other situations, an incident is described by several of the gospel writers, and each one contributes some extended passage about it. In those cases the relevant passages can be handled in units of whole sentences, and the sentences put into a sequence that makes for a sensible presentation. For example, in the description of the Great Commission to preach the gospel, Matthew reports that the disciples are to baptize all nations in the name of the Father, the Son, and the Holy Spirit. Mark reports that those who believe and are baptized will be saved. These reports can be combined in one description of Jesus' instructions. This merely requires some care to put the sentences into the most relevant order.

Finally, the most challenging situation arises when the accounts of the different gospels must be interwoven on a word-by-word basis. This situation comes up when the different accounts each provide some unique details of a single event. A good example of this is the account of the Holy Spirit descending on Jesus in the form of a dove, as discussed in the Introduction.

In selecting the passages for the harmony I have favored a general policy of inclusiveness. This has meant preserving certain familiar and well established passages, even if they are based on Greek texts now believed to have been altered or added at a later time. These questioned passages include such familiar material as the angel stirring the waters at Bethesda; the last twelve verses of Mark; and the incident of the woman taken in adultery. Although this material may not date to the very earliest manuscripts, some of it still dates to the early days of the church, and may reflect a recording of oral traditions dating back to the time of Jesus. I have taken the view that these important passages, plus a number of shorter phrases, even if not resting on the most original textual basis, have acquired their own legitimacy through their long and widespread acceptance by the Christian community. Moreover, the goal of this book is to include all the material that has been important to one or another group of Christian believers over the centuries. I have identified in footnote the principal passages that have been disputed.

Some specific issues in the harmonization

The process of combining or eliminating passages will require, of course, innumerable editorial judgments. One recurring question is when a series of descriptions from different gospels are indeed "unique facts," and when they instead overlap to such an extent that some should be dropped, even when they are not precisely the same words. This poses difficult choices, because every word has some individual connotations, but too much redundancy will make the narrative unreadable. For example, the crowd that witnessed the healing of the paralytic on the mat was variously described as "amazed" (Mark 2:12), "filled with fear" (Luke 5:26), and "awestruck" (Matthew 9:8). While this was not an easy call, I decided that the concept of being "filled with fear" was included within the broader and related term for being "filled with awe," and I therefore did not keep it as a separate description.

The harmonized text also reflects a few other editorial judgments that were made for the sake of a more complete and readable story.

First, I have included sixteen additional verses from the first two chapters of the book of Acts, which provide further details about the last days of Jesus' time on earth, and the coming of the Holy Spirit at Pentecost. Acts is generally believed to be a continuation of Luke, by the same author, and so these additions seem to be legitimately of a piece with the other gospel accounts. With a similar goal of completing the story I have also included four short verses from 1 Corinthians, which contain direct quotes from Jesus and other essential details.

A more difficult issue is posed by the middle sections of Luke. The narrative there describes some of the same incidents as in the other gospel accounts, but in a different time sequence. If these were all treated as separate incidents in the combined narrative, it would result in jarring repetition. In some cases similar things may have happened twice, of course. Jesus surely repeated his key teachings with different audiences. In other cases, however, it is likely that Luke was simply not following a rigid chronology. I have therefore made some editorial distinctions. I have retained the repetitions where Jesus may have returned to an important point in different teaching contexts. But I have consolidated the accounts where an entire extended scene is repeated in two places—for example, the "Woe to the Pharisees" speech or Jesus' denial of an alliance with Beelzebub—or where a shorter saying is repeated in circumstances where it is not obviously essential both times.

There have been many guides in the preparation of this book. Concordances and harmonies of the gospels have been prepared for virtually the entire life of the Church. One of the most useful recent ones has been Orville Daniel's scholarly and thoughtful book, *A Harmony of the Four Gospels*. That presents the four gospels in four parallel columns, coordinated chronologically, and highlights the passages that are unique to each account. Two other essential guides have been Ralph Heim's book, *A Harmony of the Gospels*, which presents the accounts in parallel columns using the Revised Standard translation, and Thomas Mumford, *Horizontal Harmony of the Four Gospels in Parallel Columns*, which uses the King James Version. Other harmonies have also been helpful in the writing here.

The present harmony is nonetheless different from its predecessors in crucial respects. Most notably, most earlier versions were committed to preserving the entire text of each of the four gospels, and they therefore set out all that material in separate columns. While this approach is excellent for students of theology and other professional users, it makes for difficult reading and a repetitive narrative. A few other harmonies do aim for a single integrated text, but these have generally involved rearrangements of the material from one standard translation only. This approach has the virtue of

248 APPENDIX 2

fidelity to a recognized account, but it leaves the reader with awkward seams and transitions.

The present book has adopted a different approach, and has made a full consolidation of the material into one story, and at the same time using new wording that smooths out the seams into a continuous narrative.

To help the reader keep track of this long and single story, I have divided the account into chapters—each under a descriptive title—recounting particular themes or events. The chapter titles are added for clarity and are not part of the original texts. Another clarifying device has been the division of each chapter into verses. These correspond to paragraphs marking the distinct segments or turning points in the account, and make it easier for the reader to follow the stages of the story. The division of verses is again my own, and is also not biblical. While I have generally followed the punctuation of earlier translations, I have felt free to alter that when it seemed to permit greater clarity.

The layout of the book will let the reader see where the material came from, and what editing decisions have been made. Directly beneath the title of each chapter is a list of the passages in the original gospels from which the material was taken. The specific edits in that material are generally not separately identified. This harmony makes so many deletions of overlaps, and so many shifts between the four gospels, that those could not be individually marked without unduly cluttering the text. Because the underlying source material is identified, the reader can easily go to the original texts if desired.

One particularly important type of edit is explicitly marked, however. Sometimes I have added words of my own. In these cases the added words are distinctively printed in italics. This is most commonly done when a transition is needed between passages that are newly brought together. Inserts in that situation can help the reader keep track of the time or place involved, such as *"Back in Jerusalem . . . ,"* or *"When Jesus returned from the wilderness . . . ."* Less commonly they will help to clarify a situation where different gospels might have pointed in different directions. Because Matthew and Luke focus on describing different aspects of the preparations for the Sermon on the Mount, for example, there may be some question of whether the sermon was addressed just to the disciples or to a larger crowd. An insert here clarifies that both groups were in Jesus' audience, and that *"his voice also carried to the crowd below."*

The general approach to translation

This harmony is also presented in a new translation. At first glance this may seem surprising, given that the Bible is already the most-translated work of all time. But there are two good reasons for a new text here.

The first is the need to make the substantive harmonization work well. The process of preparing the harmony has rearranged the gospel material, and a simple cut-and-paste will not necessarily produce a smooth text. The most appropriate English word to use in a translation will often depend on its context, and the contexts here are sometimes new as a result of movements of the text. Hence some phraseology is also new. Still, I have tried to err on the side of modesty in these changes, and wherever possible to make the adjustments few and subtle.

A second reason for a new text is that there is a need to harmonize among the stylistic approaches used in the different standard translations, just as there is a need to harmonize among the substantive accounts of the four gospels. Each of the main current approaches to translation has virtues of its own. An updated version of the King James Version has the virtue of being sufficiently modernized to be accessible to modern readers, while still preserving much of the tone of the original. Openly contemporary translations are fresh and conversational. And the King James translation itself is familiar and magisterial.

For this translation I have selected the basic approach of preparing a modernized version of the King James language. This seems to offer the best balance of qualities. It has the somewhat formal tone that one associates with the Bible, while avoiding the truly archaic phrases that can sometimes puzzle the reader of the original King James. Over ninety percent of the words in this harmony follow this approach.

Nonetheless, there are particular passages that seem better handled by one of the other approaches to translation. In those cases I have turned to an alternative method.

Some special situations call for use of contemporary language. These are generally places where the underlying thought is complex, and the language of the older translations has been unclear. In these cases a newer, freer translation can often set things right. For example, when Jesus comes to John the Baptist for his baptism, John at first resists, saying that Jesus has no need for this ceremony. In the traditional translations, Jesus responds by saying, "Let it be so now; for thus it is fitting for us to fulfill all righteousness." This is a good literal rendering, but its meaning is far from clear. But a freer version will convey the point: "Permit it for now; for in this way we each carry out the work that God has given us to do." A similar situation exists in the story of the dishonest manager. A literal translation has the master "praising" the dishonest manager who has cheated him. A more idiomatic rendering, however, makes clear that the master instead "had to acknowledge the practical shrewdness" of the dishonest manager—quite a different and more probable thing.

And in some other situations there is no substitute for the original language of the King James version. To take a few examples almost at random, we want to preserve phrases like "cast into the outer darkness," "lord and master," or "Get thee behind me, Satan!" In a similarly traditional vein, there are some phrases that are commonly remembered in a certain form, but do not actually appear in that precise form in any of the standard translations. Where the original Greek will justify the rendering, however, I have followed that informal oral tradition here. Phrases in this category include "turn the other cheek," "cast the first stone," and "Do unto others as you would have them do unto you."

In preparing this translation I have had the benefit of two thousand years of study by my predecessors, including five hundred years of prior work at casting the gospels into English. I have already mentioned my immense debt—both intellectual and stylistic—to the Revised Standard Version, the New International Version, and the original King James. Some other translations should also be recognized. The New Living Translation and God's Word editions have both provided additional insights into the practical meaning of difficult passages, by expressing these clearly in contemporary language. The Douay-Rheims translation, made from the Latin Vulgate, provides an alternative text from the same period as the King James, giving another window into the early work of rendering the Bible into English.

Throughout this translation I have applied a general principle of favoring variety of expression. I have not replaced a particular Greek word with the same English word in every case. I have sometimes used variant translations instead, in order to capture the different senses of the original word, or the different interpretations that have, at one time or another, prevailed in the Christian community. Thus, depending on the context, I have sometimes followed the patriarchal language of the King James Version, with its frequent use of the word "he," and at other times have used more gender-neutral language. Similarly, and again depending on context, I have sometimes translated a word in its primary meaning, and sometimes with its secondary connotation. Thus, for example, the Greek *charis* is usually translated in its primary meaning of "grace," but occasionally with its secondary implication of kindness or engagement.

Some specific issues in the translation

I have also followed a number of smaller and more technical conventions in the translation.

First, I have referred to a number of different Greek texts. I have made most frequent use of *The Greek New Testament According to the Majority Text* (Thomas Nelson, 2d ed. 1985), and the composite Greek text maintained on a web platform by Biblos. That latter text is based on the Westcott-Hort edition of 1881, as supplemented by Nestle-Aland variants and other additional material.

Second, I have sometimes eliminated the small interjections—such as now, well, behold, and "in those days"—that sound odd to modern ears. These words have been dropped mainly from background descriptions, and less often from direct quotations. On the other hand, I have sometimes introduced similar connectives, such as "and," "but," and "then," when they would smooth out the narrative and make sense to the modern ear. I have treated these small changes as being within the spirit of a contemporary translation, and have not usually marked them with italics.

Third, I have also substituted freely between proper names and pronouns. The process of preparing a harmony has brought together sentences that did not originally follow one another. To make these read smoothly it is sometimes necessary to substitute between names, or other specific nouns, and pronouns. Thus I have sometimes switched the text between "Jesus" and "he," or between "the disciples" and "they." I have similarly added or removed identifiers, such as John "the Baptist." I have not separately marked these changes, feeling that they too are a part of a contemporary translation.

Fourth, the term "the Jews" has been rendered in different ways depending on its context. Some of the gospels—particularly that of John—were written decades after Jesus' death, and at a time when Christians and Jews were coming to see themselves as separate communities. John in several places refers to hostile actions by "the Jews." To understand the meaning of these references, it seems useful to distinguish among different situations. In some places John is referring to the Jewish community as a whole, such as when he reports that "the Passover of the Jews was at hand." In other places, however, his reference is more probably to a subset of the community, such as to the disciples' fear of "the Jewish leaders" or of "the temple authorities." I have used these narrower terms when the context suggests that these are the intended meanings.

Disagreements among the gospels

Finally, there is the question of how to handle the points at which there is an apparent disagreement among the gospels. In most cases it has proven possible to find an approach that resolves the apparent disagreement and permits both alternatives to be used. I have taken such a course wherever possible.

Quite often the differing alternatives can be reconciled by simply recognizing that there is no contradiction in adding or juxtaposing new material. Each of the four gospels contributes a number of unique details. These different events must be interleaved in order to create the single common chronology. This task can be daunting because each gospel presents its own narrative as if it were a complete story, with one event following after another. Therefore the interleaving must sometimes take place between sentences that do not grammatically invite the addition. Luke, for example, does not describe the disciples' trip to Galilee after the resurrection, while John discusses it at length. John's details must therefore be inserted into Luke's account, at the seemingly minor break in the action from one verse to the next. But this kind of insertion is merely a recognition that each of the gospels is unique and makes its own contributions. It does not involve an actual inconsistency.

Many other apparent inconsistencies can be resolved through the dimension of time. If a situation is described in different ways by different writers, then most probably the situation itself evolved over time. So, for example, John describes the main ritual at the Last Supper as being the washing of the disciples' feet, while the other gospels describe the main ritual as the taking of bread and wine. But both are possible, and both could be done during the course of an evening. Similarly, Jesus' followers could be close to the foot of the cross at one time, and at a distance away at another time. This harmony therefore describes each action in its own place.

Still other apparent disagreements involve the lists of people present at an event. These can often be resolved by using the more comprehensive alternative. If one gospel reports that a particular person was present, and a different gospel says that two different people were present, this harmony reports that all three were there. There is no actual contradiction in this. The additional reported presence of X and Y would be inconsistent with the initially reported presence of A only if the first gospel stated that *only* A was present. This is generally not the case.

And in some cases one can propose clarifying language to state certain deduced facts that are outside of the biblical narrative but that will permit both reported accounts to be true. For example, accounts of the resurrection describe Mary Magdalene at different points as being alone and as being with other women. None of the accounts explicitly say that the group broke up and then re-formed at a later time, but the various accounts can all be true on that reasonable supposition.

Conflicts that cannot be resolved in one or another of these ways are far less frequent than one might suppose. In those cases I have either picked one or the other text, or proposed compromise language, in light of my best judgment as to the dominant theme of the different accounts as a whole. In these situations I have identified the difficulty in a footnote and have given the citations to the underlying original accounts.

If these tasks have been done properly, then, at the end of the day, all of this editing should be completely invisible. My goal is for this version of the gospels to read in a comfortable, natural way, telling the story—just a bit more clearly—in the same way that the reader already has it in mind.

Appendix 3
NOTES

Introduction. *Citizen of Heaven.* An early text, dating from the Second or Third Century, expands on the way in which Christians can build their own spiritual geography: "Every foreign land is to them as their native country, and every land of their birth as a land of strangers . . . They pass their days on earth, but they are citizens of heaven." Bass, *People's History*, 74, 322, *quoting* the Epistle to Diognetus. See Philippians 3:20 ("For our citizenship is in heaven . . . .").

Introduction. *Isaac the Syrian.* Isaac was Bishop of Nineveh in the late 7th Century. *Quoted in* Ware, *Orthodox Way*, 55.

Introduction. *Different focuses of the individual gospels.* Readers have long noted that each of the four gospel accounts has an individual tone and was probably addressed to a particular audience. Matthew, for example, was evidently writing for a Jewish audience, and his account frequently links Jesus to David and to Old Testament prophecy. Mark was apparently writing for a Roman audience, and he is careful to explain Jewish customs and phrases that would have been unfamiliar to those readers. Luke seems to have been writing to attract new members from among the Hellenized gentile communities around the eastern Mediterranean; he emphasizes how Jesus expressed broad humanity and had praised members of the despised, non-Jewish community of the Samaritans. And John, writing the last of the gospels, moved beyond the specific quotations preserved in the earlier accounts, and gives Jesus new first-person declarations ("I am the bread of life") that generalize the earlier themes and messages in terms that will be accessible to everyone. For an overview of these relationships see Metzger, *New Testament*, 106–114.

Introduction. *The value of a harmony.* Bruce Metzger has explained the benefits of reading all four gospels, each in light of the others:

> What the evangelists have preserved for us is not a photographic reproduction of all the words and all the deeds of Jesus, but something more like four interpretive portraits. Each of these portraits presents distinctive highlights of Jesus' person and

work, and, taken together, the four provide a varied and balanced account of what Jesus said and did.

Metzger, *New Testament*, 117. It is worth noting that the gospels of Matthew and Luke are already harmonies themselves, in the sense that, in addition the material known by the writers, they each apparently draw on the previously-written gospel of Mark, and on a hypothesized collection of Jesus' sayings known as "Q," from the German word *Quelle*, which means "Source."

Ch. 1. *Identity of Theophilus.* The name Theophilus means "Friend of God," and some have therefore suggested that it is a term of address to believers generally rather than to a specific person. However, the use of the adjective "most excellent" more probably suggests a known person of some rank. Bovon, *Luke*, vol.1, 23.

Ch. 2. *Grace and charis.* The notion of kindness is particularly important as a means of softening the Old Testament rigor of the Mosaic Law. The need for such softening is illustrated by the story of the woman taken in adultery. See Ch. 111.

Ch. 3. *Role of the priests.* "The people honored the priests who sacrificed animals and made offerings of products of the land—oil, flour, and wine, as stipulated by the Law—and who blessed those before them." Puig i Tarrech, *Jesus*, 86. "Sacrifice lay at the heart of the Jewish faith as a means of maintaining or reestablishing a relationship with God." Collins, *Dorling Bible*, 111.

Ch. 7. *The name of "Jesus."* It has been suggested that this passage might be more easily understood if it were translated in the following sense: "You shall call his name 'Savior' because he will save." May, *Oxford Bible*, 1172.

Ch. 10. *The two genealogies of Jesus.* Daniel-Rops, *Jesus and His Times*, 115–16. This mode of reconciliation has been proposed since the first years of the Church, beginning at least as early as Eusebius, who was Bishop of Caesarea, in what is now Israel, in the early Fourth Century.

Ch. 10. *The women in the paternal genealogy.* The four women mentioned in Matthew's genealogy (apart from Mary herself) had all had some contact with sexual irregularities. Mitchell, *The Gospel According to Jesus*, 12–13. They may have been mentioned in order to lessen any concern about the unconventional circumstances of Mary.

Ch. 11. *Descent from King David.* Metzger, *New Testament*, 79. Cf. Mitchell, *The Gospel According to Jesus*, 79.

Ch. 11. *Maternal genealogy.* Some manuscripts include an additional generation, with Admin listed as the father of Arni.

Ch. 13. *The time for purification.* The procedures for purification are described in Leviticus 12:2–4. The issue is of diminished importance in this case due to the divine nature of the birth. Nonetheless, the family's adherence to all the prescribed rituals expresses their values of "daily living true to the Law." Bovon, *Luke*, vol.1, 96.

Ch. 13. *Looking forward to the Messiah.* Literally, Simeon was looking forward to "the consolation of Israel," which was a common expression for the salvation and rescue from foreign oppression that the Messiah was expected to bring. Gundry, *Commentary*, 231.

Ch. 14. *The prophecy about Bethlehem.* See Micah 5:2.

Ch. 14. *Zoroastrian religion.* The religion itself survives in some small communities, such as among the Parsis of India.

Ch. 15. *Massacre of the Innocents.* Secular history does not record this particular massacre, but it would have been entirely consistent with what we do know of the mindset and methods of Herod. He is known to have ordered the execution of "two of his ten wives, at least three sons, a brother-in-law, and a wife's grandfather." Metzger, *New Testament*, 28. When Herod finally lay dying himself, and realized that his subjects would celebrate at being free of him, he ordered that the most highly regarded citizens of Jericho be confined in the city arena, and killed when he died. In that way he hoped to ensure that there would be widespread mourning at the time of his death, even if not precisely as a result of grief over his death. In the event, however, these final instructions were not carried out. Ibid.

Ch. 20. *The teachings of John the Baptist.* John the Baptist "preached that an apocalyptic judgment was at hand." Collins, *Apocalyptic Imagination*, 260. Apocalyptic preachings had become common at the time. While there were many reasons for this, one is that people were receptive to the notion of radical change because the political world around them had come to be seen as intolerably oppressive. "Happy people do not write apocalypses."

Fredriksen, *Jesus to Christ*, 82. An apocalyptic view became a form of protest against Roman occupation—an occupation that was especially resented
as falling on a land and people under the special protection of God. Protest
in this respect could be easily extended to protest against oppressive collaborating regimes such as that of the Herods. Horsley, *The Message*, 2–3.

By contrast, the interior aspects of John's teaching seem to have been very
traditional, calling for a return to old values of honesty and simplicity. A
valuable source on these events is Flavius Josephus, a Roman-Jewish historian of the First Century, who provides the only substantial secular history of
Judea at this time. He reports that John "was a good man, and commanded
the Jews to exercise virtue, both as to righteousness toward one another,
and piety towards God." Josephus, *Complete Works*, 581 (*Antiquities* 18.5.2).
This message was reinforced by John's own appearance. "His style was that
of an ancient prophet warning the People of Israel of the impending threat
of God's fiery vengeance." Horsley, *The Message*, 47.

Ch. 21. *Sadducees, Pharisees, and Essenes.* For a description contrasting the
origins and agendas of the Sadducees and Pharisees—one urban elite, and
the other more small-town and rural—see Metzger, *New Testament*, 26;
Duling, *New Testament*, 45–48.

The elite Sadducees eventually disappeared during the course of the Jewish Revolt of AD 66–70, about thirty-five years after Jesus' death. In the
early years of the revolt many of them were killed by the Zealots, rebels who
considered them traitors and collaborators with Rome. In the later years
of the revolt, Roman legions captured Jerusalem and razed the temple. Because sacrifices could be performed only at the temple, this deprived the
remaining Sadducees of their reason for existence. The sect disappeared
soon thereafter.

The Pharisees had long been considered the most devout and scholarly
among the Jews. Josephus describes them as "those esteemed most skillful
in the exact explication of their laws." Josephus, *Complete Works*, 729 (*Wars*
2.8.14); see Boring, *Introduction*, 101–02. Due to their loose organization
and lack of centralized institutions, the Pharisees were able to survive the
fall of Jerusalem and eventually evolved into present-day rabbinical Judaism. After the loss of the city, "the only center left to the people was the
Torah." Schurer, *History of the Jewish People*, vol. 1, 513.

The Essenes are thought by many scholars to be (or to be related to) the people who hid the Dead Sea Scrolls. Horsley, *The Message*, 32. There are some similarities between their ascetic practices and certain events mentioned in the gospels. The austere mission instructions to the apostles, for example, see Ch. 75:3–4, are not unlike the travel practices ascribed to the Essenes.

Ch. 21. *Tax gatherers.* Tax gatherers were widely hated by the general population for a variety of reasons. Some were hated for being agents of the Roman overlords. Meeks, *Harper Bible*, 1867. Others were agents for nominally-independent client monarchs, such as Herod Antipas, rather than for Rome, but those local rulers were often thought oppressive in their own right. Horsley, *The Message*, 26; Johnson, *Writings of the New Testament*, 24. And all tax gatherers "were suspect not only for collaborating with foreign powers, but also for dishonesty." Meeks, *Harper Bible*, 1966.

Ch. 22. *The Messiah.* References to the messiah are found throughout the Old Testament. For descriptions of the expected messiah's chief characteristics see Jeremiah 23:5, 33:15–16; Isaiah 11:2–5, 10–12.

The Old Testament references are difficult to interpret, however, and were perhaps supplemented by mythologies circulating among the common people, making it hard for them to know what signs would be significant. "There were those who thought the messiah would be a king, and those who thought he'd be a priest." Aslan, *Zealot*, 27. Most Jews probably thought he would possess a combination of secular and religious leadership. Most of them probably also expected that he would restore the land to its former position of power and glory. "[T]he messiah will be someone in whom are combined the traits of courage, piety, military prowess, justice, wisdom, and knowledge of Torah . . . . his duty is to inflict final defeat on the forces of evil." Fredriksen, *Jesus to Christ*, 86. Most seemed to expect that the messiah would be a human being endowed by God with special powers and abilities, but not be divine himself.

God had promised that King David's descendants would be on the throne "forever." 2 Samuel 7:16. It therefore seemed likely that the messiah would come from David's line in order to fulfill this scripture as well.

In the traditional Jewish view, the messiah was not expected to suffer. See Price, *History and Theology*, 224. Therefore, when Jesus arrived, he proved to be a messiah similar to expectations in many respects, but quite different in many others.

Ch. 22. *Elijah.* See Gundry, *Commentary*, 175. To this day a chair or cup is reserved for him at Jewish Passover dinners, one reason for this being the hope that he will come, bringing news of the messiah. Elijah had already vouched for someone in a similar way during his own lifetime, when he designated the person he chose to be his successor as a prophet, literally passing his mantle to Elisha. See 2 Kings 2:13.

Ch. 23. *Persuading John the Baptist.* Literally, Jesus said to him, "thus it is fitting for us to fulfill all righteousness."

Ch. 24. *Agnus Dei.* The notion of sacrifice for the good of the community was deeply woven into Old Testament practice. Lambs were sacrificed twice daily in the temple, at dawn and 3:00 p.m., as a sign of communal devotion to God. See Exodus 29:38–42; Numbers 28:3–8. Important annual sacrifices drew special attention to the connection between the death of the animal and the welfare of the community. The special killing of the paschal lambs, on the afternoon before Passover, was a reminder of the death of the original lambs in Egypt that provided the blood necessary for the first Passover. Their blood had been used to mark the doorposts of the homes occupied by the Israelites, and it informed the Lord to "pass over" those houses while killing the firstborn elsewhere. Once a year, on Yom Kippur, the Day of Atonement, two goats were sacrificed in another special ceremony. One was killed in the temple, and the other, the "escape goat" (later shortened to "scapegoat"), was driven out into the wilderness to die there, bearing with it the sins of the community. Later New Testament writers suggested that Jesus was, through his crucifixion, a similar sacrificial offering to atone for the sins of humanity. But unlike the sacrificial goat and the scapegoat of the Old Testament, who unknowingly bore and suffered for the sins of the community, Jesus consciously agreed to accept his own fate.

Ch. 24. *Not recognizing the Messiah.* John was a relative of Jesus, see Ch. 4:3, and so it might be expected that he would have recognized Jesus as an individual. Fitzmyer, *Catechism*, 29. John need not have immediately recognized him as the messiah, however.

Ch. 25. *The Temptation in the Wilderness.* Fred Craddock has noted that the temptations occurred at the very start of Jesus' ministry, before he had carried out any of his teachings or healings. Craddock suggests that they show Jesus in the process of resolving what it means to be about God's business:

It is important to keep in mind that a real temptation beckons us to do that about which much good can be said. Stones to bread—the hungry hope so; take political control—the oppressed hope so; leap from the temple—those longing for proof of God's power among us hope so. [But here the temptation is rejected.] Jesus has rejected the way of flaunting miracles and he will not take up the political sword. The way of God's response to human need is otherwise.

Craddock, *Luke*, 56–57.

Ch. 27. *The time of day.* Some commentators believe that John followed the Roman convention of counting the hours from midnight. This seems somewhat less likely because it would be at variance with the local practice. But if it were the case here, it would make the time about ten in the morning.

Ch. 28. *Nathaniel under the fig tree.* Jesus had "supernatural knowledge about Nathaniel." Meeks, *Harper Bible*, 2015. Some have speculated that Nathaniel meditated under the fig tree, or perhaps taught there. Whatever the particular activities, the point is that Jesus knew about them. Haenchen, *John*, vol. 1, 166.

Ch. 31. *Two cleansings and the nature of gospel chronology.* The different timing of the two accounts of cleansing the temple does not present as difficult a problem as one might at first think. John may have simply chosen to describe some events out of sequence. Many scholars believe that the gospel writers did not necessarily follow our own modern ideas about chronological narrative. Rather, the accounts are broadly chronological in their construction, but within that framework they group together some events for expositional or other purposes:

> Some of the material is organized along thematic lines, some according to a loose chronology; still other pericopes [that is, short scenes] are linked by some combination of catchwords, themes, OT attestation, genre, and logical coherence. The result is not exactly a history, biography, theology, confession, catechism, tract, homage, or letter—though it is in some respects all these. It is a 'Gospel,' a presentation of the 'good news' of Jesus the Messiah.

Carson, "Introduction to Matthew," 38–39. The Catholic Church's guide to scholarly research addresses the issue in this way:

[T]he truth of the narrative is not at all affected by the fact that the evangelists relate the words and deeds of the Lord in a different order, and express his sayings not literally but differently, while preserving their sense. For, as St. Augustine says, "It is quite probable that each evangelist believed it to have been his duty to recount what he had to in that order in which it pleased God to suggest it to his memory, in those things at least in which the order, whether it be this or that, detracts in nothing from the truth and authority of the gospel. But why the Holy Spirit, who apportions individually to each one as he wills, and who therefore undoubtedly also governed and ruled the minds of the holy (writers) . . . permitted one to compile his narrative in this way, and another in that, anyone with pious diligence may seek the reason and with divine aid will be able to find it."

Fitzmyer, *Catechism*, 158, translating *An Instruction about the Historical Truth of the Gospels*, Paragraph IX (1964). Fitzmyer suggests that the two different kinds of truth being presented—literal and illustrative—might be understood as representing the difference between "historical truth" and "gospel truth." Ibid., 140.

Ch. 32. *Verily, verily.* This phrase was "a frequent introduction to Jesus' authoritative teaching." Meeks, *Harper Bible*, 1866. Its use at important points identifies a context of "prophetic assurance." Ibid., 1923.

Ch. 32. *Son of Man.* In Old Testament writing, the phrase "son of man" was used to refer to a human being in general, or, more abstractly, to "someone." See, e.g., Numbers 23:19; Job 35:8. It seems to have been used in a similar sense in first-century secular Aramaic. Fitzmyer, *Catechism*, 107. Jesus, however, adopted the term and narrowed its meaning so as to refer to himself, and only himself. Ibid. This may have been a way of emphasizing to his listeners his human as distinguished from (or as well as) his divine nature.

Ch. 33. *The bride of Christ.* The image of Israel as God's bride is common in the Old Testament. See Isaiah 62:5 ("as a bridegroom rejoices over the bride, so shall your God rejoice over you"); Boadt, *Reading the Old Testament*, 21 (citing the Song of Songs). The gospel writers took up this image and extended it to Jesus' followers as the bride of Christ. Gundry, *Commentary*, 363.

Ch. 33. *So few accept his testimony.* Literally, "no one," but this is to be understood figuratively.

Ch. 34. *A tetrarchy*. In time this term came to be loosely used to describe any partial share of rule. Metzger, *New Testament*, 37. In the particular case of two of the three children of Herod the Great, however, it may also have had an element of literal description. Archaelaus received Judea, which represented half the value of his father's kingdom, and the younger Herod Antipas and Philip received territories that each represented about a quarter of the value. Josephus, *Complete Works*, 724 (*Wars* 2.6.3).

Ch. 34. *Herod and Herodias*. Horsley, *The Message*, 37–38. The marriage between Herod and Herodias was further complicated by the fact that Herodias was Herod's niece, which made the union incestuous as well as one involving the brother's wife. Josephus, *Complete Works*, 580 (*Antiquities* 18.5.1); Horsley, *The Message*, 44. Philip's rejected first wife learned of the lovers' plans in time to flee back to her home town, the fabled "rose red" desert city of Petra, where her father was king. Enraged by this insult to his daughter, and having his own border disputes with Herod in any event, the king began a war in which Herod's army was soundly defeated. Notwithstanding that setback, Herodias later persuaded her new husband to ask the then-reigning emperor, Caligula, for a promotion from tetrarch to the rank of king. But memory of the defeat, combined with palace intrigues led by Herodias' own brother, made Caligula suspicious of Herod's loyalty. So Herod was exiled to western Europe, possibly to the city in Gaul now known as Lyon, but more probably to Spain. Josephus, *Complete Works*, 731 (*Wars* 2.9.6) He and Herodias departed for their new lives around A.D. 39, a few years after Jesus' death. Herodias' brother took over the rule of Herod's former lands.

Herodias' first husband Philip, also known as Herod Philip or Herod II, should not be confused with another brother, Philip the tetrarch, who was introduced in Ch. 20:1 as the ruler of Ituraea and Trachonitis. The Philip in the present story had briefly been the presumptive heir of his father Herod the Great, but was later removed from his father's will and was a prominent but private citizen at the time of these events.

Ch. 34. *Herod and John the Baptist*. Josephus suggests that Herod Antipas may also have been worried that John was beginning to have a substantial following of his own: "Herod, who feared lest the great influence John had over the people might put it into his power and inclination to raise a rebellion (for they seemed ready to do anything he should advise), thought it best, by putting him to death, to prevent any mischief he might cause, and not bring himself into difficulties, by sparing a man who might make him repent of it when it should be too late." Josephus, *Complete Works*, 581 (*Antiquities* 18.5.2).

When he reproved Herod, John the Baptist would have had in mind Leviticus 20:21, which provides, "If a man shall take his brother's wife, it is an unclean thing; . . . They shall be childless." John's reproof preyed on the mind of King Henry VIII of England, who had married Catherine of Aragon, the wife of his deceased brother Arthur. Henry's marriage failed to produce a male child to inherit the realm, which he saw as a fulfillment of this scripture. Unable to persuade the Pope to grant an annulment, Henry took the church in England out from the authority of the Vatican, received an annulment from his new officials, and married Anne Boleyn.

Ch. 36. *Samaria*. Some of the estrangement between Jews and Samaritans had historical roots. These lands were on opposite sides of the border when Solomon's united kingdom split, under his successors, into the northern kingdom of Israel and the southern kingdom of Judah. The eponymous city of Samaria was the capital of Israel, and Jerusalem the capital of Judah. The two states had a testy relationship during Old Testament times, with suggestions that Samaria, under rulers such as Ahab and Jezebel, had allowed the introduction of foreign religious practices. Collins, *Dorling Bible*, 194, 208–09. Even without that complication, the Northern Kingdom maintained its own temple, separate from the temple in Jerusalem, and "the true place of worship was thus a fundamental bone of contention between Samaritans and Jews." Boring, *Introduction*, 95.

Later, in the years just before the New Testament period, there were tit-for-tat exchanges between the two states. The Jewish leader John Hyrcanus (who reigned from 134–104 BC) overran Samaria, captured the city of Sechem (known in the gospels as Sychar and known today as Nablus) and destroyed the Samaritan temple on Mount Gerizim. Metzger, *New Testament*, 27; Brown, *Introduction to the New Testament*, 57. Later, around A.D. 6–9, the Samaritans defiled the Jewish temple in Jerusalem, during the Passover festival itself, by strewing dead men's bones in the temple precincts. Ratzinger, *Jesus of Nazareth*, 196.

Ch. 36. *Jacob and Joseph*. As a mark of this favor, Jacob gave his son Joseph the "coat of many colors." Joseph's brothers became jealous and sold him into slavery in Egypt for twenty pieces of silver. Genesis 37:28. There, however, Joseph prospered, successfully interpreted dreams, and rose to become the

Pharaoh's principal advisor. During a famine the rest of the family moved to Egypt for sustenance and was reunited there. Genesis 46:30–31. 430 years later, Moses led their descendants back to Israel.

Ch. 39. *The townspeople's fury*. Scott, *Jewish Backgrounds*, 125; White, *Scripting Jesus*, 329 (discussing missions to the Gentiles).

Ch. 40. *New home in Capernaum*. Capernaum was small, but busy and significant for its size because of its role as a border crossing. Horsley, *The Message*, 46. Its population was probably about 1500, mostly "fishermen and farmers." Puig i Tàrrech, *Jesus*, 70. The town had no public buildings or defensive walls, but it did have two other facilities of general importance: a synagogue and a tax office. Ibid., 69–70.

Ch. 40. *Galilee of the Gentiles*. The province is frequently referred to in the Hebrew literature as "galil hagoyim," meaning "Galilee of the goyim" or "Galilee of the Gentiles." Barnstone, *New Covenant*, 48. This designation has historical roots. In the years 104–03 B.C., Galilee had been reconquered by the Jewish ruler Aristobulus, and its inhabitants, most of whom were Gentiles, were forced to convert to Judaism. Metzger, *New Testament*, 27. The extent or depth of some of those conversions was no doubt subject to question.

The capital cities of Galilee established by Herod Antipas were centers for a broader Mediterranean culture. The first of these cities, Sepphoris, was only about four miles from Nazareth. Duling, *New Testament*, 569. Both it and Herod's successor capital, Tiberias, on the shores of the Sea of Galilee, "were almost wholly populated with non-Galileans: Roman merchants, Greek-speaking gentiles, . . . Judean settlers." Aslan, *Zealot*, 93. There is no record of Jesus visiting either place, although it seems likely that he did.

Scholars are unsure about how the presence of these cities affected the population mix of the province as a whole. Some believe that Galilee was predominately non-Jewish. Metzger, *New Testament*, 48. Others believe it was mainly Jewish. Scott, *Jewish Backgrounds*, 48. The balance was probably close in either case.

This complex history means that we know nothing about the physical appearance of Jesus. While he unquestionably grew up in a family that was religiously and culturally Jewish, many parts of the family tree (apart from the particular lines of descent spelled out in the gospels) could have been with any of the peoples of the Mediterranean basin.

One thing that is clear is that all the people of Galilee—Jews and gentiles alike—considered themselves distinct from the cultural centers of Jerusalem and Judea. Josephus says that the rugged terrain of Galilee meant that it had "always been able to make a strong resistance on all occasions of war," Josephus, *Complete Works*, 768 (*Wars* 3.3.2), and that the Galileans seem to have always maintained a distinct self-identity.

Ch. 41. *Standing by the sea.* In this verse Luke literally speaks of the 'Lake of Gennesaret," which was another name for the Sea of Galilee.

Ch. 41. *The partners of Simon Peter.* For greater clarity this identification of James and John has been placed about three sentences earlier than it appears in Luke's account.

Ch. 41. *Catching men.* Luke records this reassurance, "Do not be afraid," and as the next point reports Jesus' promise that "from now on you will be catching men." However, a comparison with Mark makes it clear that these two things were not said at the same time. The first comment, reported by Luke, was made in the boat, and Mark specifies that the second was made while walking on the shore. Some time must have intervened between the two. The second quotation is therefore treated as part of the events in the next chapter.

Ch. 43. *Marriages among the followers.* See 1 Corinthians 9:5. The Greek word used in this passage can mean either "wife" or "woman," but most translators have concluded that in this context it means "wife." Given Jesus' concern for sexual morality, it is unlikely that any follower would have asked him to formally recognize an unsanctioned companion. Notwithstanding the evident frequency of marriages among his followers, however, the gospels do not emphasize the family ties of the people in Jesus' group. Jesus evidently favored men who had the freedom to accompany him on what was most commonly an itinerant ministry. Similarly, the gospel accounts never describe any of the women in the group as traveling with their husbands or other family members, suggesting that they exercised a similar freedom that was probably unusual for the time.

Ch. 45. *Healing leprosy*. Leprosy was viewed as "a contagious, ritual impurity, curable only by divine power." Meeks, *Harper Bible*, 1919. See also Collins, *Mark*, 179.

Ch. 48. *Scribes*. Scribes were predominately scholars and appliers of the law, rather than people engaged in the more mechanical functions that the term "scribe" or "notary" might imply today. Metger, *New Testament*, 57–58. Because the term "scribe" describes a professional function, scribes might belong to either the Pharisees or the Sadducees (or to some other group) as a matter of religious belief. But because the Sadducees generally represented the urban elite, most of the Sadducee-affiliated scribes would have been found in the larger cities such as Jerusalem, rather than in the rural parts of Galilee where Jesus was teaching. The scribes that Jesus encountered in the countryside would have been mainly Pharisees.

Ch. 50. *The angel moving the water*. The description of the angel moving the waters was part of the King James Version. Modern scholarship has concluded that this passage was probably not present in the earliest manuscripts of the gospels. It has therefore been reduced to a footnote in some recent editions. The passage is nonetheless included in this account because of its long standing in the Christian tradition, and because of its usefulness as background for understanding the later events of this chapter.

Ch. 51. *Jesus' human nature*. Jesus has two natures, human and divine, both present in one person. In his first encyclical as Pope, John Paul II explained that one consequence of Jesus' human nature was that he "fully reveals man to himself."

Ch. 53. *The apostle Bartholomew*. Bartholomew may be the man referred to as "Nathaniel" in the gospel of John, where Nathaniel appears as a disciple although not necessarily as an apostle of Jesus. See Ch. 28:3–4. Nathaniel is always mentioned together with Philip in John's gospel, while in the three synoptic gospels it is Bartholomew who is always mentioned together with Philip—a parallelism suggesting that they may be the same person. May, *Oxford Bible*, 1286.

Ch. 53. *The apostle Thaddeus*. For the suggestion that Judas Thaddeus represents the given name and the surname of the same individual, see Daniel, *Harmony*, 56 n. On the other hand, other scholars suggest that there is no sound basis for the combination. Meier, *A Marginal Jew*, vol. 3, 200

NOTES 267

("Christian imagination was quick to harmonize and produce Jude Thaddeus, a conflation that has no basis in reality.").

Ch. 53. *Simon the Zealot.* The Zealots were determined and fanatically violent. They began their resistance to Rome with a campaign of selective assassination, making use of easily hidden curved knives called *sicae*, from which they took the name of sicarii, or "daggermen," according to Josephus. "With these weapons they slew a great many; for they mingled themselves among the multitude at their festivals, when they were come up in crowds from all parts to the city to worship God . . . and easily slew those that they had a mind to slay." Josephus, *Complete Works,* 644 (*Antiquities* 20.8.10).

This violence turned into more organized terror after open rebellion broke out, and during the Roman siege of Jerusalem. "The Zealot Party took over the Temple's inner courtyard, where only the priests were permitted, and from there unleashed a wave of terror against those they deemed insufficiently loyal to the rebellion: the wealthy aristocracy and upper-class Jews; the old Herodian nobles and the Temple's former leadership; the chief priests and all those who followed the moderate camp." Aslan, *Zealot,* 64.

If Jesus could attract, among his apostles, both Matthew the former collaborator with Rome, and Simon the former Zealot, that shows the range and universality of his appeal. Metzger, *New Testament,* 55.

Ch. 55. *The poor in spirit.* The difference between the two gospels on this point may be more than just stylistic. The phrase "poor in spirit" has been said to imply an absence of self-will, going beyond just a material poverty in money. Those who are poor in spirit have been described as those who feel an "inward dependence on God." Gundry, *Commentary,* 15. Such a person might be understood as one living humbly and righteously. A classic Russian work on Christian spirituality says that the desire for unceasing interior prayer "is found in poverty of spirit and in active experience in simplicity of heart." Anonymous, *The Way of a Pilgrim,* 6. Saint Augustine described the absence of self-will even more strongly: "We see then that the two cities [or communities] were created by two kinds of love: the earthly city was created by self-love reaching the point of contempt for God, the Heavenly City by the love of God carried as far as contempt of self." Augustine, *City of God,* 593 (Book XIV, ch. 28).

Luke's contrasting reference, to "you poor," has a different focus. It is more of a piece with a general theme of concern for those who are unwillingly impoverished and outcast from society in material terms.

Ch. 55. *The Lord's Prayer.* One modern writer suggests that only a few short, key texts are needed to understand Christianity, and that this prayer is "foremost of these gifts." McGowan, *Source of Miracles*, 4. The fact that it was composed directly by Jesus gives it special weight.

Ch. 58. *"Who can accept me for what I am."* Literally, "will not be caused to stumble" by me.

Ch. 59. *The kingdom of heaven has been strongly advancing.* Several factors contribute to the difficulty of this passage. For one thing it was probably intended to be cryptic, as the final sentence of the verse suggests. More fundamentally, there is an ambiguity in the form of the Greek verbs used, which might be in either the active or the passive voice. This means that we cannot easily tell whether the kingdom of heaven is in the active mode of moving forward, or in the passive mode of suffering incursions by others.

As a result of these uncertainties there have been many different interpretations of this passage. The best guide to a correct understanding is to pay attention to the context in which the passage appears. A good reading will look back and allow the sentence to follow naturally from the previous thought about the effective work that John the Baptist had done in introducing the idea of the kingdom of heaven. And it will also look forward, so as to set the stage for Jesus' criticism, in a later chapter, of those other people, lacking vision and strength of character, who did not embrace even that clear invitation. The reading proposed here seems to do both those things. John made the kingdom attractive, and worthy people became determined to enter it.

But there are alternative readings. One alternative would interpret this passage in a consistently passive voice. The King James Version does this, and reports that "the kingdom of heaven suffereth violence, and the violent take it by force." It is hard to believe, however, that the kingdom of heaven, being protected by God, could actually be taken by violent and wicked people.

Another alternative would translate the sentence in a voice partly active and partly passive, so as to emphasize the growing conflict between the followers of Jesus and John on the one hand, and established authorities on the other. "The kingdom of heaven has been strongly advancing, but powerful forces have arisen to oppose it." This reading would take account of the growing opposition from figures like Herod and the temple authorities. It also accounts for the identification made between John and Elijah—the prophet who was to usher in a period of apocalyptic conflict. For an argument favoring such an interpretation see Hauerwas, *Matthew*, 115 (Herod "will try to defeat the kingdom heralded by John with violence, but it cannot be so overwhelmed. John the Baptist can be arrested and killed, Jesus will be crucified, but the kingdom that John proclaims comes through the peace brought by Jesus."). This reading does make sense as a statement of history. However, it focuses on a particular external conflict and does not seem to connect with the biblical passages on either side of the sentence.

The approach favored here would give a more positive interpretation to the people who are trying to enter the kingdom of heaven with force. Now these are no longer enemies seeking to overthrow it, but rather the committed believers who are marshaling the force of their faith and determination in order to make themselves worthy of admission. Luke 16:16 expresses a similar idea and provides an independent confirmation of it. This is an attractive concept, and is shared by several writers. See Luz, *Matthew*, vol. 2, 140 & nn.43-44 (noting that positive interpretations along these lines were common in the ancient church and in modern Protestantism).

Other commentary has suggested that several of these alternatives can simultaneously be true. "It has been much disputed whether the violence here is external, as against the kingdom in the persons of John the Baptist and Jesus; or that, considering the opposition of the scribes and Pharisees, only the violently resolute would press into it. Both things are true." Scofield, *Study Bible*, 1009 n.3.

For the useful linking text sentence in italics, I am grateful for a suggestion in the New Living Translation, Luke 16:17.

Ch. 59. *John the Baptist is Elijah.* "On the basis of Malachi 4:5-6, some expected Elijah (or an Elijah-like figure) to be the forerunner who would prepare the way for the Messiah. Others seem to have expected Elijah to come back to life to be the Messiah. Justin Martyr preserves a tradition that the Elijah-forerunner would actually anoint the Messiah." Scott, *Jewish Backgrounds*, 318-19.

Ch. 62. *Mary Magdalene*. No fewer than three different female figures in the gospels might represent different aspects of Mary Magdalene—Mary Magdalene herself, Mary of Bethany, and the penitent sinner. These may be the same person under different descriptions, or they may be separate individuals.

First of all, there is some logic in identifying Mary of Bethany with Mary Magdalene. Mary of Bethany receives Jesus on several occasions, most notably when he is making his final journey to Jerusalem. See Ch. 154. This Mary abruptly drops out of the narrative after this encounter, while Mary Magdalene abruptly reenters it a few days later at the time of the crucifixion. Yet there is a thematic continuity between the actions of these two characters. Mary of Bethany symbolically anoints Jesus in a way that foretells his burial, while Mary Magdalene brings spices to anoint his body in the tomb. It is possible that these two Marys are the same person.

There is also some logic in combining this dual figure with the earlier, unnamed penitent woman. See Ch. 61. This woman anointed Jesus' feet and dried them with her hair—an unusual gesture that was later made by Mary of Bethany as well. It would be a symmetrical and harmonious image to think that a deeply worried Mary of Bethany would reenact the earlier anointing in this context, reminding Jesus, now so threatened on all sides, of the innocent days of his early ministry.

On the other hand, other considerations suggest that these may be separate women. Mary Magdalene evidently came from Galilee. "Magdala" is a town there and is mentioned in Ch. 88:1. It would be surprising to find her so soon afterwards living as Mary of Bethany, in the town of Bethany, near Jerusalem, 60 miles to the south. The penitent woman might likewise be a separate person. The gospel of Luke first introduces Mary Magdalene in the chapter immediately following his description of the penitent woman. Luke introduces Mary Magdalene as if she were a new character, describing her as a person out of whom Jesus had cast seven demons. If this Mary were in fact the penitent woman, he would presumably have referred to her as the person that the reader has just met in the immediately preceding incident.

There is no reason to believe that a fourth individual—the woman taken in adultery—is Mary Magdalene.

Whatever conclusion is reached on these issues, it should not be strongly driven by a sense that it would be demeaning or disrespectful to Mary

Magdalene to characterize her as a former prostitute or other reformed sinner. That view does not really reflect the philosophy of the gospels. The core
message of Jesus' ministry was one of repentance and forgiveness of sins. It
suited his mission for reformed sinners to be among his closest followers.
Matthew the collaborationist tax-gatherer was one such; Mary Magdalene
could have been—although she need not have been—another.

Ch. 62. *Women as disciples.* Thurston, *Women in the New Testament*, 105–06;
Meier, *A Marginal Jew*, vol. 3, 80 ("Whatever the problems of vocabulary,
the most probable conclusion is that Jesus viewed and treated these women
as disciples"). Jesus' openness to women was also shown in his earlier interactions with the Woman at the Well. See Ch. 36:9. "It was against the social
customs of that time for a Jewish religious teacher to be speaking with a
woman in public." Meeks, *Harper Bible*, 2020.

Ch. 66. *"Not in his right mind."* Another, more benign reading of this passage
would have the family members say that, due to the strains of his work, "He
is too distracted to take care of himself."

Ch. 67. *Beelzebub.* Barnstone, *The New Covenant*, 249. Beelzebub may also
be another name for Satan himself. Pagels, *Origin of Satan*, xvii, 34.

Ch. 67. *Binding the strong man.* For this interpretation of the passage see
Luz, *Matthew*, vol. 2, 205 ("Jesus suggests that the devil is already bound;
only then can one enter his house and liberate people who are ruled by
him.").

Ch. 68. *The kingdom of God.* "[T]he conception of the Kingdom comes as
near to being the key element in the New Testament as any that could be
named." Gunn, *Gospel of the Kingdom*, 136. The kingdom of God has an
external aspect, an internal aspect, and, perhaps, the possibility of combining these elements into one harmonious whole.

One part of the kingdom of God is to be external to the individual. It will
be characterized by different and better relationships among people, and
by people's acceptance of a better relationship with God. It might perhaps
be termed "the reign of God" in order to free it from any suggestion that it
refers to a defined territory.

Jesus does not describe this external aspect of the kingdom in detail, as-
suming instead that his listeners are already familiar with the concept. We

must deduce its features from the specific examples that Jesus gives. One prominent Protestant theologian believes Jesus taught his hearers "to recognize God's sovereignty as a present reality, to be acknowledged by a personal response, and . . . he also led them to hope for a new age in which human hardness of heart would no longer prevent God's sovereignty from finding universal and complete response." Metzger, *New Testament*, 173. Many of the parables in this chapter fit this message, showing how a new and beneficent influence of this kind can work its way, slowly but surely, through a mass of material. This external influence may lead in the end to a complete change in attitude, as believers come to recognize all people as "brothers and sisters under God." Horsley, *The Message*, 54.

This external aspect of the kingdom is not simply benign, however. It also contains an element of judgment—even of apocalyptic judgment. At some future time "there will be a glorious manifestation of the power of the kingdom when the Son of Man will come with his angels in the glory of his Father." Metzger, *New Testament*, 174. And this element of sternness and judgment is, in the view of a prominent Catholic theologian, an essential part of the vision of the kingdom. It helps "to prevent a naive understanding of it, as if it were a mere inward reality, an attitude of the human heart." Fitzmyer, *Catechism*, 149.

Preaching on these themes naturally leads to calls for repentance. The current ruling powers on earth are to be overthrown—perhaps in the very near future—and replaced by heavenly rule. Hence the urgency behind the literal message to "repent, for the kingdom of heaven is at hand."

Because it is possible that the rulers are to be changed, the Kingdom of God in this sense has a political, insurrectionist air about it. Or at least it can be so perceived by secular rulers, including the rulers of Jesus' own day, who could become worried about the strengths and purposes of this kind of revivalist movement. For one historically documented example of such concern see the endnote on Ch. 34, "Herod and John the Baptist."

On the other hand, the Kingdom of God also has a second element that is primarily internal to the individual. It is similar to attaining a state of enlightenment. One writer describes it this way:

> When Jesus talked about the kingdom of God, he was not prophesying about some easy, danger-free perfection that will someday appear. He was talking about a state of being, a way

of living at ease among the joys and sorrows of *our* world. It is possible, he said, to be as simple and beautiful as the birds of the sky or the lilies of the field, who are always within the eternal Now. This state of being is not something alien or mystical. We don't need to earn it. It is already ours.

Mitchell, *The Gospel According to Jesus*, 11.

The kingdom of God was described in similar terms in the non-canonical but historically important Coptic Gospel of Thomas. This is a very early document purporting to collect Jesus' sayings. It was known only by name until a copy was rediscovered in 1945. That manuscript itself probably dates to the early second century, and it may incorporate material that is genuinely from the time of Jesus. Ehrman, *Lost Scriptures*, 19. Teaching 3 in the list of sayings focuses on the interior aspects of the kingdom:

> Jesus said, "If those who lead you say to you, 'See, the Kingdom is in the sky,' then the birds of the sky will precede you. If they say to you, 'It is in the sea,' then the fish will precede you. Rather, the Kingdom is inside of you, and it is outside of you. When you come to know yourselves, then you will become known, and you will realize that it is you who are the sons of the living Father. But if you will not know yourselves, you dwell in poverty and it is you who are that poverty."

Teaching 113 provides some further details as follows:

> His disciples said to him, "When will the Kingdom come?" Jesus said, "It will not come by waiting for it. It will not be a matter of saying 'here it is' or 'there it is.' Rather, the Kingdom of the Father is spread out upon the earth, and men do not see it."

Koester, "The Gospel of Thomas," 118, 129–30. Stephen Mitchell suggests that the interior aspects of the Kingdom of God can also be thought of as the network—the archipelago—of places that are inhabited or influenced by people who have attained that state of enlightenment.

These two aspects of the kingdom of God are no doubt parts of a single harmonious whole. Finding the right words to describe the combination is a challenge, but some commentary seems particularly helpful in understanding the Kingdom in its entirety:

> The 'Kingdom of God' is a phrase that does not appear in the Old Testament, although the notion of God's authority over all of his creation runs throughout. The kingdom that Jesus spoke about,

> and which is mentioned many times in the Gospels of Matthew,
> Mark, and Luke, is not a physical place, but is God's dynamic
> rule where his grace, power, and mercy are experienced. The
> New Testament writers looked forward to this kingdom com-
> ing in its fullness, and yet they reported that the kingdom was
> already present in Jesus' ministry, steadily at work, just as yeast
> turns dough into bread.

Collins, *Dorling Bible*, 297. The paradoxical combination of these two qualities has been summed up in the phrase that the Kingdom of God exists "already" and at the same time "not yet." Meier, *A Marginal Jew*, vol. 2, 451.

Ch. 68. *To those who have, more will be given.* "The reference here is not
to money or material gains, but to the word of God." Meeks, *Harper Bible*,
1973.

Ch. 69. *Calming the waves.* In Matthew, Jesus asks his fellow passengers why
they are fearful, before calming the sea. In Mark and Luke he poses the
question afterwards, asking why they had been afraid. This text uses the
earlier timing. Asking the question beforehand seems to suggest a higher
level of self-assurance that he will in fact be able to calm the waves.

Ch. 70. *Two demon-possessed men.* Matthew reports that there were two
demon-possessed men. Mark and Luke describe the conduct of only one
man. Presumably this was the more violent and intimidating of the two. For
this mode of reconciliation see Daniel, *Harmony*, 76 n.

Ch. 70. *The demons putting a spell on Jesus.* For a discussion of this feature
of the passage see White, *Scripting Jesus*, 171. The demons call on the power
of God by saying that they "command" Jesus in God's name; and they do so
in an effort to prevent Jesus from subjecting them to questioning or cross-
examination. Under the legal rules of the day a cross-examination might
involve torture, something presumably unattractive even to a demon. Their
main concern, however, was that the questioning might force them to reveal
their true identity and name. That would make them vulnerable to exorcism
themselves—as in fact happens in the next verse.

Ch. 71. *The woman with the flow of blood.* See Leviticus 15:19–30; Thurston,
Women in the New Testament, 71. A woman with a continuing flow of blood
would be "ritually unclean and defiling to others." Gundry, *Commentary*, 37.
The main lesson to be drawn from this incident is probably that Jesus was

willing to amend the old rules on ritual purity when human needs required this. Alternatively, one might take the view that the curing power of Jesus was such as to remove the underlying impurity in the first place. Still others have argued that the Jewish tradition contained enough flexibility to allow Jesus to perform all (or most) of his cures without violating Jewish law. Vermes, *Religion of Jesus*, 22–24.

Ch. 71. *When the woman was healed.* There a difference in emphasis between two of the gospels on this point. Mark reports that the woman felt free of her suffering the moment she first touched the garments, while Matthew says she was made well at the later moment when Jesus spoke to her. This is not an actual inconsistency, however. The woman may have felt better with the initial touch, but became lastingly healed only when Jesus focused his attention on her.

Ch. 73. *The final rejection.* A simple change of emphasis would make the even first line sarcastic: "Where does *this* man get special powers?" At whatever point it took place, there has been a change in mood.

Ch. 73. *The parentage of Jesus.* For the suggestion that Jesus could have been thought illegitimate by the townspeople, see Collins, *Mark*, 290 ("It was usual in Semitic cultures to refer to a man as the son of his father, even when the father was dead."). So the crowd's reference to the son of Mary may have meant "that the mother is named and not the father because the father was unknown and the son illegitimate." Ibid., 291. Jesus himself was quoted as expressing similar concerns in Teaching 105 of the ancient although non-canonical Gospel of Thomas: "Jesus said, 'He who knows the father and the mother will be called the son of a harlot.'" Koester, "The Gospel of Thomas," 129. For a more benign interpretation of the crowd's reactions, see Meier, *A Marginal Jew*, vol. 1, 227: "Since Mary was presumably the only surviving parent, the raucous, ad hoc attack on Jesus in the synagogue would naturally point to her standing right there, rather than to a dead and therefore absent father."

Ch. 73. *Brothers and sisters of Jesus.* Some evidence can be cited for each of the possible identifications of these "brothers" and "sisters." Brown, *Birth of the Messiah*, 605–06.

Treating them as blood siblings has the virtues of directness and simplicity of interpretation. Moreover, the contexts in which the terms are used are ones that most naturally suggest a reference to blood relations. Here, the

townspeople are referring to relatives with whom they are quite familiar—
which suggests that they have known the relatives for years, which in turn
suggests siblings. Another reference to relatives of Jesus can be found in Ch.
66:3, where his "mother and his brothers" arrived in an effort to dissuade
him from his teaching. In that situation Jesus contrasted those relatives with
his followers and disciples, which suggests that the reference to "brother"
referred to an actual family member rather than to a "fellow follower in
God." And the secular historian Josephus makes reference to James "the
the brother of Jesus, who was called Christ," without any suggestion that he
was making an allegorical use of the word. Josephus, *Complete Works*, 645
(*Antiquities* 20.9.1).

There is also warrant for treating these brothers and sisters as children of
Joseph, born from a prior marriage. It has been pointed out that the skeptical view of the brothers seems to express an attitude common among older
half-siblings. Such an attitude would have been on display not only in Ch.
66:3, but also in Ch. 98:2 ("For even his brothers did not believe in him.").

And there are grounds for thinking that these must be some more distant
relations—cousins, or perhaps just brothers in faith. Jesus' dying instruction
to John to take Mary into his house seems unlikely if there were more closely-
related natural children on the scene, who would ordinarily be expected to
care for their mother. The disputed references to "brothers" or "sisters" must
then arguably mean something other than those close relatives. The Greek
vocabulary permits this argument. To be sure, the New Testament does already have a distinct word for cousin, *anepsios*, see Colossians 4:10, so this
meaning is not easily read into the present word *adelphos*, or brother; but,
on the other hand, that meaning is certainly not precluded either. Fitzmyer,
Catechism, 37–38. Moreover, the Catholic and Orthodox Churches hold to
the perpetual virginity of Mary, which would as a matter of doctrine rule
out other blood children of Mary.

If the people mentioned in this gospel passage were in fact later-born children of Joseph and Mary, then it is likely that a number of direct descendants
of the Virgin Mary are living today. Unlike living descendants of Jesus, who
are a product of fictional speculation, the possibility of living descendants of
Mary would have support in the historical record.

Ch. 75. *Sandals and staffs.* The distinction between "shoes" and "sandals"
in the gospel instructions was expressly incorporated in the King James
Version, and has been noted in the commentary. Luz, *Matthew*, vol. 2, 77

& n.49. Similarly, the instructions with respect to walking sticks probably implies a distinction between the "staffs" in daily use, and the heavier "staves" carried by travelers "to protect themselves from attacking animals and human beings." Collins, *Mark*, 299. Both formulations emphasize that the apostles are to avoid acquiring any expensive or elaborate gear, and are instead to set off just as they are.

A number of writers have noted that these instructions were not aimed at imposing austerity for austerity's sake alone, but rather to keep the apostles light and swift in their journey, and equipped with a simplicity and trustfulness that would keep them in touch with ordinary people. Bovon, *Luke*, vol.1, 347; Donahue, *Mark*, 194.

Ch. 75. *Conflict and division.* The reference to bringing not peace but a sword suggests "'cutting' old family ties." Meeks, *Harper Bible*, 1876.

Ch. 75. *The modest followers.* In this context, "little ones" probably refers to "disciples who don't occupy positions of leadership in the church." Gundry, *Commentary*, 44. See also Luz, *Matthew*, vol. 2, 121 ("ordinary, insignificant Christians").

Ch. 78. *Eight months' wages.* In the original, "two hundred denarii."

Ch. 79. *Avoiding offer of the kingship.* By avoiding this offer, Jesus headed off any expectation that he might be a Messiah of the expected type—a military king who would deliver the land of the Jews from its Roman occupation. Metzger, *New Testament*, 139. Later, however, when Jesus entered Jerusalem, he did allow the crowd to give him the honors due to a Messiah—although he was still a Messiah of a different type. See Ch. 156:6–7.

Ch. 79. *Going by way of Bethsaida.* Davis, *Dictionary of the Bible*, 93. Davis considers and rejects the suggestion that there was a second town, also called Bethsaida, on the western side of the lake. He thinks it unlikely that there would be two places so close together sharing the same name.

Ch. 81. *The hem of the garment.* The Greek word *kraspedon* can be variously translated as "tassel," "fringe," or "edge." Longman, *Bible Dictionary*, 618–19. Tassels may have been a part of the particular garment involved here. The tassels of an outer garment are "a required part of the dress of a Jewish man." Meeks, *Harper Bible*, 1874 (citing Numbers 15:37–41). For a possible connection with the tassels on a prayer shawl see Kaiser, *Archaeological Bible*,

217; Collins, *Dorling Bible*, 318. This feature of the gospel account under-scores the fact that Jesus grew up in, and was rooted in, the Jewish tradition. Levine, *The Misunderstood Jew*, 23–24.

Ch. 82. *Teachings on immortality.* Scott, *Jewish Backgrounds*, 18. The period recorded in the canonical Old Testament ended about 435 B.C., with an account of how the descendants of the former exiles, now returned from their captivity in Babylon, went about re-creating Jewish practices in Jeru-salem. Ibid.; Stanley, *The Hebrew Bible*, 276, 474–75 (describing the books of Nehemiah and Malachi). Jewish culture and beliefs continued to evolve during the four centuries between the Old and New Testaments, however. By the time of Jesus, at least some Jews believed in the immortality of the soul. See Ch. 167:1.

Ch. 84. *Talmud and traditions.* The oral tradition thus set a protective "fence" around the law. Scott, *Jewish Backgrounds*, 129. The first written compilation of the tradition resulted in a document called the *Mishnah*. This runs about 800 printed pages. Later a further commentary and analysis was made on the Mishnah and other subjects. This too was eventually written down, and the combination of that commentary, together with the original Mishnah, is called the Talmud. Two different versions of the Talmud emerged, grow-ing from the work of the rabbinical centers in Jerusalem and Babylon. Of the two, the Babylonian Talmud is the later and more highly regarded. In a standard printed format it is over 6000 pages long. For a description see Metzger, *New Testament*, 63–64.

Ch. 84. *Baptism and dining couches.* For a reference to sprinkling certain hard-to-immerse objects such as tents and swords, see Aslan, *Zealot*, 83. Other authorities believe that the law was more rigorous than that, and even couches and beds were intended to be dismantled and immersed. Collins, *Mark*, 349.

Ch. 85. *Jewish and Greek ethnic groups.* For the use of the designation "Greek" to describe non-Jews generally, see Collins, *Mark*, 364; Gundry, *Commentary*, 419.

Ch. 89. *The unwholesome yeast.* Meeks, *Harper Bible*, 1983.

Ch. 92. *Grace versus works.* "If Paul knew that one is saved by faith alone, he knew also that the faith that saves does not remain alone—it is followed by good works that testify to its vitality." Metzger, *New Testament*, 278. Paul spoke, for example, of "faith working through love." Galatians 5:6. The letter of James also plays a role in showing that both qualities are important: "faith by itself, without works, is dead." James 2:17; see also James 2:24. There have been long periods when salvation though such works has been emphasized by some churches. Prichard, *Nature of Salvation*, 137.

Ch. 93. *The Mount of the Transfiguration.* Collins, *Dorling Bible*, 131. Another possible location is Mount Hermon, on the border between Syria and Lebanon. Ibid., 354. This latter location is supported by the fact that Mount Hermon is close to Caesarea Philippi, where Jesus and the disciples had been shortly before.

Ch. 98. *Jesus' relatives in the early church.* The book of Acts records how some of Jesus' family members came to play a role in the church. However, any potential for leadership by the family was snuffed out by the early deaths of the most plausible candidates. Jesus' brother, James the Just, was a prominent leader of the early church. Then in a incident eerily reminiscent of Jesus' own death, James was killed through the intrigues of the high priest Annas, who was a son of the former high priest of the same name and the brother-in-law of Caiaphas, who used the opportunity presented by an interregnum between Roman governors. These events were recorded by Josephus:

> [T]his younger Annas, who . . . took the high priesthood, was a bold man in his temper, and very insolent; he was also of the sect of the Sadducees, who are very rigid in judging offenders, above all the rest of the Jews; . . . [W]hen, therefore, Annas was of this disposition, he thought he had now a proper opportunity to exercise his authority. [The Roman prefect] Festus was now dead, and [his successor] Albinus was but upon the road; so he assembled the Sanhedrin of judges, and brought before them the brother of Jesus, who was called Christ, whose name was James, and some of his companions; and when he had formed an accusation against them as breakers of the law, he delivered them to be stoned.

Josephus, *Complete Works*, 645 (*Antiquities* 20.9.1). Jerusalem's Jewish community was outraged and complained to the incoming governor, and Annas was quickly deposed. Ibid., 645–46.

After James' execution, Eusebius reports that the leadership of the Jerusalem assembly was conferred "with one consent" on another member of Jesus' extended family, his cousin Simeon the son of Clopas. However, the fact that the relatives were concentrated in the visible and important religious center of Jerusalem would have left them especially vulnerable during the Jewish revolt. There is a tradition holding that some parts of the original Jerusalem church found safety in exile in the city of Pella across the Jordan. Mitchell, *Cambridge History*, vol. 1, 99. Still, many members of the Jerusalem family are likely to have perished in the sack of A.D. 70.

Whatever the particulars, at some point around this time the leadership of the church passed into the hands of the Gentile converts, who were well positioned to spread the word because they spoke and wrote in Greek, the common language of the region. Ibid., 100–01, 106. The earliest known versions of all four gospels are written in Greek.

There is, it will be recalled, a dispute about whether the "brothers" of Jesus named in the gospels are literal blood brothers, or people of some more remote connection. See Ch. 73, endnote on brothers and sisters. Insofar as they may have been more remote connections, then authority would probably have shifted away from the family still more quickly.

Ch. 99. *Salting every sacrifice.* The second half of this sentence is omitted from many manuscripts, although the substance of the thought is certainly implied.

Ch. 100. *The great sum of money.* According to the text, the servant owed the king "ten thousand talents," a talent being about 100 or 130 pounds' weight of gold or silver. This is figurative language intended to suggest a huge debt.

Ch. 103. *Burying the dead.* This passage refers to "the spiritually dead, who are not alive to the greater demands of the Kingdom of God." May, *Oxford Bible*, 1180. See Bruce, *Hard Sayings of Jesus*, 162. Jesus was, in general, inclined to downplay the importance of family ties. Mitchell, *The Gospel According to Jesus*, 44.

Ch. 105. *Denouncing the unreceptive cities.* Matthew records this denunciation at an earlier point in his narrative, just after Jesus claims the mantle of John the Baptist in Chapter 59. The gospel writers therefore did not fix a precise time for it. It seems more likely, however, that the denunciation was delivered at the time when Jesus was leaving the cities.

Ch. 110. *No prophet from Galilee.* Galilee was an isolated and poor part of the Jewish world. Horsley, *The Message,* 24. It also had a reputation for rebelliousness, being frequently overrun with rebels or "bandits." Josephus, *Complete Works,* 680 (*Wars* 1.16.2) (robbers based in caves around Sepphoris "overran a great deal of the country, and did as great mischief to its inhabitants as a war itself could have done"); ibid., 761 (*Wars* 2.21.1) (a rebel leader "laid waste all Galilee").

Ch. 111. *The woman taken in adultery.* This chapter is included in the text here because it is, by the widespread judgment of the Christian community, considered representative of Jesus' teachings. Scholars generally agree that the story is "a later insertion," but, nonetheless, that "a good case can be argued that the story had its origins in the East and is truly ancient." Brown, *Gospel of John,* 335.

Ch. 112. *Traditional Jewish teachings.* Leviticus 19:18 provides as follows: "Thou shalt not avenge, nor bear any grudge against the children of thy people, but thou shalt love thy neighbor as thyself." Jesus elaborates further on both traditional teachings in Ch. 168, below.

Ch. 114. *Jesus asserts his divine status.* Jesus often expressly refers to himself as the Son of God, and sometimes as the Messiah, but only occasionally as God. However, this is one of several occasions on which he does announce that he is not merely a man endowed with special powers by God, but that he has divine status himself. Ratzinger, *Jesus of Nazareth,* 350; Fitzmyer, *Catechism,* 84. In Ch. 114:13 Jesus claims not only a life beyond a human span, but also the distinctive designation "I am," a term used in the Old Testament to describe God. See Exodus 3:14. See also May, *Oxford Bible,* 1298 ("The *I am* is the divine name, a claim to pre-existence and oneness with God"). In Chapter 125:2 Jesus states that "I and my Father are one." And in Ch. 214:2 he receives, without contradiction, Doubting Thomas' address as "My Lord and my God." In addition, Jesus sometimes indirectly suggests his divinity, as in the description of his supernatural powers and attributes at the second coming. See Ch. 173:18.

Ch. 116. *"Give God the praise."* This is "a command to tell the truth." Meeks, *Harper Bible,* 2032. It is not an instruction to give the praise to God rather than to the person who worked the cure—at least not in so many words.

Ch. 116. *Those who are blind and those who see.* Literally, "For judgment I came into this world, so that those who do not see may see, and that those who see may become blind." The wording in text attempts to convey the meaning of this passage. It is clear enough that those who are unaware of the path of righteousness may have it shown to them; thus the blind may see. The more difficult concept is how and why those who think they see should be shown that they are blind. The idea here seems to be that the wise among that group will then realize their blindness and reform, even if the more stubborn are reinforced in their errors.

Ch. 117. *The Book of Mormon.* See 3 Nephi 15–16. The Book of Mormon holds that Jesus appeared to a group of Nephites after his resurrection and identified them as "other sheep" referred to in John 10:16. See 3 Nephi 15:21. In addition, Jesus spoke of the lost tribes of Israel as "other sheep." See 3 Nephi 16:1.

Ch. 118. *The Lord's Prayer in Luke.* As given in Luke 11:2–4, the prayer reads as follows:

> Our Father in heaven,
> hallowed be thy name.
> Thy kingdom come.
> Give us each day our daily bread;
> and forgive us our sins,
> for we ourselves forgive all those
> who are indebted to us;
> and lead us not into temptation,
> but deliver us from evil.

Ch. 118. *Prayer instructions and Beelzebub.* At the end of his instructions on prayer, Luke gives a description of the incident in which Jesus denied an alliance with Beelzebub. In this volume that is combined with the earlier description by Matthew in Ch. 67. The incident seems more likely to have come at the earlier point in Jesus' career, when he was still defining the nature of his ministry.

Ch. 121. *Girding up the loins.* Bailey, *Jesus Through Middle Eastern Eyes*, 369. The phrase that the King James Version renders as "gird up thy loins" is translated in the New International Version as "tuck your cloak into your belt." See, e.g., 2 Kings 9:1.

Ch. 123. *Mixed blood in sacrifice.* "Pilate was known for brutal reprisals and disdain for local religious practices." Meeks, *Harper Bible*, 1986. While the particular incident in text is not recorded in secular history, Josephus reports two similar events from this same period. In one, Pilate ordered Roman soldiers to enter Jerusalem carrying military standards with images that he knew the local population considered idolatrous, "whereas our law forbids us the very making of images." Josephus, *Complete Works*, 575 (*Antiquities* 18.3.1). On another occasion Pilate appropriated sacred money from the temple treasury in order to build a needed aqueduct. When the people protested, he had soldiers mingle with the crowd and then strike about them, and "there were a great number of them slain by these means." Ibid., 576 (*Antiquities* 18.3.2).

Pilate's nature may not have been as inflexible as these examples initially suggest, however. On neither occasion did he seem to have intended actual bloodshed. In the incident with the objectionable legionary standards, Pilate "was deeply affected with their firm resolution to keep their laws inviolable," and eventually ordered the standards to be withdrawn. In the incident involving the protests over taking money from the temple, Josephus reports that the deaths resulted because the soldiers dealt out "much greater blows than Pilate had commanded." Ibid. (*Antiquities* 18.3.1–2).

Ch.127. *The circuit in Perea.* The trip must have been circular, even though this is not explicitly stated. We know from John's description that Jesus was in Jerusalem at the Feast of Dedication, and then had to leave. Ch. 126. We know from Luke that Jesus was subsequently in the north, near the border between Samaria and Galilee, at the time he healed the ten lepers. Ch. 140. Then we learn from all three synoptic writers of his final approach to Jerusalem once more, on the third occasion that he predicted his death and resurrection. Ch. 148.

Ch. 131. *The anointing by Mary.* Meyers, *Women in Scripture*, 119–20. See also Ch. 62, endnote on Mary Magdalene.

Ch. 131. *Dying with him.* The reference here is to dying with Jesus. Lazarus was already dead, but Jesus was still at risk; and the disciples believed that a trip to Judea was dangerous to him.

Ch. 131. *Dead four days.* "Jewish belief also held that the soul lingered near the body for three days, so that death was truly final on the fourth day." Meeks, *Harper Bible*, 2035.

Ch. 132. *The prophecy of Caiaphas.* Caiaphas made "an unwitting prophecy." Gundry, *Commentary*, 416. When Caiaphas spoke, "like other opponents of Jesus, he spoke more truly than he knew." Meeks, *Harper Bible*, 2037.

Ch. 132. *The Sadducees were more dangerous than the Pharisees.* In New Testament times the Sanhedrin was dominated by Sadducees, who, as the political-religious establishment, had not only religious principles at stake, but also secular interests to defend. Scott, *Jewish Backgrounds*, 207–08. Those interests included both the privileged relationship with the Romans, and also their standing and income within the temple. As a result, the elders and chief priests "constitute the primary opposition to Jesus during the final days in Jerusalem." Meeks, *Harper Bible*, 1888. "It is the high priest Caiaphas, who will become the main instigator of the plot to execute Jesus precisely because of the threat he posed to the Temple's authority." Aslan, *Zealot*, 100. "From now on, they [the Pharisees] seem to subordinate themselves to the priestly caste, whose business indeed it was, for once the matter passed into the realm of law and politics the Pharisees were no longer concerned in it." Daniel-Rops, *Jesus and His Times*, 433.

Ch. 137. *Using wealth to make friends.* Literally, "make friends for yourselves by the mammon of unrighteousness."

Ch. 138. *Meaning of the name Lazarus.* Bailey, *Jesus Through Middle Eastern Eyes*, 383 (name means "the one whom God helps"). The rich man in this story is not named, but he is often referred to as Dives, which is simply Latin for "rich man." May, *Oxford Bible*, 1269.

Ch. 141. *Where is the kingdom of God?* This is the only place in this book that resolves an ambiguity in the language by presenting both possible translations in the text. At first sight this is a troublesome exercise. Only a single word was used in the original text, and it is obvious that the two translations cannot both be correct. On the other hand, over the years the original connotations of the word have been lost, and each interpretation has been developed into its own line of thought. By now both seem to be parts of the collective wisdom of the Christian church. It is also possible that Jesus was deliberately using an ambiguous phrase in order to make his listeners consider both possible meanings.

Ch. 143. *That I am not as other men.* The Pharisees had a reputation for strict and self-conscious observance of the religious laws. Josephus noted that the Pharisees "are a certain sect of the Jews that appear more religious than others." Josephus, *Complete Works*, 662 (*Wars* 1.5.2). Despite their strictness, many Pharisees, such as Hillel, were people of broad and humane temperament. Others were more judgmental, however. Some would not eat with or marry the less observant Jews who made up the great majority of the population. Metzger, *New Testament*, 56; Fredriksen, *King of the Jews*, 64 (Pharisees were no more than 1.2 percent of the population).

Ch. 144. *Lands beyond the Jordan.* Literally, "and went to the region of Judea beyond the Jordan." This phrase evidently describes the route rather than the destination, however, because Judea itself lies entirely on the closer, western side of the Jordan.

Ch. 144. *Made themselves eunuchs.* This phrase is "probably hyperbole for practicing celibacy." Meeks, *Harper Bible*, 1892. Jesus may have thought of this as a "calling" or a "gift." Loader, *New Testament on Sexuality*, 483.

Ch. 145. *Receiving like a little child.* The idea is that the person must "depend in trustful simplicity on what God offers." May, *Oxford Bible*, 1227.

Ch. 146. *Revival of the twelve tribes.* Meier, *A Marginal Jew*, vol. 3, 131; Horsley, *The Message*, 63. The number twelve evidently had a broader significance to Jesus for this reason. He may have selected twelve apostles in the first place in order to match the number of tribes, or the number of minor prophets.

Ch. 149. *The ambitious request.* Mark describes this request as coming from the two sons. Matthew describes the initial request as coming from the mother, with the sons participating in the subsequent discussion.

Ch. 149. *Sacrifice, ransom, and the plan of salvation.* "Ransom, originally a compensation required to release (or 'redeem') something or someone, was subsequently developed as a metaphor for the reclamation or redemption of God's people, particularly through Christ." Meeks, *Harper Bible*, 1938.

Sacrifice and ransom had roots in Jewish law. Certain animals and individuals were to be dedicated to the Lord, either through sacrifice or, as in the case of first-born sons, through service. They could be redeemed or excused from this obligation, however, by providing an alternative sacrifice. Thus "the firstborn son was presented in the Temple and then 'redeemed' from priestly duties by the payment of five silver shekels." Ibid., 319. See Numbers 18:16; Numbers 3:47–48; Exodus 13:13–15.

In Christian thinking, the sacrifice involved in Jesus' life and death have paid the ransom to free humanity from more fundamental burdens. These begin with the obligation of death incurred as a consequence of Adam's fall. See Genesis 3:3, 19. Other burdens include sin, physical or mental illness, and disasters in nature. Those still exist, but now "a counterforce is present among human beings to cope with such evil." Fitzmyer, *Catechism*, 61.

This teaching of sacrifice and salvation was later more fully explained in the letters of Paul, and now may be more familiar to Christians from those letters than it is from the gospels themselves. See Hebrews 9:1—10:10; Romans 5:12–19; Romans 8:21. The subject is addressed in gospel passages such as this one and Ch. 32:3, however. In addition, Jesus alluded to salvation at the time he instituted the Eucharist, when he referred to his blood as shed for the forgiveness of sins. Ch. 179:3.

Ch. 150. *Sycamore tree.* Vincent, *Word Studies*, vol. 1, 408.

Ch. 151. *Ten pounds of silver.* Literally "ten minas." A mina was about three months' wages. Daniel, *Harmony*, 146.

Ch. 151. *The cruelty of Archelaus.* Metzger, *New Testament*, 30. Archelaus once reportedly killed "thousands" of pilgrims who were coming to Jerusalem for Passover. Horsley, *The Message*, 19. On another occasion, a Roman provincial governor, acting on his behalf, crucified "about two thousand" rebels in Jerusalem. Ibid., 86. Notwithstanding his willingness to resort to extreme measures, however, Archelaus was not an effective administrator, and the Emperor Augustus eventually deposed him.

Ch. 152. *Old and new Jericho.* For the possibility that these were two separate places, see Bovon, *Luke*, vol. 2, 584. The administrative complex of New Jericho was one of Herod the Great's favorite palaces, and the place where he died in 4 B.C. See Scott, *Jewish Backgrounds*, 96. The intended victims for his funeral observances would have been nearby in the arena of Old Jericho. See Ch. 15, endnote on The Massacre of the Innocents.

Ch. 152. *Two blind beggars.* Matthew reports that there were two blind men. Mark and Luke describe Jesus' interactions with only one person—Bartimaeus. Presumably he was the more notable of the two, perhaps because he was himself well known to pilgrims, or perhaps because his father, mentioned here by name, had been a prominent member of the community. Collins, *Mark*, 508; Daniel, *Harmony*, 145.

Ch. 153. *Attendance at Passover.* Scott, *Jewish Backgrounds*, 69.

Ch. 154. *Bethany as the last stop along the way.* The existence of an expatriate community from Galilee would make it possible for Mary of Bethany and Mary Magdalene to be the same person, even though Mary Magdalene was evidently of Galilean origin. Other features of Bethany also contributed to making it a suitable stop for Jesus. The origins of the name are disputed, but the most common view is that it means "House of the poor," or "House of affliction." It appears that the sect of the Essenes operated a shelter here for the poor and sick, taking in travelers as well as local people, much as the Knights Hospitaller did during the Crusades. This might account for the presence of Simon the Leper. Capper, "Essene Community Houses," 498.

Ch. 154. *The date of the dinner in Bethany.* Both of the possible dates are reasonable. However, it seems more likely that Jesus would have taken this last opportunity to have a comfortable meal among friends, before entering the potentially dangerous precincts of Jerusalem. Jesus also returned to Bethany for the night on several occasions during Holy Week.

Ch. 154. *Bypassing Samaria.* Bailey, *Jesus Through Middle Eastern Eyes*, 201. Other Jews still took the direct route, however. Boring, *Introduction*, 95.

Ch. 156. *The unridden colt.* The description in the text here is "reminiscent of the unyoked, consecrated animals in the Old Testament." Meeks, *Harper Bible*, 1939.

Ch. 156. *Implications of "Hosanna!"* See Collins, *Mark*, 520. "Jesus' triumphant entry into Jerusalem was an unmistakable political act. He has come to be acknowledged as king. He is the son of David, the one long expected, to free Jerusalem from foreign domination." Hauerwas, *Matthew*, 182. With the triumphal entry into Jerusalem, Jesus is now accepting the role of Messiah that he had previously sidestepped, see Ch. 79, when he avoided the offer of the kingship. Metzger, *New Testament*, 142.

Ch. 156. *The destruction of Jerusalem.* The temple was destroyed as part of the sack of Jerusalem. With it was lost the only permissible place to conduct the temple ceremonies and carry out sacrifices. The practice of Judaism therefore underwent a fundamental change at this point, and thereafter concentrated on synagogue teaching and the observance of the Mosaic laws.

The last refugees held out for another three years on the fortified mesa of Masada, in the wilderness near the Dead Sea. When the Romans finally breached the walls, they found that virtually all of the defenders—960 men, women, and children—had killed themselves rather than be captured. Just two women and five children were found hiding in a cave. Josephus, *Complete Works*, 922 (*Wars* 7.9.1). Our knowledge of the last events inside Masada comes from their testimony.

Ch. 157. *Cursing the fig tree.* This was an atypical incident. In his dealings with human beings, Jesus used his powers solely to heal rather than to inflict harm. He limited his actions in this way even though others in the New Testament did use special powers to punish people when the circumstances called for it. Fitzmyer, *Catechism*, 61. See Ch. 3:4 (the angel making Zechariah unable to speak); Acts 13:10–11 (Paul blinding Elymas the magician).

Ch. 158. *Cleansing the temple.* "Market merchants would have been outside the restricted temple, in the adjacent courtyards . . . where non-Jews were permitted to buy and sell." Barnstone, *New Covenant*, 83.

Ch. 159. *Satan will be cast out.* The reference is not to the final judgment, but rather to a turning point, a decisive moment. Henceforth mankind will deal on new terms with the former "ruler of this world"—that is, with Satan.

Ch. 162. *Delegation of the elders.* The three classes named here (chief priests, scribes, and elders) are "the three classes making up the Sanhedrin," and so the present group may have been a delegation from it. Gundry, *Commentary*, 192. It would be understandable for emissaries to be sent to challenge Jesus' recent provocative actions. Collins, *Mark*, 539; Wells, *Who Was Jesus?*, 117 ("the challenge to 'these things' can refer only to his violent behavior in the temple the previous day"). This group's status as the representatives of the establishment would give their visit special weight.

Ch. 162. *John's power to perform baptisms.* John's teaching was not wholly unprecedented. Other groups and figures, often on the margins of society, had also preached baptism. The Essenes believed in self-administered full immersion baths "at least once a day." Collins, *Mark*, 140. Josephus himself had spent a period of apprenticeship with an ascetic known as Bannus, or "the Bather." Horsley, *The Message*, 31. However, John's teaching was new in

the sense that it called for an open, public, voluntary, lifetime commitment
to a new mode of thinking. Ibid., 32–33.

Ch. 164. *Return of the vineyard owner.* The gospels disagree as to whether
the response to Jesus' rhetorical question about the vineyard owner's return
comes from Jesus himself or from the crowd. This harmony takes a compromise position, attributing some part of the response to each. It seems clear
that the concluding proposal to re-let the vineyard to others most probably
comes from Jesus. That would best account for the crowd's reaction against
the thought, saying "God forbid!" The last two sentences of this chapter are
reversed from the order in which they appear in Matthew. In this way the
narrative appears in a more natural sequence.

Ch. 168. *The question about the commandment.* Matthew suggests that the
Pharisees had heard about the final result of Jesus' dispute with the Sadducees before the legal scholar went over. Mark suggests that the scholar was
present for all or much of the dispute. The words in italics balance these two
accounts by suggesting that the scholar heard how the discussion was going
and went over in time to hear the end of it.

Ch. 169. *Tuesday to Wednesday.* The gospels do not specify where the break
between Tuesday night and Wednesday morning took place. The time
here seems like a probable start for Wednesday however, because Jesus is
expressly described as engaged in teaching in the temple precincts, and we
know that this was part of his morning routine. See Ch. 169:2. A break here
will also permit an approximately equal number of events on each day.

Ch. 170. *The son of David.* "[T]he meaning here is that this title, though
correct, is not adequate, especially insofar as it suggests Jesus' subordination
to David." Meeks, *Harper Bible,* 2000.

Ch. 170. *No further questions.* The end result that no one dared to ask Jesus
any further questions is reported by different gospel writers after different
events during this day. Luke reports it when Jesus answered the question
about the resurrection (Ch. 167); Mark after Jesus answered the question
about the greatest commandment (Ch. 168); and Matthew after the question about the ancestry of the Christ (Ch. 170). The reports of the silenced
questioners are all consolidated here in the context of the last incident to
appear in the combined narrative.

Ch. 172. *The widow's mite.* In Greek this small coin was called a *lepton*. Our modern name for a class of very small subatomic particles is derived from the same root word.

Ch. 173. *This generation will not pass away.* The words of Jesus may have been incorrectly noted by a scribe. Or Jesus may have used the term "generation" to mean something other than the normal human interval from parent to child. May, *Oxford Bible*, 1204. To many readers, however, this prophecy seems not to have come true. The fact that it was nonetheless retained in the later manuscripts of the gospels, despite this difficulty, is cited as evidence that the later copyists were careful to preserve accurate copies of the record. Metzger, *New Testament*, 105–06.

Ch. 173. *Eagles or vultures?* In the apt formula of one commentator, "where the sin is, there will the punishment be." Clarke, *Commentary*, at Luke 17:37. Jesus may also have intended a double entendre in the ambiguity between the two kinds of birds. The eagle was the emblem of the Roman legions, and so this could have been a further reference to how the Roman armies would gather around the sinful metropolis of Jerusalem.

Ch. 173. *Parable of the talents.* The use of the word "talent" in this passage, as a measure of weight, was misunderstood by the readers of the King James and eventually gave rise to our current use of the word as a reference to natural skills. Metzger, *New Testament*, 166.

Ch. 173. *The last judgment.* "The theme of judgment is foundational to Christianity, although Christians remain divided about the exact number and character of these judgments." Longman, *Bible Dictionary*, 520.

Ch. 174. *Potential for trouble.* Trouble was especially likely on this holiday because it commemorated an earlier deliverance of the people from foreign rule.

Ch. 175. *Thirty pieces of silver.* Because several different types of minted silver coins were in circulation at the time of Jesus, other specific valuations might also have been meant. In any event, the sum is "shamefully low." Luz, *Matthew*, vol. 2, 345.

Ch. 176. *Maundy Thursday.* Other explanations for the name have also been suggested. One is that the term is derived from the "maundy purses" of alms which English monarchs were in the custom of distributing to the poor on this day. Under this theory, the name of the day would have been derived ultimately from the Latin *mendicare* and the Old French *mendier*, both of which mean "to beg," as in our present word "mendicant." These terms evolved into the English *maund*, which also meant to beg. By extension the word "maund" came to refer to the small baskets carried by beggars, and from that to the purses given out on this day as an act of charity, and from that eventually to the day itself. For discussions of various possible origins of the name see Brewer, *Phrase and Fable*, 821; Murray, *Oxford English Dictionary*, 1747–48.

Ch. 176. *Sacrificing lambs at the temple.* Even the lambs intended for private household dinners were sacrificed in public at the temple. "On the day of preparation for the Passover at noon the Passover lambs began to be slaughtered in the Temple (since the large number of Passover pilgrims prevented Ex. 12:6 from being followed literally)." Meeks, *Harper Bible*, 2050.

Ch. 176. *A Passover seder?* The gospel texts do not clearly establish the nature of the Last Supper. Preparations of the lamb for the dinner normally took place on the day before the celebration, and later that same evening, after sunset, when it would have become the next day by the Jewish calendar, the seder was held. The events in this chapter fit this description, which suggests that the Last Supper was in fact a Passover meal. On the other hand, the gospel of John, which is incorporated into Chapter 193:1 below, suggests a different chronology. John reports that on the next day, after Jesus had been taken and brought before Pilate, the Jewish leaders were anxious to avoid certain forms of uncleanness, because they wanted to be able to take the Passover that evening. By this account the Passover was still to come, and so the Last Supper must have taken place one day before the Passover dinner.

Because John's dating is explicit, while the identification with Passover in the other gospels is more inferential, the traditional Christian resolution has been to accept John's chronology. This means that the Last Supper took place one day before the regular Jewish Passover. This could have come about in any of several ways. The Last Supper may have been an important preparatory meal, but not the Passover itself. Or Jesus may have moved his observance of the Passover forward by a day, so that his death the next day, as a sacrifice for humanity, would take place at the same time as the community's sacrifice of the lambs for the regular Passover. Or Jesus and his followers may have belonged to a minority tradition within Judaism that calculated the dates of the Passover according to a non-standard calendar. Metzger, *New Testament*, 126.

This conventional interpretation has also been disputed, however. Several features of the traditional Jewish culture around Jesus tend to support the view that the Last Supper was a seder after all. A formal dinner during this period, observed with this much ceremony and planning, would most naturally be the seder. Also, the words in the Eucharist are a variation of the Passover ritual, which at the time said: "This is the bread of affliction which our fathers ate in the land of Egypt. Let everyone who hungers come and eat; let everyone who is in need come and eat the Passover meal." Ibid., 145.

On the other hand, other cultural factors count against it being a seder. The Last Supper would have been unconventional for a Passover meal, because Jesus did not celebrate it with his family, as Jewish tradition called for, but rather with his disciples. Feeley-Harnik, *The Lord's Table*, 144. Moreover, if the Last Supper were a seder, then the worldly events of the next twenty-four hours, including Jesus' appearance before the Sanhedrin, would also have been irregular, and not the kind of conduct expected during Passover. Levine, *The Misunderstood Jew*, 208. In particular, the Jewish establishment was not likely to have favored a capital trial and execution during this period. Harrington, *Gospel of Matthew*, 370; Meier, *A Marginal Jew*, vol. 1, 396. On the other hand, other authors believe that Jewish practice did permit the execution of serious religious offenders even on holy days. Hoehner, *Chronological Aspects of the Life of Christ*, 79.

Perhaps the best way of resolving this uncertainty is to assess events in light of the emerging Christian culture around Jesus, rather than the received Jewish culture. Assigning different dates to the two events tends to differentiate the Christian Last Supper from the Jewish Passover. It also tends to reinforce the theological message of Christian redemption. If the Last Supper took place the night before Passover, then Jesus would have died on the cross the next afternoon, at the same time that the Passover lambs were being sacrificed in memory of their deaths for the common good. Boring, *Introduction to the New Testament*, 697–98. So under this interpretation the Last Supper would have been a solemn meal, made on the eve of the Passover, but not actually a seder.

The few existing independent sources tend to support this dating. Later, somewhat ambiguous Jewish writing describes the life of a person called "Yeshu," who "practiced magic and led Israel into apostasy, had disciples, and was 'hanged on the eve of Passover.'" Fitzmyer, *Catechism*, 13 (quoting the Babylonian Talmud at Sanhedrin 43a). Some other writers concur in

Fitzmyer's interpretation that the reference to the "eve of" Passover in this passage means the evening before. Hoehner, *Chronological Aspects of the Life of Christ*, 75.

Ch. 178. *Leaning on the chest of Jesus.* "On special occasions, meals were eaten while lying on couches around a low central table. Those eating lay on their left sides; the disciple reclining next to Jesus would be to Jesus' right." Meeks, *Harper Bible*, 2041.

Some older Bibles translate this passage in ways that can have an unwarranted sensual tone to modern ears. In the King James Version it begins, "Now there was leaning on Jesus' bosom one of his disciples, whom Jesus loved." And when this disciple asked his question it was described in this way: "He then lying on Jesus' breast saith unto him, Lord, who is it?"

The intended sense of the passages is likely to have been fairly matter-of-fact, however, in two respects. First, the leaning "on the bosom" in the first sentence is best understood as a standard idiom, referring to people lying in close proximity on the dining couches. A similar phrase was used in an earlier chapter, where the King James translation describes the beggar Lazarus being carried by angels into heaven and "into Abraham's bosom." Ch. 138:2. And in the second sentence, the reference to asking a question while "lying on Jesus' breast" involves too literal a translation. This phrase most probably refers simply to the position temporarily taken on the dining couches for a close, quiet exchange of words.

Ch. 179. *Institution of the Eucharist.* "[W]e have good evidence that this ritual of the Eucharist became very early the principal way in which Christians marked their gatherings weekly . . . ." Farwell, *Liturgy Explained*, 7.

Ch. 180. *Sifting Peter like wheat.* See Job 1:7–12. Wheat is shaken when it is being separated from the chaff, and so too Peter will be shaken to test his commitment and mettle. Bovon, *Luke*, vol. 3, 177.

Ch. 180. *Two swords.* The two swords are sufficient for Jesus' purposes, even though they will not be sufficient to prevent his imminent arrest. Gundry, *Commentary*, 333.

Ch. 182. *The "spirit of truth" in Islam.* The first verse of this chapter is significant in Islamic thought. Islam does not recognize Jesus as divine or as the son of God. It does, however, honor him as an important prophet; he is mentioned about twenty-five times in the Koran. Moslems believe that Jesus foretold the later coming of Mohammad. This passage is interpreted by many Moslems as such a prophecy.

Ch. 182. *"The Father is greater than I."* This short phrase has led to numerous heresies, and to the clarifying declaration of the Nicene Creed. Belief in the Trinity is basic to Christianity, but some theologians have put a special emphasis on the role of God the Father. Such beliefs often found popular support—although not doctrinal acceptance—in the first centuries of the church. An early example is the so-called Arian Heresy, named after its most conspicuous proponent, Arius, a priest in Alexandria, Egypt, around 300 A.D. Arianism held that Jesus was an exalted being but was not fully God, that he was instead created by God, and that he had a definite beginning point in time. Brown, *Heresies*, 104–05. Many of the Germanic tribes that invaded western Europe, including the Vandals, Lombards, and Visigoths, later adopted the Arian Heresy and held it for some centuries. The first Council of Nicaea was called to resolve the dispute, and it resulted in the Nicene Creed of 325, which rejected Arius' views and held that Jesus was co-eternal with God the Father and of the same substance. That view eventually prevailed.

Ch. 183. *The time of departure.* John 14:31 implies that the departure happened at this point, because the suggestion that the group "be on its way" would most naturally come at the end of dinner. Consistent with this, Luke 22:39 places the departure just before his description of events at Gethsemane. On the other hand, Matthew 26:30 and Mark 14:26 both describe the departure as taking place earlier, immediately after the institution of the Eucharist, and before Jesus' prediction of Peter's disavowal. This harmony adopts the chronology of Luke and John, with its implication of a later departure and a longer conversation beforehand at the table during the Last Supper. The topics during that post-Eucharist conversation included Jesus' instructions to his disciples to fetch their wallets, bags, and cloaks, and those instructions most naturally suggest that the group was then still in the upper room, where they had been staying and where they would have access to those things. Conversely, if the departure had been at an earlier time instead, then most of the prolonged and complex discourses would have been held while the group was walking at night on unlit streets. This is certainly possible, but some discussion set around the dinner table seems more likely.

Ch. 183. *The Spirit as teacher.* Verse 15 of this chapter has used a relatively free translation in order to communicate a difficult concept. Jesus actually described personal attributes in a more terse and abstract form, saying that the Spirit "will take of what is mine, and make it known to you." This harmony preserves the more literal translation when Jesus reiterates the point in the next sentence. In either rendering, it is clear that the Spirit will aid the faithful in understanding the teachings of Jesus and in applying them to the varied and changing circumstances of life. Battle, *To Set Our Hope*, 19.

Ch. 186. *The crowd led by Judas.* This party was probably sent from the Sanhedrin, which was made up of the groups listed in verse 1. See Ch. 162, endnote on the delegation of the elders.

Ch. 186. *The crowd backs away.* Meeks, *Harper Bible*, 2029, 2048.

Ch. 187. *The priesthood of Annas.* To head off possible unrest in Judea, the Romans made a special point of controlling the office of high priest, and establishing their power to install and remove its occupants. This explains such facts as Caiaphas being "high priest that year." Ch. 132:3. Scott, *Jewish Backgrounds*, 92. Although now out of that office himself, Annas is still referred to as "the high priest" as a courtesy title.

Ch. 188. *The visits to Annas and the high priest.* The difficulty in sequencing these two interviews has led some to speculate that Annas' house and Caiaphas' may have been located in the same compound, so that reaching either one of them would be tantamount to reaching the other. For a discussion of the issues here see Zarley, *Gospels Interwoven*, 355–59.

Ch. 190. *Jesus looked at Peter.* "Those who frequent law courts know that groups are waiting in the corridors, that paths cross and looks are exchanged between those who are leaving a session and those who are waiting outside." Bovon, *Luke*, vol. 3, 232. Another possibility is that Jesus looked out at Peter through an open window. Collins, *Dorling Bible*, 394.

Ch. 191. *The Sadducees as collaborators with Rome.* As the elite class and the dominant faction within the Sanhedrin, the Sadducees represented Judea in its formal dealings with Rome, and were quite aware of their mutual interests. The Sadducees shared a common Hellenized culture with Rome. And "as a good working relationship with Rome helped guarantee the uninterrupted operation of the Temple, these aristocrats inclined toward the governing powers politically as well." Fredriksen, *Jesus to Christ*, 87. At the temple the Sadducees made "a daily sacrifice for the well-being of the emperor." Horsley, *The Message*, 75. Their role has been described as follows: "The main difference [in the political orientation of the Sadducees and the Pharisees] was that the Sadducees were willing to cooperate *actively* with the Romans, even if this meant handing over troublemakers to them for execution." Maccoby, *Mythmaker*, 58. See also Mitchell, *The Gospel According to Jesus*, 266.

Ch. 191. *The authority of the Roman governor.* Jerusalem had been conquered for Rome by Pompey in 63 BC, but for some time afterwards was left to be administered by the local rulers, although those were ultimately subject to Rome. Metzger, *New Testament*, 27. This arrangement ended about twenty years before the events described here. Archelaus "was the least competent of Herod's sons." Boring, *Introduction*, 81. "Because of his incompetence and the severity of his rule Jewish and Samaritan officials appealed to Caesar for relief. Archelaus was deposed in A.D. 6 and the area placed under procurators appointed by the emperor." Scott, *Jewish Backgrounds*, 97. Like his brother Herod Antipas, Archelaus ended his days in exile, in his case at Vienne, "a city of Gaul." Josephus, *Complete Works*, 725 (*Wars* 2.7.3).

Ch. 192. *The death of Judas.* One tradition in the church is that the limb from which Judas hanged himself broke, perhaps during the earthquake at the time of Jesus' death. Zarley, *Gospels Interwoven*, 367. However, the simpler and more natural supposition is that he was cut down by human action.

Ch. 192. *Who bought the potter's field?* The two accounts "are reconciled by understanding that Luke means Judas bought the field only in the sense that it was his money. It is not necessary to translate Luke's word *ektesato* as 'bought.' The word means 'procure for oneself, acquire, get.' The NASB translates it: 'Now this man acquired a field,' i.e., by proxy." Zarley, *Gospels Interwoven*, 366–67.

Ch. 192. *Prophecies about the field.* The quotation attributed to Jeremiah is actually a free rendering of Zechariah 11:13. Gundry, *Commentary*, 126.

Ch. 193. *A Gentile's house.* May, *Oxford Bible*, 1311. In the book of Acts, Peter described the beliefs and customs of the day in the following terms: "You yourselves know that it is unlawful for a Jew to associate with or to visit a Gentile . . . ." Acts 10:28. Even if there were no absolute prohibition, Jewish ritual law is not followed in such a house, and so "[a] Jew who came under a Gentile's roof would risk defilement." Meeks, *Harper Bible*, 1970.

This defilement involved only purity for ceremonial purposes, and was not a matter of sin, but it could have been seen as important nonetheless.

Ch. 193. *Pontius Pilate.* "There [is] almost nothing to go on. We do not even know his *praenomen*, the name his mother and wife and friends called him by. The only physical evidence we have of this man is one inscribed stone and a few small coins." Wroe, *Pontius Pilate*, xii. A family background in warfare seems likely. A probable ancestor, Gavius Pontius, had defeated the Romans at the Battle of the Caudine Forks, and made their soldiers pass under a yoke as a symbol of submission. Ibid., 13–14. At some point the family acquired the name "Pilatus," meaning "skilled with the javelin (the *pilium*)." Ibid., 16. Long before Pontius Pilate's birth, however, the Samnites had been crushed during the civil war between Marius and Sulla, in 86 B.C. When Pilate was born, he was probably born into a family with a proud martial tradition but, due to the local changes of fortune, only a modest social standing.

Ch. 193. *"Are you the king of the Jews?"* Stanley Hauerwas has shrewd insights on this question: "Pilate's question . . . is a question of a Gentile. He does not ask if Jesus is the son of David, but rather if he is the king of the Jews. He wants to know if Jesus may be a rival to Herod. One suspects that it would never occur to Pilate that, in reality, Jesus is a rival to Caesar." Hauerwas, *Matthew*, 231.

Ch. 194. *Tension with Herod.* Meeks, *Harper Bible*, 1961; Horsley, *The Message*, 55.

Ch. 196. *Barabbas as a robber.* Josephus regularly used the term "bandit" or "robber" when referring to the Zealots. Mitchell, *Gospel According to Jesus*, 269. He also used the term when referring to participants in rural unrest. Scott, *Jewish Backgrounds*, 212, 245. The Greek word for bandit or robber "had become a synonym for 'resistance fighter.'" Ratzinger, *Jesus of Nazareth*, 40. Barabbas was probably a violent freedom fighter of one of these kinds, and perhaps the actual leader of an uprising. If he had been a mere mercenary brigand he is unlikely to have had the kind of public support that he did. One can speculate that in the restive climate of the day, the violent activist Barabbas might have had more widespread popular appeal than the nonviolent Jesus did. Ibid., 41.

Ch. 197. *Collective responsibility.* See Paul VI, *Nostra Aetate*, Section 4. Insofar as the sentence from the crowd has been used to assign responsibility for the death of Jesus, this would be proper only as to the group of people actively participating in the demands for crucifixion at that particular time and place—the people, in other words, who assumed responsibility through their individual actions.

Ch. 199. *The hour of Pilate's verdict.* Another resolution would also be plausible. One might accept John's account of the time, and say that Pilate gave his verdict sometime close to midday. This would be quite plausible in practical terms. A careful governor, trying to understand and to hear out all the different factions, and sending Jesus over to Herod for a time, could very well have spent the entire morning on the case. A crucifixion shortly after that would also accord with the reported darkness that began at noon. The problem with this view, however, is that it is inconsistent with Mark's statement that Jesus was crucified at nine in the morning. Zarley, *Gospels Interwoven*, 372. This may create an unnecessary conflict between the gospels, when it is possible to reconcile them in the manner suggested in the footnote. For a general discussion of the issue of timing in this context see Metzger, *New Testament*, 126–27.

Ch. 199. *The penalty of crucifixion.* Although the Jewish leadership played a role in bringing about Jesus' execution for reasons of their own, the execution itself was carried out by Romans acting under Roman law. Crucifixion was a Roman means of execution, and was the usual punishment for political rebellion.

Ch. 200. *When the tree is dry.* May, *Oxford Bible*, 1281.

Ch. 201. *Numbered with the transgressors.* This sentence is confined to footnote in some editions of the Bible.

Ch. 202. *Casting lots for the clothing.* The most literal reading of the gospel accounts supports the construction in text—that the soldiers cast lots twice, once to determine which share of clothes each would get, and the second time to decide who would take the tunic as a single item. It is possible, however, that they cast lots only for the tunic, and that this act was then reported as affecting the allocation of the clothing as a whole. The accounts do not provide enough detail to give us a firm answer to this question.

Ch. 203. *Sour wine.* See May, *Oxford Bible*, 1211.

Ch. 203. *The veil of the temple.* Tearing the curtain would have opened up the inmost and holiest part of the temple to public view. The Holy of Holies, behind the veil, was at this time an empty room. Puig i Tarrech, *Jesus*, 86. This is where the Ark of the Covenant had been kept before it was lost. The area was still deeply sacrosanct, however. The Holy of Holies "could be entered only by the high priest, wearing special clothes," and only once a year, on Yom Kippur, the Day of Atonement. Ibid. Pompey had sparked outrage when he passed behind the curtain on an inspection after first conquering Judea.

Tearing this curtain clearly had a symbolic import, although it is not certain what precise meaning is best attached to it. It may have meant that the secrets of the old covenant were now open to gentiles and Jews alike, or that the way to heaven was now open to all believers, or that the special authority of the high priest and the Mosaic Law were withdrawn. Luz, *Matthew*, vol. 3, 562, 565–66.

Ch. 208. *Two apostles visit the tomb.* The gospels differ as to which apostle performed certain actions during the visit to the tomb. Luke reports that it was Peter who stooped to look into the tomb, while John says it was the other who did so. This divergence probably stems from the different lengths of the accounts. John provides a more detailed narrative describing the actions of both apostles, while Luke's report is fairly short and stylized, following only one actor. This harmony follows the principle of inclusion on this point and attributes the reported actions to both of the apostles who are identified in John.

Ch. 208. *The apostles are confused.* The text at this point does not specify whether the disciples believed that Jesus' body had been stolen, as Mary Magdalene had reported, or that Jesus had been bodily resurrected. However, some disciples' later doubts about the resurrection, described in Ch. 209:6, suggest that at this time they had only a general conviction that something unusual had happened.

Ch. 210. *Josephus' description of Jesus.* Flavius Josephus, should, in principle, be a particularly reliable source of information on these matters. He was a secular historian, a near-contemporary of the events, and, as a product of Roman-Jewish culture, had no direct stake either way in the early Christian controversies that he mentions in passing. Yet as it happens his accounts have provoked considerable disagreement. A much-disputed passage gives his description of the life and death of Jesus. This is the so-called "Testimonium Flavianum," which reads as follows:

> Now, there was about this time Jesus, a wise man, if it be lawful to call him a man, for he was a doer of wonderful works—a teacher of such men as receive the truth with pleasure. He drew over to him both many of the Jews, and many of the Gentiles. He was [the] Christ; and when Pilate, at the suggestion of the principal men amongst us, had condemned him to the cross, those that loved him at the first did not forsake him, for he appeared to them alive again the third day, as the divine prophets had foretold these and ten thousand other wonderful things concerning him; and the tribe of Christians, so named from him, are not extinct at this day.

Josephus, *Complete Works*, 576 (*Antiquities* 18.3.3). This passage is a challenge to the historian and the critical reader alike. It contains several phrases that are obvious interpolations by a later Christian scribe. A Roman-Jewish aristocrat such as Josephus would not state that Jesus "was the Christ," nor worry about whether it was "lawful to call him a man." For this reason many skeptics have dismissed the entire paragraph.

That seems too simple, however. Other phrases are things that no pious Christian is likely to have written either, and so are probably original to Josephus. Among these is the cool assessment that the followers of Jesus "are not extinct at this day"—with the implication that they might become so at any time. Moreover, it would be surprising for Josephus to have written paragraph-length passages on John the Baptist and James the Just, neither of which is much challenged by scholars, but to have written nothing about Jesus. All things considered, it seems best to read this paragraph phrase by phrase, provisionally accepting those elements that are consistent with Josephus' perspective as a secular historian, and rejecting those that are not. See Kee, *Jesus in History*, 44 ("It seems very unlikely that the passage in its entirety is a Christian interpolation"); Duling, *New Testament*, 518. For another line of reasoning supporting the basic historicity of the passage, see Metzger, *New Testament*, 91 (discussing a tenth century Arabic version of Josephus, which lacks many of the questioned Christian features but still contains the core passage).

John Meier's well-regarded attempt to retrieve the original substance of the Testimonium Flavianum, after deleting the probable interpolations and updating the translation, has led him to suggest that it originally read as follows:

> At this time there appeared Jesus, a wise man. For he was a doer of startling deeds, a teacher of people who receive the truth with pleasure. And he gained a following both among Jews and among many of Greek origin. And when Pilate, because of an accusation made by the leading men among us, condemned him to the cross, those who had loved him previously did not cease to do so. And up until this very day the tribe of Christians (named after him) has not died out.

Meier, *A Marginal Jew*, vol. 1, 61. While disputes remain, most scholarly opinion now seems to believe that the core parts of this passage are original to Josephus. See Whealey, *Josephus on Jesus*, 194; Mykytiuk, "Did Jesus Exist?" 44.

Ch. 213. *Appearance to five hundred.* Although the site of this appearance is not specified, some suggest that it was at the same mountain in Galilee where Jesus delivered the Great Commission. See Ch. 217. They reason that Jesus had more followers in Galilee as a result of his ministry there, and that the remote location would allow them to assemble there in relative safety.

Ch. 213. *Appearances to James and the apostles.* The "James" referred to here is probably the brother of Jesus. Jesus had already appeared to the original twelve apostles, including the other plausible James—the son of Zebedee—prior to the time of his appearance to this James. The term "apostles" is evidently used here to suggest a group beyond the original twelve, and so it may include such others as the seventy or seventy-two who had been sent out to prepare Jesus' way to Jerusalem. See Ch. 104.

Ch. 215. *Third appearance to the disciples.* Jesus had previously made two appearances to his followers in the upper room. Presumably his additional appearances, to Simon Peter and to the walkers on the road to Emmaus, had not been made to the collective group of "the disciples" in this same sense.

Ch. 216. *Making up for prior denials.* "The triple question is reminiscent of Peter's triple denial." May, *Oxford Bible*, 1315.

Ch. 217. *The mission to the Gentiles.* "Go. Make disciples. Baptize. Teach. These are highly active words." Gortner, *Transforming Evangelism*, 2. The mission to all nations represented a broadening of traditional Jewish

practice, which had previously avoided proselytizing or efforts to win converts. The architecture of the Jerusalem temple had made this inward focus
clear. Separate inner courtyards were established for Jewish priests, for men,
and for women. An outer courtyard was open to all, but notices warned of
the consequences of venturing further in: "Any Gentile passing this wall will
have only himself to blame for his ensuing death."

Ch. 217. *The long ending of Mark.* This long ending of Mark, verses 9–20, is
thought to be most probably a later addition. Boring, *Introduction*, 533. It is,
nonetheless, still canonical. Focant, *Mark*, 667.

Ch. 219. *Sabbath day's journey.* This is about three-fifths of a mile. Metzger,
New Testament, 59.

Ch. 220. *Arrival of the Holy Spirit.* Acts 2:4 goes on to describe how the disciples then became able to speak and preach forcefully in many languages.
The Pentecostal movement among evangelical Protestants is named after
this day, and emphasizes its followers' direct personal contact with God
through the Holy Spirit, in addition to the knowledge they acquire through
the study of scripture. Tickle, *The Great Emergence*, 146.

ACKNOWLEDGEMENTS

Innumerable people have helped this book along the way. Some of them lived centuries ago, while others are friends and colleagues in daily life. All are remembered and gratefully acknowledged.

The initial thanks must go to the monks of Mount Athos in Greece. They have maintained a religious tradition for over a thousand years, and also carry on the tradition of hospitality toward even wayfaring and skeptical visitors. It was on such a visit there that I first saw the potential of a life lived according to faith, and decided to set out on this project of creating a more accessible version of the gospels. Father Maximos of Simonospetra monastery provided just the right introduction to that world—academic and committed, yet also relaxed and peaceful about it. Through him I met Fathers Makarios and Iakavos, who gave additional guidance. And in time I came to meet helpful people affiliated with other monasteries as well, including Father Matthew of Vatopedi, who opened the doors to the icon collection, Father Barnabas of Karakalou, and Father Zosimos of Xenophontos, all of whom took the time to talk.

In the years since then an energetic English group, the Friends of Mount Athos, has kept me in touch with the place through its programs of pilgrimage and trail maintenance.

Back home in the States, I turned to the work of assembling the text, and then adding an ever-increasing number of footnotes to keep things clear for new readers. Fortunately, I was able to meet a number of established biblical scholars, who were encouraging and generous with their time and counsel. These included Alan Mitchell of Georgetown, a scholar of First Century Jewish culture; George Parsenios of Princeton Theological Seminary, who gave me my first interlinear translation; Carole Burnett, who worked diligently to teach me Greek; Charles Hoffacker, who shepherds an Episcopal congregation in Maryland when he is not writing books; and Katherine Grieb of the Virginia Theological Seminary, who pointed me toward the right reference books. Special thanks go to Father Stephen Ryan of the Dominican House of Studies in Washington, who carefully reviewed the footnotes and made helpful comments, even while recognizing, with a sigh, that an ecumenical Christian book could not always be fully consistent with Catholic teachings.

Not even these excellent people can be everywhere at once, however, and so the responsibility for any errors in this book is mine alone, and not to be laid at their door.

Next came the task of reviewing the draft text, polishing the language, and identifying points that had remained stubbornly obscure. Here I had help from a number of civilian friends and bystanders, who, either willingly or through conscription, took the time to read the product and comment on issues large and small. These included Sonja Albin, Nick Frederick, Lorraine Ledford, Tim Sharman, Eleanor Sims, and my sister Edith Strate.

All these steps brought us to the point of finding a publisher. And here special thanks must go to Ian Markham, the Dean of the Virginia Theological Seminary in Alexandria, Virginia, and an all-around good fellow. Dean Markham had already been independently thinking about the value of a consolidated gospel, and was instrumental in introducing this work to the religious houses. It was through him that I met the talented staff at Wipf and Stock.

Many people at Wipf and Stock collaborated to bring this book to light, most notably my editor, Matthew Wimer, and typesetter, Ian Creeger. My friend Louisa Woodville became involved in the publishing process at this point and gave valuable advice on the selection of illustrative art, while Richard Stanley helped devise the layout and formatting of the text. Mary Lou Steptoe provided two careful reads and edits of the finished manuscript.

Throughout this work I have had essential help on the home front from my well-loved wife, Kirstin Downey. She discussed, reviewed, and edited all phases of the project. She also provided the invaluable ability to see me for who I am, and to understand and share the spiritual journey that underlies this book. Her insights were essential in framing the Introduction, and her own deep sympathy for and connection with the teachings of Jesus helped in numerous ways to frame the language that you see here.

Our five children—John, Elizabeth, and Amelia Averitt; and Alex and Rachel Grimsley—bore up patiently through all the distractions of writing and contributed shrewd thoughts where needed.

Behind all these individual efforts are the institutions that provide archives of resources and continuity of purpose. Some of those too deserve special thanks. The Virginia Theological Seminary, the Dominican House of Studies, and Washington College were all particularly generous in making their collections available.

And, of course, the largest and most complex institution is the Christian community as a whole. For two thousand years now it has preserved, rearranged, and studied its sacred texts. Generations of anonymous scribes preserved the manuscripts through all the vagaries of war, plague, and neglect. Saint Jerome prepared the standard Latin text of the Bible; Desiderius Erasmus compiled the standard Greek text of the New Testament; and William Tyndale translated both these works into English, creating in the process most of the language used in the King James Version. Tatian prepared the first composite gospel in the Second Century AD, beginning a genre of religious writing that continues to this day. This work rests on all their shoulders.

INDEX OF VERSE
LOCATIONS

LUKE

JOHN

ɣ

BIBLIOGRAPHY

Alexander, Eden. *Proof of Heaven*. New York: Simon & Schuster, 2012.

Anonymous. *The Way of a Pilgrim*. Translated by R.M. French. Pasadena: Hope, 1993.

Aslan, Reza. *Zealot: The Life and Times of Jesus of Nazareth*. New York: Random House, 2013.

Augustine of Hippo, Saint. *City of God*. New York: Penguin Classics, 1984.

Bailey, Kenneth E. *Jesus Through Middle Eastern Eyes*. Downer's Grove, IL: InterVarsity, 2008.

Barnes, Albert. *Notes on the New Testament*. Grand Rapids MI: Kregel, 1962.

Barnstone, Willis. *The New Covenant: Commonly Called the New Testament*. New York: Riverhead, 2002.

Bass, Diana Butler. *A People's History of Christianity*. New York: HarperOne, 2009.

Battle, Michael, et al. *To Set our Hope on Christ*. New York: The Episcopal Church Center, 2005.

Biblos. Bible Suite. http://www.biblecc.com.

Boadt, Lawrence. *Reading the Old Testament*. New York: Paulist Press, 1984.

Boring, M. Eugene. *An Introduction to the New Testament: History, Literature, Theology*. Louisville, KY: John Knox, 2012.

——— and Fred Craddock. *The People's New Testament Commentary*. Louisville, KY: John Knox, 2004.

Botti, Joe, et al. "The Problem of Apparent Chronological Contradictions in the Synoptics." http://www.xenos.org/essays/problem-apparent-chronological-contradictions-synoptics.

Bovon, Francois. *A Commentary on the Gospel of Luke* (3 vols.). Translated by James Crouch. Minneapolis: Fortress, 2002–2012.

Brewer, E. Cobham. *The Dictionary of Phrase and Fable*. New York: Avenel, 1978.

Brown, Harold. *Heresies*. Garden City, NY: Doubleday, 1984.

Brown, Raymond E. *The Birth of the Messiah*. New York: Doubleday, 1993.

———. *The Gospel According to John* (3 vols.). Garden City, NY: Doubleday, 1966.

———. *An Introduction to the New Testament*. New York: Doubleday, 1997.

Bruce, F.F. *The Hard Sayings of Jesus*. Downers Grove, IL: InterVarsity, 1983.

Capper, Brian J. "Essene Community Houses and Jesus' Early Community." In *Jesus and Archaeology*, edited by James H. Charlesworth. Grand Rapids, MI: Eerdmans, 2006.

Carson, D.A. "Introduction to Matthew." In *The Expositor's Bible Commentary*, Vol. VIII, edited by Frank Gaebelein. Grand Rapids, MI: Zondervan, 1984.

Chopra, Deepak. *The Third Jesus.* New York: Harmony, 2008.

Clarke, Adam. *Commentary on the Bible* (1831). http://biblehub.com/matthew/1-1. htm passim.

Collins, Adela. *Mark: A Commentary.* Minneapolis: Fortress, 2007.

Collins, John J. *The Apocalyptic Imagination: an Introduction to Jewish Apocalyptic Literature.* 2nd ed. Hermeneia. Grand Rapids, MI: Eerdmans, 1998.

Collins, Michael, ed. *The Illustrated Bible.* New York: Dorling Kindersley, 2012.

Craddock, Fred B. *Luke.* Louisville, KY: John Knox, 1990.

Crossan, John Dominic. *The Historical Jesus: The Life of a Mediterranean Jewish Peasant.* San Francisco: HarperSanFrancisco, 1991.

Daniel, Orville E. *A Harmony of the Four Gospels: The New International Version.* 2nd ed. Grand Rapids, MI: Baker, 1996.

Daniel-Rops, Henri. *Jesus and his Times.* New York: Dutton, 1954.

Davis, John. *A Dictionary of the Bible.* Philadelphia: Westminster, 1942.

Donahue, John R. and Daniel J. Harrington. *The Gospel of Mark.* Collegeville, MN: Liturgical, 2002.

Duling, Dennis C. *The New Testament: History, Literature, and Social Context.* 4th ed. Belmont, CA: Wadsworth/Thompson, 2003.

Ehrman, Bart D. *Lost Scriptures: Books that Did Not Make It into the New Testament.* New York: Oxford University Press, 2003.

———. *Misquoting Jesus: The Story Behind Who Changed the Bible and Why.* New York: HarperCollins, 2005.

Farstad, Arthur, et al., eds. *The NKJV Greek-English Interlinear New Testament.* Nashville, TN: Nelson, 1994.

Farwell, James. *The Liturgy Explained.* New York: Morehouse, 2013.

———. *This is the Night: Suffering, Salvation, and the Liturgies of Holy Week.* New York: t&t clark, 2005.

Feeley-Harnik, Gillian. *The Lord's Table: The Meaning of Food in Early Judaism and Christianity.* Washington, DC: Smithsonian, 1994.

Fitzmyer, Joseph A. *A Christological Catechism.* Mahwah, NJ: Paulist, 1991.

Focant, Camille. *The Gospel According to Mark: A Commentary.* Translated by Leslie Keylock. Eugene, OR: Pickwick, 2012.

Fredriksen, Paula. *From Jesus to Christ: The Origins of the New Testament Images of Jesus.* New Haven: Yale University Press, 1988.

———. *Jesus of Nazareth, King of the Jews.* New York: Knopf, 2000.

Gill, John. *Exposition on the Entire Bible* (1746–48). http://biblehub.com/matthew/1-1. htm passim.

Gloer, Hulitt, ed. *Eschatology and the New Testament.* Peabody, MA: Hendrickson, 1988.

Gortner, David. *Transforming Evangelism.* New York: Church, 2008.

Gundry, Robert H. *Commentary on the New Testament.* Peabody, MA: Hendrickson, 2010.

Gunn, George. *This Gospel of the Kingdom.* London: James Clarke, 1964.

Haenchen, Ernst. *A Commentary on the Gospel of John* (2 vols.). Translated by Robert Funk. Philadelphia: Fortress, 1984.

Harrington, Daniel J. *The Gospel of Matthew.* Collegeville, MN: Liturgical, 1991.

Hauerwas, Stanley. *Matthew.* Grand Rapids, MI: Brazos, 2006.

Heim, Ralph D. *A Harmony of the Gospels: According to the Text of the Revised Standard Version*. Philadelphia: Fortress, 1947.

Henry, Matthew. *Concise Commentary on the Whole Bible* (1706). http://biblehub.com/matthew/1-1.htm passim.

Hill, Jonathan. *Zondervan Handbook to the History of Christianity*. Oxford: Lion, 2006.

Hoehner, Harold W. *Chronological Aspects of the Life of Christ*. Grand Rapids, MI: Zondervan, 1977.

Horsley, Richard and Neil Silberman. *The Message and the Kingdom*. New York: Grosset/Putnam, 1997.

Hurtado, Larry W. *Lord Jesus Christ: Devotion to Jesus in Earliest Christianity*. Grand Rapids, MI: Eerdmans, 2003.

Johnson, Luke Timothy. *The Writings of the New Testament*. 3rd ed. Minneapolis: Fortress, 2010.

Josephus, Flavius. *The Complete Works* [including *Antiquities of the Jews* and *The Jewish Wars*]. William Whiston, translator. Nashville: Nelson, 1998.

Kaiser, Walter C. Jr. et al., eds. *The Archaeological Study Bible*. Grand Rapids, MI: Zondervan, 2005.

Kee, Howard Clark. *Jesus in History: An Approach to the Study of the Gospels*. Fort Worth: Harcourt, 1996.

Keith, Chris and Larry Hurtado, eds. *Jesus Among Friends and Enemies: A Historical and Literary Introduction to Jesus in the Gospels*. Grand Rapids, MI: Baker Academic, 2011.

Koenig, John. *New Testament Hospitality*. Philadelphia: Fortress, 1985.

Koester, Helmut and Thomas Lambdin. "The Gospel of Thomas." In *The Nag Hammadi Library in English*, edited by James Robinson. San Francisco: Harper & Row, 1977.

Levine, Amy-Jill. The *Misunderstood Jew: The Church and the Scandal of the Jewish Jesus*. New York: HarperOne, 2006.

Loader, William. *The New Testament on Sexuality*. Grand Rapids, MI: Eerdmans, 2012.

Longman, Tremper III et al., eds. *The Baker Illustrated Bible Dictionary*. Grand Rapids, MI: Baker, 2013.

Luz, Ulrich. *Matthew: A Commentary* (3 vols.). Translated by James Crouch. Minneapolis: Fortress, 2001–2007.

Maccoby, Hyam. *The Mythmaker: Paul and the Invention of Christianity*. New York: Harper & Row, 1986.

Mahoney, William F.E. "On Taking the Kingdom by Force." *New Oxford Review* 29 (Dec. 2012).

May, Herbert G. and Bruce M. Metzger. *The Oxford Annotated Bible, Revised Standard Version*. New York: Oxford University Press, 1965.

McGowan, Kathleen. *The Source of Miracles*. New York: Simon & Schuster, 2009.

Meeks, Wayne A. et al., eds. *The HarperCollins Study Bible*. San Francisco: HarperCollins, 1993.

Meier, John P. *A Marginal Jew* (3 vols.). New York: Doubleday Anchor, 1991.

Metzger, Bruce M. *The New Testament: Its Background, Growth, and Content*. 3rd ed. Nashville, TN: Abingdon, 2003.

Meyers, Carol, ed. *Women in Scripture*. Boston: Houghton Mifflin, 2000.

Mitchell, Margaret and Frances Young, eds. *The Cambridge History of Christianity* (4 vols.). Cambridge UK: Cambridge University Press, 2006.

Mitchell, Stephen. *The Gospel According to Jesus*. New York: Harper Perennial, 1993.

Mumford, Thomas M. *Horizontal Harmony of the Four Gospels in Parallel Columns: King James Version*. Salt Lake City, UT: Deseret, 1976.

Murray, J.A.H. et al., eds. *Oxford English Dictionary, Compact Edition* (2 vols.). Oxford, UK: Oxford University Press, 1971.

Mykytiuk, Lawrence. "Did Jesus Exist?" *Biblical Archeology Review* 44 (Jan/Feb 2015).

Neufeld, Dietmar and Richard E. DeMaris, eds. *Understanding the Social World of the New Testament*. New York: Routledge, 2010.

Pagels, Elaine. *The Origin of Satan*. New York: Vintage, 1996.

Paul VI (Pope). *Nostra Aetate ("In Our Time")*. Vatican City: Council documents, 1965. http://www.vatican.va/archive/hist_councils/ii_vatican_council/documents/vat-ii_decl_19651028_nostra-aetate_en.html

Price, James L. *The New Testament: Its History and Theology*. New York: Macmillan, 1987.

Prichard, Robert W. *The Nature of Salvation: Theological Consensus in the Episcopal Church, 1801–73*. Urbana, IL: University of Illinois Press, 1997.

Puig i Tarrech, Armand. *Jesus: A Biography*. Waco, TX: Baylor University Press, 2011.

Ratzinger, Joseph (Pope Benedict XVI). *Jesus of Nazareth: From the Baptism in the Jordan to the Transfiguration*. New York: Doubleday, 2007.

Schurer, Emil. *The History of the Jewish People in the Age of Jesus Christ* (4 vols.). Revised and edited by Geza Vermes and Fergus Millar. Edinburgh: T&T Clark, 1973.

Scofield, C.I., ed. *The New Scofield Study Bible*. New York: Oxford University Press, 1967.

Scott, J. Julius Jr. *Jewish Backgrounds of the New Testament*. Grand Rapids, MI: Baker Academic, 1995.

Stanley, Christopher D. *The Hebrew Bible: A Comparative Approach*. Minneapolis: Fortress, 2010.

Thurston, Bonnie. *Women in the New Testament*. New York: Crossroad, 1998.

Tickle, Phyllis. *The Great Emergence: How Christianity is Changing and Why*. Grand Rapids, MI: Baker, 2008.

Tomson, Peter J. *Paul and the Jewish Law: Halakha in the Letters of the Apostle to the Gentiles*. Minneapolis: Fortress, 1990.

Vermes, Geza. *The Religion of Jesus the Jew*. Minneapolis: Fortress, 1993.

Vincent, Marvin R. *Word Studies in the New Testament* (4 vols.). New York: Scribner's, 1906.

Ware, Kallistos. *The Orthodox Way*. Crestwood, NY: St Vladimir's Seminary Press, rev'd 1995.

Wells, G.A. *Who Was Jesus? A Critique of the New Testament Record*. LaSalle, IL: Open Court, 1989.

Whealey, Alice. *Josephus on Jesus: The Testimonium Flavianum Controversy from Late Antiquity to Modern Times*. New York: Peter Lang, 2003.

White, L. Michael. *Scripting Jesus: The Gospels in Rewrite*. New York: Harper Collins, 2010.

Wikipedia. http://www.wikipedia.org.

Witherington, Ben III. *Jesus and Money*. Grand Rapids, MI: Brazos, 2010.

Wroe, Ann. *Pontius Pilate*. New York: Modern Library, 2001.

Zarley, Kermit. *The Gospels Interwoven*. Wheaton, IL: Victor, 1987.

Bible translations consulted

Revised Standard Version
New International Version
King James Version
New Living Translation
God's Word Translation
Douay-Rheims Bible
The New Covenant
Aramaic Bible in Plain English
New Revised Standard Version
Young's Literal Translation
English Standard Version
New American Standard Bible
Holman Christian Standard Bible
International Standard Version
NET Bible
American Standard Version
New King James Bible
Darby Bible Translation
English Revised Version
Webster's Bible Translation
Jubilee Bible 2000
King James 2000 Bible
American King James Version
Weymouth New Testament
World English Bible

Made in the USA
Las Vegas, NV
14 January 2025

16389955R00193